Classics of Russian Literature
Part II

Professor Irwin Weil

THE TEACHING COMPANY ®

PUBLISHED BY:

THE TEACHING COMPANY
4151 Lafayette Center Drive, Suite 100
Chantilly, Virginia 20151-1232
1-800-TEACH-12
Fax—703-378-3819
www.teach12.com

ISBN 1-59803-187-2

Irwin Weil, Ph.D.

Professor of Russian and Russian Literature, Northwestern University

Irwin Weil is professor of Russian and Russian Literature at Northwestern University, where he has been teaching since 1966. Previously, he taught at Harvard and Brandeis Universities. He was born and raised in Cincinnati, Ohio, in a family that speaks only Midwestern American English; his father was formerly the owner of the Cincinnati Reds baseball team. At the age of 19, as a student at the University of Chicago, the young Weil encountered the powerful talent of Dostoevsky and decided to learn how to read that literary powerhouse in his native language. When Soviet diplomats laughed at the young American's desire to enter the USSR in Stalinist days, he settled for learning, reading, and speaking Russian in the United States. Twelve years later, when Kennedy and Khrushchev agreed to open the gates slightly, he made a beeline for Moscow, only to hear from natives that he spoke Russian "too well, like a character from Tolstoy"—shades of his reading!

Dr. Weil has been going to the USSR (later Russia) for more than 45 years—lecturing at Russian universities and academies, talking up a storm with colleagues and friends by the hundreds, if not by the thousands. He knows the Russian language and its culture as well as any person born in the United States.

Dr. Weil's students come to him in groups that number more than 500 every year. He has received dozens of teaching awards from universities and national associations. He is a laureate of the International Pushkin Medal for Outstanding Service to Russian Language and Literature and the possessor of an honorary doctorate from the prestigious St. Petersburg Nevsky Institute for the Humanities. He now speaks six or seven European languages, and he reads biblical Hebrew.

Dr. Weil's written work covers the field of Russian literature and culture, with special attention to the classics of 19th-century Russian literature and the Soviet period. He has done a great deal of work on the relations between Russian literature and music, and neither he nor his students are strangers to musical notes.

To this very day, students and colleagues continue to ask him: "So, what are *your* Russians up to now?"

Table of Contents
Classics of Russian Literature
Part II

Classics of Russian Literature

Scope:

Throughout the entire world, Russian culture—and most especially its 19th-century literature—has acquired an enormous reputation. Like the heydays of other cultures—the Golden Age of Athens, the biblical period of the Hebrews, the Renaissance of the Italians, the Elizabethan period in England—the century of Tolstoy, Dostoevsky, Pushkin, and other great Russian writers seems, to many readers, like a great moral and spiritual compass, pointing the way toward deeper and wider understanding of what some call "the Russian soul," but many others would call the soul of every human being.

How did this culture come about, within the context of a huge continental country, perched on the cusp between European and Asiatic civilizations, taking part in all of them yet not becoming completely subject to or involved in any of them? What were the origins of this culture? How did it grow and exert its influence, first on its neighbors, then on countries and civilizations far from its borders? What influences did it feel from without, and how did it adapt and shape these influences for Russian ends? What were its inner sources of strength and understanding that allowed it to touch—and sometimes to clash with—these other cultures and still come out with something distinctively Russian? What wider implications does this process have for the entire human race?

Such are the questions and musings of the mind and the heart that these lectures will attempt to arouse and entertain. No final solutions can possibly be claimed, but some amusement and, perhaps, instruction and enlightenment may well be encountered.

Some consideration will be given to the very first predecessors of the contemporary Russians and their so-called "era of Rus'," which occurred in the Eastern European territory around the ancient city of Kiev. The origin and rise of these predecessors, together with their discovery of Eastern Orthodox Christianity—their attempt to coalesce and their fatal clash with the eastern Tatar invaders, from the 9th to the 13th centuries A.D.—produced two impressive literary languages and documents well worthy of serious study.

Subsequent history contributed to a literature that reflected human life and its nature and spirit. That history included the formation of a huge empire, starting around the city of Moscow in the 14th century and expanding under the rule of a government located in the more recent city of St. Petersburg from the early 18th century. Two cataclysmic 20th-century revolutions, which led first to the formation of the USSR in the early 1920s, then to the reestablishment of Russia as a federation in 1991, also greatly influenced the shape of literature.

After a consideration of the early formation of Russia and some of its basic documents, which provide important direction for the centuries ahead, we shall move to the 19th and 20th centuries.

We shall look at Pushkin, touted as the poetic "Sun of Russian Literature" and the "Mozart of the 19th century." Then we will examine the art of Gogol', with its remarkable combination of humor and the grotesque. The two prose giants of Russia will follow: Dostoevsky, with his dialectic between the depths of human pathology and the heights of religious inspiration, and Tolstoy, with his enormous universe of creatures, both animal and human, no two of whom are alike. Between these two giants came a very fine writer, Turgenev, who found himself, as a Russian liberal of the 1860s, caught between the radicals and the conservatives, the Westernizers and the Slavophile admirers of old Russian culture, not to mention the fierce emotions of his fellow writers. We will then turn to two immediate shapers of the 20th century: Chekhov, who has become the god of the American and British theater, and Gorky, who stood on the edge of the Russian Revolution of 1917 and survived to become the icon of Soviet ideology in literature.

From the time of the USSR, we will examine Maiakovsky, who saw the Russian Revolution as the greatest and most humane achievement of human history; Sholokhov, whose prize-winning novel saw the revolution as a tragedy that destroyed the Cossack world that he loved so well; Zoshchenko, who saw the revolution as food for parody and satire; Pasternak, one of the greatest poets of the 20th century, who also wrote a Nobel prize-winning novel; Solzhenitsyn, who first exposed the reality of the Soviet forced labor camps and continued to speak prophetically until he reached what he considered enlightened new nationalism.

We will conclude with the situation in post-Soviet Russia. In what ways can it become the worthy inheritor of such a powerful and all-embracing literary culture?

Notes on the Course

Russian Names:

Traditionally, when a Russian met another Russian, each would almost always address the other by his or her first name plus the patronymic, formed by using the first name of the person's father with the suffix -*ich* or -*vich* for a man, and -*ovna* or -*evna* for a woman. Examples: Fedor Mikhailovich Dostoevsky (Theodore, the son of Michael), Anna Arkad'evna Karenina (Anna, the daughter of Arkadii).

The use of the first name and the patronymic was a way of showing respect, in the same way that we say "Mr. Jones" or "Ms. Smith." Presently in Russia, this custom is in the process of dying out, although students still almost universally address their teachers in this way. In the 19th and early 20th centuries, the practice was ubiquitous.

Transliteration:

The Russian language uses the Cyrillic alphabet, somewhat altered after the 1917 revolution. In the sections quoted directly from literary texts, I have used the Library of Congress system of transliteration. Although it is not totally internally consistent, it is—among all those currently in use—the closest to an English speaker's sense of spelling and pronunciation. There are other systems that are more consistent internally, but they seem stiff and pretentious to the non-specialist.

In the use of proper names, I have used the spellings most familiar to English speakers.

In the bibliography, I have used the spelling employed by individual authors, many of whom deviate from the Library of Congress standard. In every case, I have tried to follow what seemed to me the dictates of common sense.

Lecture Thirteen
Inside the Troubled Mind of a Criminal

Scope:

The tortured mind and heart of the intelligent young criminal leads us through the gallery of psychological doubles, mates to various sides of Raskol'nikov's fractured personality: Svidrigailov, the apogee of evil and malice, who yet turns out to have a better side; Sonya, a young girl forced into prostitution to support her family, uses the great Russian version of the New Testament to push Raskol'nikov in a very different direction, toward salvation; Porfiry Petrovich, the investigating prosecutor looms like an almost supernatural doom over the protagonist, yet offers a kind of legal salvation in the end. All of them, together with other penetrating psychological portraits, make *Crime and Punishment* a conflagration of passions and arguments that hypnotize the reader.

Outline

I. As Raskol'nikov evades those who arrive on the murder scene, our hearts pound with the fears and passions of the murderer. But our apprehensions are nothing compared with the building anxiety within the murderer himself.

  A. Raskol'nikov lies in a tortured, half-delirious state in his cramped room. His friends, including Razumikhin ("the rational one"), vainly try to bring the young man out of what seems like an irrational state close to insanity.

  B. Dostoevsky is skilled at involving his readers in the madness of this scene, as the horror of what he has done repeats itself over and over in Raskol'nikov's mind.

  C. We soon learn that the young man is not totally irrational when Luzhin, the obnoxious man who is engaged to Dunya, comes to visit him. Not only is there a complete absence of politeness, but Raskol'nikov threatens to throw Luzhin down the stairs. Raskol'nikov has now made an enemy of Luzhin.

  D. Meanwhile, Raskol'nikov's mother and sister arrive. Again, this scene illustrates Dostoevsky's mastery of suspense. Razumikhin tries to assuage their worries. He becomes attracted to Dunya, who, in turn, becomes attracted to

Razumikhin, because his decency shows through his clumsy attempts to assuage her concerns and to hide his attraction to her.

II. In a marvelous scene of psychological torture, Raskol'nikov pays a visit to Porfiry Petrovich, the investigating prosecutor of the murder case.

A. The experienced older man is suspicious of Raskol'nikov. He mentions one of the articles that Raskol'nikov has written, in which he argues that certain rare and extraordinary individuals have the moral right to commit crimes, even murders, if they are done to bring benefit to humankind; these people are the Napoleons of the world of ideas.

B. Petrovich then asks Raskol'nikov how one would recognize such a person—and, by the way, did he consider himself one of them?

C. The suggestion is planted as an extraordinary explanation for an extraordinary murder.

D. It resounds with terrible resonance after the 20th century, when dictators ordered the murder of millions, simply because they were supposedly of a lesser order of humanity.

III. Dostoevsky is brilliant at increasing tension at the very moment it seems it could not get worse. Raskol'nikov gets into more and more hot water. Eventually, near the end of part 3, with all of these passions and fears boiling within him, Raskol'nikov returns to his small room.

A. Suddenly, he is back in the old woman's apartment; she is cackling away, he lifts the axe with frenzy and strikes her head again and again, only to hear her laughing so hard that she is shaking. He tries to scream and half awakes. Again, Dostoevsky has trapped us into a nightmare, barely distinguished from reality. But this time it is different.

B. He is aware of a presence in the room. A man is sitting on a chair, staring at him. The intruder is Arkady Ivanovich Svidrigailov, who tells Raskol'nikov that they have something in common.

1. In the face of Raskol'nikov's denial, Svidrigailov talks about seeing a ghost.

2. Remembering his own nightmare, Raskol'nikov tries to suggest that Svidrigailov is mentally ill.
3. The reply: Oh yes, but the fact that only ill people see ghosts is no proof that ghosts do not exist. It proves that you must be sick to see them.
4. Raskol'nikov begins to see why Svidrigailov states that they have something in common.

C. The conversation turns to the subject of eternity, which Svidrigailov describes as a dusty public bathhouse with spider webs in the corners.
   1. The bleakness of his vision reinforces Raskol'nikov's own feelings of guilt and estrangement—from his family, friends, and the world of reality around him.
   2. The bond between them becomes even stronger, emphasizing how tightly they are now connected.

IV. Raskol'nikov remembers a promise he made to visit Sonya, the daughter of Marmeladov, who had died after an accident, leaving his family totally dependent on her.

A. In their encounter, we see Raskol'nikov challenged by the better side of his own nature, which we have previously witnessed in his impulsive acts of generosity toward the Marmeladov family.

B. He starts by almost torturing Sonya with the knowledge of her family's difficulties. The mother is on the verge of madness and will probably die soon.

C. Sonya's response is to fall back on her religion; she repeats that God will not allow such injustice to happen. Raskol'nikov then, with malicious enjoyment, repeats the opinion common among the Russian radicals of his day: Perhaps God does not exist!

D. Raskol'nikov suddenly falls to the ground and kisses her feet. Here, we see both sides of Raskol'nikov: his malice and his ability to appreciate decency and faith.

E. He asks Sonya to read from the New Testament about the resurrection of Lazarus. She reads the part where Jesus tells the people to remove the stone from the grave.

1. Earlier, Dostoevsky had made quite a point about Raskol'nikov hiding the valuables and money taken from the old woman's apartment under a stone.
2. Just as the stone on the grave of Lazarus must be removed for his resurrection, so must the stone be taken away from the valuables stolen from the murdered old woman.
3. Raskol'nikov must work his way toward salvation through the expiation and confession of his crime.

F. Dostoevsky compounds the strong feeling of the scene by letting us know that Svidrigailov, in the next room, has overheard the whole conversation and now believes Raskol'nikov to be the pawnbroker's murderer.

V. News comes that Katerina Ivanovna is dying.

A. Raskol'nikov is forced to deal with Svidrigailov once more, when Svidrigailov exhibits generosity to Katerina's orphans, then lets Raskol'nikov know that his conversations with Sonya have been overheard.

B. Svidrigailov uses his knowledge of Raskol'nikov's crime to tempt Dunya to meet him—for the good of her brother.
1. Svidrigailov convinces Dunya to come to a room where they can be alone, whereupon he threatens her with rape.
2. She pulls out a pistol that he had given her at the time she was on his estate.
3. Undeterred, he walks toward her, and she shoots twice, barely missing him. He continues to walk toward her—this time, she cannot possibly miss, yet she drops the revolver.
4. Unlike her brother, she cannot kill another human being, even an evil one.

C. Once again, Dunya proves herself the strongest person in the novel.
1. In the contest of pride with her brother, she is the winner.
2. Svidrigailov understands, and he unlocks the door to the room, letting her escape unharmed.

D. This scene is the end for Svidrigailov. He commits suicide.

E. It is only after Raskol'nikov hears of the suicide, while he is at the police station, where he has gone to confess his crime, that he actually has the courage to make the confession.

F. Clearly, Svidrigailov must be gone before Raskol'nikov can take the first step toward redemption.

VI. The novel finishes with an epilogue, claiming to portray the redemption of Raskol'nikov in a Siberian prison.

    A. Many readers and critics have rejected the epilogue, insisting that Dostoevsky lost his literary power when he strove too easily to untie the knot of human problems.

    B. Yet it was clear that his imagination was beginning to work in another direction, one to which he would give the full range of his powers in his last novel, written more than 13 years after *Crime and Punishment*.

Suggested Reading:

Joseph Frank, *Dostoevsky—The Miraculous Years, 1865–71*, vol. 4.

Questions to Consider:

1. In the struggle between Dunya, Raskol'nikov's sister, and Svidrigailov, her would-be seducer—and a diabolical presence in the novel—who actually has the upper hand, both morally and physically?

2. Sonya Marmeladova, the daughter of the drunkard and the consoler of Raskol'nikov, is often seen as an angelic presence in the novel. To what extent is she a convincing force for the protagonist's redemption? Is that force believable?

Lecture Thirteen—Transcript
Inside the Troubled Mind of a Criminal

In talking about the murder in the last lecture, I just gave you a brief synopsis of the crime. The actual killing was really quite horrible, with Raskol'nikov struggling to wrest a purse from the old pawnbroker's neck, finding a key to open the strongbox, filling his pockets with the gold jewelry inside, and so on.

There was also, of course, another aspect to the horror, at least from the point of view of the criminal, from the fact that there were people who came down the hall and came to realize that somebody had locked himself in the room. Raskol'nikov, in trying to get out of the room, had to take advantage of several incidences of good luck in order not to be seen as he left the house. He ran down the stairs, and there were people coming up the stairs; he managed to duck into a room that was being painted. And, of course, these details came back later on to haunt him because the painters realized later on that somebody had been in that room. As a matter of fact, something was even dropped.

These details, plus the terrible knowledge of what he has just done, are things, of course, that go through the murderer's mind, go through Raskol'nikov's mind over and over again after he gets back into his room. We begin to get inside the mind of somebody who has committed such a terrible crime. The first thing he does, of course, is to try to hide the parts of his clothing that are covered with blood. Then he falls down on the bed and gets into a position that's almost close to insanity. He ends up on the bed, pitifully clutching some socks together because he's afraid that these socks might have some spot of blood on them that might be seen.

His friends come in. Of course, the landlady and the people living in the house report to some of his friends that he seems to be in a terrible condition. The two friends, who come in, of course become very important characters in the novel. One of them is Razumikhin—in Russian, the word *razum* means intelligence or rationality—Razumikhin is the one who stands for a somewhat calmer rationality, a somewhat calmer kind of decency and, later on, will be attracted to the sister of Raskol'nikov, Dunya. He brings in a little bit later a man named Zametov, who is something of a psychologist, who tries to deal with Raskol'nikov, and they realize that something is prying on his mind. They can't understand; they think he's a sick man. And, of course, they notice that as soon as they start talking about the murder, which, of course, has tremendous resonance now in the city of Petersburg, he gets terribly upset, so they realize they have to avoid talking about it with him. Of course, they have no idea that he would be involved in something like that; furthermore, they know that his family is coming. He realizes that his mother and his sister are coming to visit him in Petersburg and, of course, he's terribly worried about the impression that he'll make on them, and he doesn't dare let them know that he's been involved in such a terrible murder. This goes on and on and goes through the mind of Raskol'nikov over and over again, almost as if there is some kind of a spike that has been put through his brain.

And I must say that when you read this particular part of the novel, in Part Two, the reader feels a little bit as if a spike has been put through his own brain as well. Dostoevsky is quite skilled at getting you to be involved in the madness and irrationality of the scene. In the middle of all of this, all of a sudden, another character shows up in Raskol'nikov's room. This is Luzhin; as you may remember, I explained that *luzhin* means a mud puddle in Russian. Luzhin is the man who had decided to take advantage of Raskol'nikov's sister, whom we called Dunya, when she had been accused of bad behavior on the estate of Svidrigailov. He realized that she was in a very bad position, and particularly when her name was cleared, he decided that he would propose marriage to her. He realized she was unusually strong and an unusually attractive woman and he thought his taking her up when she was very, very poor would mean that she would be completely under his control. As a matter of fact, he even made the statement, which was quoted in the mother's letter, that it was, "very good to marry a woman who is poor because then she will appreciate what I give to her." Of course, he kind of let the cat out of the bag there, explaining that he expected her to be totally subservient to him in the marriage. Raskol'nikov is furious, of course, at Luzhin, for taking advantage of the situation like this.

Dunya is doing this partly because she believes that Luzhin, who is a lawyer in St. Petersburg, can help her brother in the early stages with his career, after he finishes the university. And Raskol'nikov is very angry that his sister would think of sacrificing herself for him; he wants to sacrifice himself for humanity. Of course, the fact that she might have the same kind of pride that he has is something that gets him very upset. So when Luzhin comes in, hoping to kind of lord it over Raskol'nikov, as he hopes to lord it over his sister, he is quite shocked that Raskol'nikov greets him with enormous rudeness, with enormous impoliteness, and even quotes to him the statement that he got from the mother's letter and, of course, Luzhin is very angry. He feels that he has been misinterpreted in this letter, and he says, "I am going to talk to your mother about this." And Raskol'nikov says, "If you mention my mother again I'll throw you down the stairs." Razumikhin is quite shocked by this, that he would behave towards the fiancé of his own sister in such a rude way. He says, "Rodya, Rodya, calm down. Try to bring it..." and of course the more he tries to calm him down, the angrier Raskol'nikov becomes. Finally, Dr. Zametov tries to tell Luzhin, "Look, can't you see you're upsetting the man? He's my patient. Kindly try to get of here as graciously as you possibly can." Luzhin is deeply insulted. Of course, Raskol'nikov has built up against himself an enemy that will try to do all kinds of nasty things to him.

Meanwhile, Raskol'nikov is waiting for the approach of his sister and his mother. And, of course, this is a very difficult thing for him because he realizes they'll see him and they'll see what kind of a state he's in. Finally, Dostoevsky builds up the suspense. He's a marvelous master of suspense in his novels; he believes in suspense just as strongly as Tolstoy is against suspense. Suddenly, the family appears and he tries very, very hard to be kind to them, not to give them the impression of the terrible state that he's in. Of course, they immediately notice, "What's this? He's acting as if this was some kind of official meeting. Why is my son"—and in Dunya's case "my brother"—"behaving in such a formal, stiff, inflexible kind of way?" They can't quite understand it. Razumikhin desperately tries to get them out of the room to try to explain to them that their brother has obviously been attacked by some kind of sickness, that they shouldn't irritate him.

Eventually they do go out of the room and, of course, by this time Razumikhin is tremendously attracted by the beauty of Dunya, Raskol'nikov's sister, and on the one hand, he realizes that she is a woman who is betrothed to another man, but he doesn't dare act towards her in proposing some kind of love between them; on the other hand, he can't restrain himself. In the struggle, he turns out to be sort of clumsy like a bear, and the more clumsy like a bear he becomes, the more they realize that this is a very decent man; it's a wonderful paradox. You would think that in meeting somebody, it would be good manners that would attract that other person to you, but in this particular case, Razumikhin's bear-like qualities, Razumikhin's inept and clumsy kind of qualities, only endear him more to Dunya, and you realize that a relationship will grow up between them in the novel in spite of the fact that she is betrothed to another man.

In short, the whole situation around Raskol'nikov is terribly upset. Of course, Dostoevsky is trying to get across to you what happens inside a person when that person is engaged in some kind of violence and some kind of terrible scheme. It turns out that the prosecuting attorney in Russia in those days, the person who investigated the crime and the one who prosecuted in the trial, was one and the same person; so that the character of Porfiry Petrovich is a kind of a cross between an examining magistrate and a prosecuting attorney. The very name, Porfiry, of course, implies something because *porphyry* is "purple" in Greek and, of course, the idea of the purple, that is the emperor. The Emperor of the Byzantine Empire was somebody who was always born in the purple room and who always wore the purple. There is something royal, there is something majestic, about Porfiry Petrovich.

And Porfiry Petrovich, of course, is increasingly suspicious of Raskol'nikov and he tells his relative, Razumikhin, that he would like to talk to this young man. He finds him very interesting, a very unusual case. There is nothing less that Raskol'nikov would like to do than to encounter Porfiry Petrovich at this point, but he realizes that if he refuses it would look very suspicious; so he agrees to go with Razumikhin to meet Porfiry Petrovich. Dostoevsky gives you a marvelous scene of psychological torture. Porfiry Petrovich very quickly understands that there is something off with this man, that his behavior is very, very suspicious, and Raskol'nikov is bound and determined to appear before him as a totally normal man who, in no sense, could be possibly be guilty of a crime of which, as a matter of fact, he was very guilty.

So, of course, he goes in, almost laughing, as if he's making some kind of joke. Porfiry Petrovich responds to the bait and says, "Oh, well, I see you're a very happy man. That's very, very nice." He said, "You know, I find you a tremendously interesting young man,

Mr. Raskol'nikov." He says, "Really? Why?" He said, "Well do you know that article of yours?" He says, "Well, what article? What are you talking about?" He said, "But surely you must remember. You wrote an article that was published." Raskol'nikov did not even know that the article had been published. And, of course, in the article, he had evidently written that there are two classes of people in the world. There are ordinary people who are bound by ordinary rules of behavior and laws of the land and then there are, occasionally, there are some people who are very, very special, people like Napoleon, people like Mohammed, who were entitled— not only do they take actions which are illegal but they are entitled to take such actions because they bear such an enormously new idea and such an enormously different approach to the possibilities for humankind that they are entitled to step across any boundaries. They can commit murders; they can commit atrocities. Would Napoleon hesitate to take any action that he considered necessary in order for him to become emperor? Would Mohammed hesitate at taking any action to found a new religion to make people see the universe in the way that he wanted them to see the universe? Such people were extraordinary people and they have extraordinary privileges. They could even commit crimes.

Raskol'nikov said, "Really? That article was published?" He said, "For goodness sake, young man, you don't seem to take care of your own affairs very well. They would give you money for this article; you should go and collect the fee for having been published." He said, "I find this extraordinarily interesting"—this is Porfiry Petrovich talking. "I find this extraordinarily interesting. Now tell me a little bit more about these people. Is there a way of recognizing such people? Is there perhaps an inscription on the forehead? Are they perhaps built in a particular way?" And, of course, Raskol'nikov realizes that Porfiry Petrovich's suspicions are getting closer and closer to him. He says, "Oh, nonsense, these days everybody considers himself a Napoleon. These days everybody considers himself an extraordinary person." And Porfiry Petrovich says, "You wouldn't by any chance yourself, perhaps, consider yourself a Napoleon?" Raskol'nikov realizes that he is getting very close. "Oh, nonsense, and even if I did consider myself such a person, I certainly wouldn't tell you."

Now, of course, stop to think for a moment about this theory that Raskol'nikov has propounded. Think of it in terms of the 20th century. He has killed a woman whom he considers less than human, a kind of insect, a kind of louse. Think of the dictators of the 20th century who are responsible for the deaths of tens of millions of people because they consider them somehow less than human, somehow not part of the human race. Think of the foresight of what Dostoevsky is seeing here, the future history of the 20th century. This is a very powerful and a very troubling part of the novel.

Raskol'nikov realizes that he is in big trouble with the law and with Porfiry Petrovich and he's going to have to be very, very clever to escape the suspicions of Porfiry. If he was in bad shape when we saw him at the beginning of Part Two, after the murder, he is in much, much worse shape now. And, of course, Dostoevsky builds up all kinds of incidents, together with Porfiry Petrovich in all kinds of conversations, which only build the tension of the novel. If there is anything that Dostoevsky is brilliant at, it's increasing tension. When you think it has got to such a point it couldn't possibly get even worse, he makes it worse.

And Raskol'nikov, of course, is a victim. You understand that he's been a criminal, that he has exercised a murder on somebody who is his victim; but he, in turn, has also made himself a victim. There is no victim who is more suffering in this novel than Raskol'nikov himself, although, one thinks, of course, that he is trying to reduce an old woman to the category of a louse or an insect. That's also a terrible kind of suffering.

In any case, he mulls over this; he gets involved in situations which only get him in more and more hot water. He goes back to visit the scene of the crime and he meets a person, even calls him to his face "a murderer." When he's at the height of tension and the height of guilt and the height of worry, he suddenly falls onto his bed in his room and, all of a sudden, he sees the old woman before him and he takes the axe and he hits her over the head again and again and again. And the more he hits her, the more she laughs, the less she goes down. In the beginning of the description of the scene, you think this is actually happening, and it takes a while for you to realize that you are, once again, in a nightmare of Raskol'nikov. Sometimes it's very, very difficult to distinguish when it's a dream and when it's true.

Dostoevsky makes you realize exactly what it feels like to go through a terrible dream. He is a past master at that kind of thing.

And so he is hitting this old woman again and again and again over the head. He is beginning to sweat. He's getting desperate, he is getting anxious, and the more he strikes, the more she laughs at him. And suddenly, through this dream, it's as if he's almost half awake. You know, when sometimes you're having a nightmare, you get to the most terrible part of the nightmare, you suddenly want to wake up; you struggle to wake up. Sometimes you can't wake up and sometimes, suddenly, you do wake up. Here he is, struggling to wake up, and he's aware vaguely that there is some presence in the room. It's standing like a supernatural presence in the room. He can't get over it. He goes back into the dream; again, he tries to wake. And suddenly, he wakes up. And there is a man, dressed as a traveling German professor perhaps, dressed very, very well, sitting in front of him, sitting in a chair with his two hands upon a walking stick. And Raskol'nikov, of course, pretends as if he doesn't—maybe this is a hallucination, maybe this is the devil. What is this? He opens his eyes and, again, the man is sitting there.

Suddenly he sits straight up and says, "Who are you anyway?" And the man, not at all flustered, not at all bothered by the tone that Raskol'nikov takes says, "Allow me to introduce myself. My name is Arkady Ivanovich Svidrigailov." You remember Svidrigailov in the letter from the mother. Here is that terrible man whom Raskol'nikov considered, on the basis of the letter from the mother, the corruptor of Dunya, the corruptor of his sister and the source of a tremendous amount of nastiness in this novel.

This is the face of the old lecher that I talked about, you remember, in *Poor Folk*, the first example of whom you got in a much cleaner man by the name of Devushkin. This is a man who represents a tremendous amount of evil, a lecher, a cardsharp, a murderer, because it seems that he might well have murdered his own wife. And this is Svidrigailov. Raskol'nikov is virtually speechless. "How would you dare come to a place like mine?" He says, "Oh, you know there is something in common between you and me." "No, no, there's nothing in common; there is absolutely nothing that you and I could possibly—" "Oh, no," he said. "Tell me, do you sometimes see ghosts?" Remember the dream Raskol'nikov had. He said, "You must be a sick man. You are hallucinating and seeing ghosts." He said, "Oh, I know. They say that those who see ghosts are sick people and the ghosts are hallucinations of a sick imagination. But you know there is some logic to that, of course, but there's an equal logic to say, well, ghosts really exist; you simply have to be sick to see them. After all, what could be more natural? Sick people are much closer to the other world. Well people are furthest away from the other world, so it's quite logical that sick people would be the ones who would be privileged to see the ghosts." You'd have to think about that for a while and see how well you sleep in the evening.

And then they go on to talk about eternity. Svidrigailov says, "Suppose eternity is nothing but a Russian bathhouse that's dried up with cobwebs in the corner. And, of course, this view, this bleakness, the view of eternity, fits in very well with the world that Raskol'nikov has built for himself, estranged from the whole world because of the terrible crime he has committed and because of his notions about being a superior person, about being a Napoleon. It's equivalent to that empty, dusty bathhouse with cobwebs in the corner.

Raskol'nikov is forced to recognize, of course, at this particular part of the novel, subconsciously, that there is indeed something in common between him and Svidrigailov. And, of course, we now very well understand that Svidrigailov is that evil side of Raskol'nikov, representing him very well. At that point, Raskol'nikov remembers that he had made a promise to Sonya, the daughter of Marmeladov, who had died after an accident in the street; he had promised to visit her. Because, you remember, he had left some coins for the children, they saw him as a kind of a benefactor. And so there's a famous scene where Raskol'nikov goes to the room of Sonya and tries to understand who is she. What enables her to be the noble kind of a person who would sacrifice her entire life to help her own family, which as a matter of fact, may die very soon? And, of course, what will she do, what will the children do when the mother dies? Sonya says, "No, no, no, they couldn't suffer when my mother dies. God will take care of them; I believe in God. God will see them." And Raskol'nikov turns and looks at her and he says, "And suppose there is no God?" This deeply upsets Sonya. She virtually attacks him physically, says, "No, you must not talk like that. That's impossible to think that way. There must be a God; there is a God. I won't listen to you." And Raskol'nikov thinks to himself, "She must be mad. There must be some kind of illness—almost insanity—in her case."

It's interesting that he had been previously betrothed to the daughter of the landlady in his apartment. And at one point he said, "I don't know why I was attracted to her. Perhaps I was attracted to her by the very fact that she was ill, that she was sick." And, of course, that seems to say something about Sonya in the novel. This angelic character who Dostoevsky presents is nevertheless perhaps sick; perhaps there is some kind of sickness here. Dostoevsky plays with this in the world of Raskol'nikov and you begin to realize how the human mind works, how the human spirit works.

He taunts her and, of course, she gets extremely upset and she tries very, very hard to make him understand what it means to have faith. And all of a sudden, when she talks about the possible fate of her siblings, of her younger siblings, Raskol'nikov falls to the ground and kisses her feet. And, of course, here you see absolutely both sides of Raskol'nikov. You see that part that really does have something in common with Svidrigailov. We have something deeply evil and, on the other hand, someone who can deeply appreciate decency and faith, as Dostoevsky sees it.

At one point he asks her to read from the New Testament and she reads about the resurrection of Lazarus. And, of course, you get that scene where it says, sm"rdit—that's Old Church Slavonic—"he stinketh," as it's translated in the New Testament, the *King James* edition, to make the point that he really is dead and now he's resurrected. And in trying to see that Lazarus is resurrected in the scene in the New Testament, they have to roll away the stone. Of course, that's very important for Dostoevsky. Raskol'nikov had buried the money that he had stolen under a stone, and just as that stone had to be rolled away from Lazarus's tomb, so the stone would eventually have to be rolled away from the place that he had hidden the money. There is an implication there, of course, of resurrection and of salvation, even for a criminal like Raskol'nikov.

At the end of the scene, we suddenly realize that somebody has set up a chair in the apartment next to where this is all going on. Of course, he set up a chair so he could put his ear more comfortably against the wall to listen to what was going on. That somebody was Svidrigailov. And we suddenly realize that Svidrigailov now has a very good hint of what's bothering Raskol'nikov, of who committed that crime. Svidrigailov uses this to go to Dunya, the sister, and to get her to see him. But before he can do that, Katerina Ivanovna, the mother of Sonya and the mother of the children, has sort of gone out of her mind. And because she can't get any money, she dresses the children up in costumes and pushes them out on the street where they have to sing the song, *Marlborough s'en va-t-en guerre*, for all passers-by. Of course, the passers-by who see this terrible scene, this grotesque and comic scene, don't know what the devil is going on. The kids are terrified when people are following them; they try to run away. Katerina Ivanovna runs after them, trips over a stone and falls, knocks her head against the stone and realizes that she is going to die.

The prediction that Raskol'nikov made in the apartment of Sonya has come to pass. Now she really is going to die, and here the children are left hopeless. At that moment, who should step in but Svidrigailov, telling him—of course, he's been following Raskol'nikov—telling him, "Look, don't worry, I'll take care of these children. I'll put several thousand rubles in trust for each one of them and they'll be taken care of." Of course, Raskol'nikov is tremendously shocked that Svidrigailov, of all people, would do something like this. People are very complicated in Dostoevsky; they don't have just one side. And, of course, that too also puts him in parallel, as he said before, with Raskol'nikov because Raskol'nikov had done something exactly comparable to that in leaving his last coins for those people when he visited the house of Marmeladov.

The psychology gets very complicated and very penetrating. At this point, Svidrigailov insists that he wants to see Dunya. Raskol'nikov, of course, will not let him get anywhere near Dunya because of the reputation of what he's done before, but he manages to catch her on the street. And, of course, she greets him with revulsion. He says, "Look, I know something very important about your brother. I'm going to tell you something about your brother; this is for his benefit." And, of course, she is willing to sacrifice herself to the extent for her brother that she'll even go with Svidrigailov. And he gets her to come to his apartment, where he locks the door. And he tells her the business about the murder. She can hardly believe it. But he says, "Look, I can arrange it so that he can get away. I can arrange it so he won't be subject to justice, but you'll have to do something for me first." And she realizes that he has trapped her in this room for very nasty purposes; essentially, he is ready to rape her.

She accuses him of rape. He says, "Look, Miss Raskol'nikov, rape is a very hard thing to prove." It is so nasty that finally she pulls out a gun, a gun which, as a matter of fact, he had given her when she was on his estate earlier, earlier events in the novel. She said, "Take a step towards me and I'll shoot." He said, "Oh, if that's the case, that's just what I want. I was planning a trip to America." You begin to realize what the trip to America was. He takes a step, and she shoots and only grazes his head. Of course, this is a flesh wound and blood that comes from the top. He said, "Oh, I see you were aiming at my head. Well, that's interesting." He takes another step and she shoots again, and this time barely missing him. He said, "That's all right, take your time; reload. I'll keep on coming." And she realizes this time, if she shoots again, she really will kill him. And she makes a decision, quite different from the decision of her brother; she drops the pistol. She refuses to kill a human being, even an evil human being.

And, of course, in the contest of wills, in the contest of pride, you realize that it's Dunya who is the stronger one. In spite of Raskol'nikov's diabolical pride, his sister is even more powerful. Svidrigailov too, understands this, and quickly he looks at her and he says, "Quick, go. Get out of here." A storm is brewing over St. Petersburg and you realize that you're coming to the last moments of Svidrigailov. He picks up the pistol, puts it in his pocket, and goes to a terrible ratty hotel in the city of Petersburg, where Dostoevsky takes us through a series of nightmares, of terrible nightmares, and you realize that if anybody understands the nature of dreams, it's Dostoevsky. And all of these dreams are centered around his sensuality. He sees what looks like a French harlot in a coffin who suddenly wakes up from the coffin and starts laughing at him, starts appealing for him to come to her. He comes to her, and he suddenly wakes up. As he wakes up, of course, he hears somebody bullying a friend of his in the other room. And then he goes back to sleep, and when he goes back to sleep again, he sees these terrible sensual images and he doesn't know what to do. He's tortured in sleep; he's tortured awake. The skies have burst in Petersburg; there's a terrible rain going on. And you understand this is the first time in the novel that there's been rain. It's summertime, and it's been very hot and very dusty in Petersburg and all of a sudden there's rain, clearly a rain of redemption. Dostoevsky has brought a rain of redemption into the novel at a time when Svidrigailov is at his worst and his most troubled.

Finally, Svidrigailov can stand it no longer. He goes out into the square and begins to put the gun to his head. At this point, a rather curious scene occurs in the novel. He is being observed by a man who is talking in clearly a very heavy Jewish accent, a Jewish fellow with a strange casque on his head, and Dostoevsky identifies him as a Jew. He says, "Hey, wait a minute," in a rather heavy accent. "You can't do that here. You can't do that here. This is not the place." He says, "Well, brother, it's quite all right. I'm only going to America." And, of course, as though this Jew is a witness, he shoots himself. And this has something to do with Dostoevsky's attitude towards the Jews; this would come up at a time like that.

Raskol'nikov has been convinced by Sonya that he should go and confess the crime. He goes to the police station. Of course, the police have been keeping an eye on him. And he wants to say something, but he can't do it. He suddenly leaves the police station; as he leaves he hears that Svidrigailov has committed suicide and now, clearly, he's free to do it. He comes back into the station and says, "It was I who killed." Dostoevsky has an epilog where he has the resurrection of Raskol'nikov. Whether or not this is believable is something that critics have argued about to a great extent and very, very fiercely. But the real solution to this problem will come in the novels that we'll be talking about in the next lectures.

Lecture Fourteen
The Generation of the Karamazovs

Scope:

Throughout the 1870s, Dostoevsky became ever more deeply obsessed with what the Russians called "the eternal questions": the relationship between the eternal human desire for freedom and the desire for love; the wellsprings of human attachment and, equally, human hate; the problem of passing on humankind's greatest achievements from one generation to another. Underlying all these issues lay the question of God's existence and his order in the universe. In the process of wrestling with these problems, Dostoevsky created the Karamazov family, whose lives, passions, and lusts vividly grasped the creative imagination not only of the 19th century but of many centuries to come. Dmitrii Karamazov, the sensualist among the brothers, puts it very succinctly: "In this world there is nothing higher than the ideal of the Madonna, and nothing lower than the Karamazov conscience." Ivan Karamazov, the intellectual, puts forward the greatest doubts that puzzle the Christian believer.

Outline

I. All through the 1870s, Dostoevsky was concerned with the many problems connected with sin and with Christian faith.

    A. By that time, he had become an ardent supporter of the tsarist regime and its close ally, the Russian Orthodox Church. Yet, at the same time, few people understood as well or as deeply as Dostoevsky the force of the atheist argument so popular among the Russian intelligentsia at that time.

    B. He gave a great deal of thought and energy to the notion of constructing a literary character who would be a great sinner yet would eventually transcend that sin in finding Christ. In order to do this, Dostoevsky went back to the *Lives of the Saints* and the concept of the two different kinds of saints: the kind who was saintly throughout his life and the kind who sinned his way to sainthood.

II. In May of 1878, Dostoevsky faced a terrible loss: His favorite child, the three-year-old Aleksei, whom he called Alyosha, suddenly fell into terrible convulsions and died before the eyes of his parents. It turned out that the child suffered from epilepsy, inherited from his father.

A. Dostoevsky's grief was profound, and Anna Grigor'evna feared for his health, which was rather weak at that time. She decided that he needed to go to a monastery, Optina Pustyn', famous for its connections with many Russian writers.

B. The monastery was the home of a Russian monk called an "elder"—a person widely reputed both for holiness and psychological insight into troubled people who came to visit.

C. The monk's name was Father Amvrosii, and he gave Dostoevsky several private audiences. Dostoevsky returned from the visit in a much more settled frame of mind, ready to continue work on his great novel.

D. It is clear that Father Amvrosii was the model for the character of Father Zosima, the elder in *The Brothers Karamazov.*

E. It is equally clear that the character of Alyosha Karamazov has a connection with Dostoevsky's young son.

III. The opening of the novel tells us a great deal. After his dedication to Anna Grigor'evna, Dostoevsky presents an epigraph quoted from the New Testament book of John. It is a famous preachment by Jesus, concerning a seed of wheat that will render a rich harvest only if it first dies in the ground. Clearly, the novel concerns, among other things, the Christological issue of resurrection.

A. Dostoevsky takes great care to introduce his hero, Aleksei Fedorovich Karamazov (to be called Alyosha), with a certain amount of ironic humor. Among critics, there has been considerable controversy about which brother is the central protagonist in the novel.

1. In the initial words from the author, Dostoevsky makes it clear that Alyosha is the hero, and many critics will react negatively, because he will seem so virtuous and bland.

2. Dostoevsky says he is talking about a certain kind of "clarity" of character. But the kind of clarity that was accepted in Pushkin's time was no longer accepted in Dostoevsky's time.

B. The novel opens with the introduction of Fedor Pavlovich Karamazov, the father of the family. He is a debauched sensualist, with many repulsive human traits. Yet he is the most intelligent character in the novel. He has four sons: Dmitrii, Ivan, Alyosha, and Smerdiakov.

C. Dmitrii, the eldest son, is a sensualist like his father. He is in love with a woman with whom his father is also in love, creating a conflict between the two men. This will cast suspicions on Dmitrii after the father is found murdered.

D. Smerdiakov ("the stinking one") is named after his mother, a holy fool called Smerdiashchaia ("Stinking") Lizaveta. Fedor had fathered this son on a dare from his companions.

E. The focus is on the third son, Alyosha, who wants to be a monk. Curiously, he becomes the favorite of his profligate father. Yet even Alyosha shows the Karamazov side of his character, when he refuses to do anything to prevent the murder that is being plotted within his family.

F. The old man asks whether God exists. Alyosha answers yes; Ivan says no. The old man acts as if he is in a quandary: "Whom, then, am I to believe?" This question, of course, continues throughout the book.

IV. Dmitrii seeks out his brother Alyosha to talk about some of the terrible things he has done. He speaks the famous words:

> Beauty! I can't bear the fact that a person with the best heart and the highest mind begins with the ideal of the Madonna and ends up with Sodom. It's even more terrible that a person with the ideal of Sodom in his soul does not reject the ideal of the Madonna. His soul burns with that ideal, truly, truly it burns as it did in his younger, innocent years. No, the human creature is broad, even way too broad. I would make him narrower.

A. Here, we have the height of Dostoevsky's statement about the moral and psychological complexity of human reality, the deep divisions in the human personality, with which every one of us struggles.

B. As Dmitrii struggles with his own passion and lust, Alyosha sees the decent side of his brother, even as he sees his deep weaknesses. All of these things take place inside a part of the novel called "The Sensualists."

C. Later, in another part of the novel called "Pro and Contra," Alyosha is witness to the passions of his brother.

D. Ivan has been very eager to see his brother Alyosha, from whom he has been separated for some years. They meet in a tavern, and Ivan begins to test his brother's faith.

    1. Ivan says that he does not reject the idea of paradise; he simply refuses to accept the ticket at the cost of even one drop of innocent human blood.

    2. Alyosha argues that there is one figure in history who could find forgiveness for even the most horrendous of crimes. Ivan immediately counters with his "Tale of the Grand Inquisitor."

V. This tale is perhaps the most commonly quoted and studied fragment of any novel. It is gripping, puzzling, and—for most readers—impossible to put down.

A. The story takes place in 15th-century Seville, Spain, after an *auto-da-fé*, during which people have been tortured and killed because the Church deemed them heretics. All was done *ad maiorem gloriam Dei*, for the greater glory of God.

B. On the public square is a coffin, containing the body of a dead young girl. Suddenly, Jesus appears and is immediately recognized by everyone. Assuaging the grief of the family, Jesus pronounces the biblical words "*Talifa kumi*" ("maiden arise"), and she does just that. The crowd joyfully hails the appearance of the Savior.

C. Suddenly, an old man, the Grand Inquisitor, arrives on his way back from the executions. Frowningly, he orders the immediate arrest of Jesus. Such is his authority that no one dares oppose him.

D. The scene then shifts to the holding cell in the prison, where the old man confronts Jesus with the curious accusation that the Savior has been obstructing the work of the Christian Church.

1. How could it be that Jesus Christ himself could be a stumbling block to those who call themselves Christians?

2. In many ways, it is a question useful to the very atheists whom Dostoevsky is presumably attacking in the novel.

E. It turns out that the Grand Inquisitor is attacking Christ because the Savior wanted people to come to him and his teachings freely, without coercion. He wanted to attract them neither by miracle nor by guilt, but only by the purest of human love.

F. The Grand Inquisitor claims to know humankind, with all our weaknesses, far better than Christ knows us. The old man claims that human creatures are weak; the masses require and always worship those who dominate them.

G. It is not hard to understand why this book is considered so prescient toward the 20th century, and—let us hope not!—possibly for the 21st. Dostoevsky sensed, to a degree virtually unparalleled among his peers, the threats of totalitarianism in our times.

H. The Grand Inquisitor proceeds to use the famous New Testament story that describes how the devil attempts to seduce Christ by urging the great teacher to use bread, miracles, and authority. In every case, Jesus refuses, saying, "not by bread alone," "Tempt not the Lord thy God," and finally, "Get thee behind me, Satan." These are great words.

I. But the Grand Inquisitor tells Jesus that he was all wrong.

J. Through all of this brilliant harangue, Jesus sits silent. He then kisses the Grand Inquisitor on the lips and departs, silently.

K. Alyosha responds to Ivan's tale with great excitement but without much understanding: Is this praise of Jesus, an attack on the Church, a sick fantasy, or what? Ivan replies with irony, about how people are unable to digest fantasy and imagination.

L. But Dostoevsky gives Alyosha his ironic revenge: He kisses his brother's lips and silently departs. "Plagiarism!" shouts Ivan. Seldom has modern literature reached such a height of emotion or spiritual penetration.

Suggested Reading:

Fedor Dostoevsky, *The Brothers Karamazov*.

Robert L. Jackson, ed., *A New Word on the Brothers Karamazov*.

Questions to Consider:

1. In what ways does Dostoevsky make the saintly brother, Alyosha, a genuine part of the sinning and sensual Karamazov nature? Does this lower his moral status in the eyes of the reader?

2. Why is the Grand Inquisitor so confident that he can correct the mistakes of Jesus, the founder of the church that gives the old man his authority? Is Dostoevsky saying something here about the nature of human self-confidence?

Lecture Fourteen—Transcript
The Generation of the Karamazovs

Crime and Punishment was published in the middle of the 1860s, and from that time onward, all the way through the 1870s, Dostoevsky was very much concerned with problems of sin and Christian faith. Of course, by that time he had become an ardent supporter of the tsarist regime and the Russian Orthodox Church, which is very closely connected with the tsarist regime. And yet, at the very same time, he understood the force of the atheist argument which was so popular among the Russian intelligentsia at that time. He gave a tremendous amount of thought and energy to the notion of constructing a character who would somehow cut through this problem, who would, by the force of his own personality or the force of his own psychology, make an expression that would be convincing both in terms of Christian faith and also as an answer to the arguments of the atheists and the intellectuals who were becoming increasingly impressive and powerful in Russia at that time.

In order to do this, he went back to a form that was very popular in Russia earlier. You remember, when we dealt with Kievan Rus', we talked a little bit about this. He went back to the notion of the lives of the saints. You understand there were two different kinds of saints that they dealt with in those days. On the one hand there was the saint who, as it were, was born with the halo nailed to his head from birth, even whose parents realized they had someone very holy among them, whose playmates bowed down to him because they realized that he was holy. His sainthood went with him through his entire life. He was always the same. On the other hand, there was a very different kind of saint, who started out as almost a kind of a little devil, who, as a young child, was very badly behaved, who, as a young man, engaged in debauchery, engaged in all the terrible things that the church teaches against, who lived what might be called a life of sin and then, all of a sudden, at a particular time, usually in adolescence or in early adulthood, was suddenly faced with a blinding insight of what faith was.

And as bad a person as that person had previously been, that much of a saint he was in the future. And, of course, that person who, as it were, sinned his way to sainthood, was a character that appealed deeply to Dostoevsky because he thought this was the kind of a person who could really understand what human life was about and how to bring sanctity to human life, in spite of the fact that part of his personality also included those terribly sinful things that belonged in the character of any human being.

While he was going through this and going through all kinds of experiments of the kind of a novel that he might write when dealing with this—by the way, recorded in a series of articles called, *Diary of a Writer*, which has become very popular in modern times; it's a kind of a workshop of Dostoevsky's ideas—a terrible thing happened.

In May of 1878, he faced a terrible loss. He had had a young son named Aleksei. Of course, the nickname for Aleksei is Alyosha. And for some reason or other—I don't quite know why—Dostoevsky believed that this child was the one who had inherited the talent of the father. He gave enormous attention to the child; he felt very close to the child. He liked to play with him, even as a very small infant. And that particular day in May, he had been playing with him for an hour or so, and then the child was tired so he laid him down in the crib so he would go to sleep. And while the child was just about to go to sleep, suddenly he was struck with terrible convulsions and he died before the eyes of his parents. When the doctors came, they realized that these convulsions were caused by epilepsy, obviously a disease inherited directly from Dostoevsky.

Dostoevsky's grief was profound and Anna Grigor'evna really feared for his sanity, feared for his health, which, even without this, was not the very best at that time, given the life that he had led. And so she took him to a very famous monastery in Russia in those days, a place named Optina Pustyn, which was connected not only with Dostoevsky but with quite a few major Russian writers at that time.

At that monastery, Dostoevsky made the acquaintance of an elder. In those days, the Russian Orthodox Church gave place and position to people who were called "elders." They seemed to have a particular kind of sanctity, a particular understanding of human beings, a particular ability to deal with troubled people and to bring them to faith, things like that. The man's name was Father Amvrosii, and, of course, naturally he had heard a great deal about Dostoevsky. He was a very famous writer by that time. He gave him quite a bit of time and they talked about Dostoevsky's troubles at considerable length.

Evidently Amvrosii was a very acute psychologist and he knew how to deal with people in grief.

When Dostoevsky returned from the visit, he came back in a much more settled frame of mind, ready to continue work on what was going to become probably his greatest novel. As a matter of fact, many of the words of Father Amvrosii show up in the character of Father Zosima, the elder in *The Brothers Karamazov*. In the scene where troubled women are coming to visit him, some of the things that he tells them are exactly what Father Amvrosii had told Dostoevsky. Clearly, many of the experiences that Dostoevsky experienced in the late 1870s come into the novel and obviously the character of Alyosha, to a certain extent at least, has some connection with the Alyosha who was Dostoevsky's young son and who died of epilepsy.

The novel is dedicated—and quite rightly so, I think—to Anna Grigor'evna, Dostoevsky's wife, Dostoevsky's second wife, that is. It seems to be very clear that without her love, without her constancy, and without all of the things that she did for him, in spite of the fact that she was 20 years younger than he was, without that, I doubt very much that he would have written his great novels. She certainly deserves what she got in having that great novel dedicated to her. Later on, rather sadly, at the time of the revolution, she died after having been very, very hungry in a place where there was famine for a week. Somebody found a loaf of freshly baked bread, hot freshly baked bread. They gave it to her—of course, this was many years later, in 1917—they gave it to her. She fell upon it as only a hungry person would fall upon it, and she died from the expansion of that hot bread inside of her stomach. It's a very sad story and a very sad ending to really a great individual, a great woman.

The epigraph is very important; the epigraph is taken from the book of John, the Gospel, Chapter 12, Verse 24, a very famous sentence where he says, "Unless a seed of wheat falls into the ground and dies, it abides alone. But if it dies, it will bring forth much fruit." Of course, what he's referring to there is the phenomenon of winter wheat, which is planted just before the winter comes on. What he is saying is that as long as it lies under the ground, fallow, and doesn't sprout, it will come up at the proper time. But, of course, if there's an early thaw, if there's an unexpected warm spell, suddenly that seed will sprout and, of course, when the cold comes again it will kill it. So in order to bring forth fruit, in order to bring forth the wheat, it has to die, it has to seem to die, that is, lying under the ground, fallow, for three or perhaps even four months until the spring comes, and then it suddenly comes up. Clearly, this is a parable, with which the Gospel tries to handle the theme of resurrection. And, of course, the theme of resurrection is enormously important in the course of this novel.

Furthermore, there's a rather ironic introduction in the author's introduction of the man he calls his protagonist, Alyosha Karamazov. Now among critics there has been a tremendous amount of argument as to just exactly who is the real protagonist in this novel, which one of the four brothers is the real protagonist. And many people go for Ivan and for Dmitrii, but Dostoevsky says it's Alyosha, and I am one who tends to take an author at his word. I know there are critics who think that they know much more about the novel than the author does, but I am not among those people. It seems to me that it's the author who wrote the novel and he knows what he wants to do, particularly when he has the intelligence of Dostoevsky.

But it is interesting that Dostoevsky introduces the man he calls Geroi—that's the Russian word for hero—with irony. He says, "Well, so people will ask me, 'What has he done to make him a hero? Has he done something great? to whom and by what? Why do you call him your hero? Why do you call him a special person?'" And Dostoevsky says, "Well, I'm talking about a certain kind of clarity, but, of course, it's very difficult to talk about clarity in our times." You may remember the verse that I quoted from Pushkin about clarity. His song was clear, the idea of clarity was something that was very much accepted in Pushkin's time, was nowhere nearly so well accepted in Dostoevsky's time.

In the beginning of the novel, Dostoevsky introduces us to one of the central characters, Fedor Pavlovich Karamazov, that is, the father of these three sons. He's a debauched sensualist, he's a man who is evil in many ways, and, yet, I think it's very clear that he is the most intelligent character in the novel. As nasty as he is, his intelligence manages to cut through all of the deceiving parts, all of the places that aren't clear in the novel. And, of course, he had two wives, one of them a kind of blue stocking, who kind of lorded it over him; a highly intelligent woman who eventually flees from the old man because she has sense enough to get away. The second is a much weaker woman, a somewhat sickly woman, but, nevertheless, a very, very religious woman to whom, for some reason or other, he is attracted. The blue stocking was the mother of Dmitrii, the oldest son, the one who turns out to be a sensualist like his father. The second one, Sophia, the weaker one, the one who is in some ways kind of half mad, in some ways almost a holy fool, is the mother both of Ivan, the second son, and Alyosha, the third son.

And then, of course, there is also a fourth son, but before I talk about that, I think I should say something about Dmitrii. Dmitrii, of course, is a sensualist, a very strong sensualist. And he falls in love with a woman for whom the father is also falling in love, in spite of the fact he has been married several times. And, of course, there is a conflict between them over the same woman. This has a lot to do with his suspicions about Dmitrii after the father is found murdered.

Then, of course, there is a fourth son called Smerdiakov. You remember in the previous lecture I talked about the body of Lazarus smelling in the tomb; the Old Church Slavic form of the bible uses the word *sm"rdit* [modern: *smerdiat*], a particular kind of stench that a dead body has. And this young man is called Smerdiakov, or the "stinking one," because he is the son of a woman who is a holy fool, one of the *iurodivyi* that we talked about before, holy fool in Christ, stinking Lizaveta, or Smerdiashchaia Lizaveta; that's why he is Smerdiakov. On a dare, the old man, Fedor Pavlovich says, "There is no such thing as an ugly woman; there is no such thing as a woman who lacks attractiveness. Womanhood means to be attractive." They said, "Well, could you have sexual relations with that stinking Lizaveta over there?" He said, "Yes, I can," and he actually did it. And the result of that was the birth of his fourth son. She dies in childbirth, but she gets close to his house to give birth to the child, so they know that it's Fedor Pavlovich's son, Smerdiakov, the fourth son.

There's a time in the novel, in the beginning of the novel when the brothers come together; they all come back after many, many years of growing up. They come back to their father's house, and somehow the focus of all their attentions is on Alyosha. Alyosha is a strange sort of person to be found in a family like the Karamazovs. As a matter of fact, Alyosha wants to be a monk, and he is already a novice in the monastery that's near the house of the father.

Curiously, the old man, Fedor Pavlovich, this sensualist, this lecher; this old man who, in many ways, is a very ugly kind of personality, sees the goodness of Alyosha. Alyosha becomes his favorite. He realizes that among all of his sons, Alyosha is the one who will be kind to him; Alyosha is the one who will be kind to the world and this evil Karamazov sees in Alyosha the decent sort of a person he actually is. It's remarkable the way his intelligence comes through at that point.

Dmitrii, on the other hand—there is, of course, one other important thing about Alyosha. At one point he is asked by a skeptic, a man named Rakitin, "Alyosha, don't you realize that there is a murder brewing in your family?" Alyosha says, "Yes, I do." He said, "Aha, so you're not quite the kindly, naive young man they take you for. Well, why don't you do something about it?" Alyosha replies, "I can't. I won't." "Aha," says Rakitin, "you're a Karamazov too." Dostoevsky goes out of his way to show that even the saintly Alyosha Karamazov, as kind as he is, is nevertheless a Karamazov.

Dmitrii is a sensualist, as I said before, who competes with his father for the infernal woman, the *infernal'nitsa* of a novel, a woman named Grushen'ka, or a woman nicknamed Grushen'ka, which means a particularly succulent kind of a pear. At one point there is a quarrel in the house where Dmitrii actually physically attacks his father and beats him, beats him so that the father bleeds, and you realize that there is really bad blood between father and son.

Later on, when the old man is talking to Ivan about Dmitrii and complaining about the way Dmitrii deals with him, he also talks about the mother of Alyosha. He says, "You know, the mother was just like Alyosha. She could get into a sort of holy fit and then the only way I could bring her back to normality was to spit in her face, was to spit water upon her." And Ivan turns; he says, "You seem to forget that that woman is not only the mother of Alyosha but also my mother." And the old man says, "Now, wait a minute. Oh, yes, that's right," as he realizes how angry Ivan is at him and he fears Ivan— and it turns out rightfully so—fears Ivan very deeply.

In any case, the two of them get together and the old man is drinking cognac and he says, "Now, look, I ask Alyosha, 'Alyosha, does God exist?' And Alyosha says, '*Da*, yes.' I ask Ivan, 'Does God exist?' And Ivan says, '*Nyet*, no, God does not exist.' Well, whom am I to believe? Am I to believe Ivan, the skeptic? Am I to believe my son,

Alyosha, the religious one? Whom am I to believe?" That the problem of the existence of God, the problem with the existence of divinity in the world, is put very, very starkly by Dostoevsky in this novel. And then Dmitrii, the sensualist, seeks out his very religious brother, Alyosha, and he goes into a long, long story about some of the terrible things that he's done with women in the past. And then he says a very famous phrase, often quoted from Dostoevsky:

> Beauty! I can't bear the fact that a person with the best heart, the highest mind, begins with the greatest idea that humankind ever had, the idea of the Madonna, and then, step by step, ends up with Sodom, with a Karamazov conscience. It is even more terrible that a person with the ideal of Sodom in his soul does not reject the idea of the Madonna. His soul burns with that ideal. Truly, truly it burns as it did in his younger innocent years. No, the human creature is too broad, even way too broad. I would make him narrower.

...shirok chelovek, slishkom dazhe shirok, ia by suzil—"Too broad is humankind. [If I had created him,] I would have made him more narrow." Here we have the height of Dostoevsky's statement about the moral and psychological complexity of human reality, the deep divisions in the human personality with which every single one of us struggles. And, of course, as Dmitrii struggles with his own passion and lust, Alyosha sees the decent side of his brother, even as he sees his deep weaknesses. All these things take place in a section called "The Sensualists."

But, of course, for most readers, the most powerful part of the novel occurs after Alyosha meets with Dmitrii. He meets with his brother Ivan and the section is called "Pro and Contra," "For and Against." And, of course, again Alyosha is the witness to the passions of his brother. Ivan is tremendously eager to see his brother, whom he hasn't seen for a long time. He knows he's religious and he knows he believes deeply in Christ, and he begins to taunt him. He says, "Look, you know something about the existence of evil in the world." Alyosha says, "Yes, I've seen some of that."

You know that people are capable of terrible passions, are capable of terrible hatred. Let me tell you about some of the things that happened in this world. You know there are certain Russian landowners who are terribly crazy, who misuse the power they have over their serfs in a hideous way.

He said:

> The famous case, for example, of course, there are people who beat little children. You understand what it means to beat people who are totally innocent, the kind of sadism that's involved in the suffering of the innocent. But in this particular case, here was a landowner who had some hunting dogs of which he was very fond, and there was a little kid; the son of one of the serfs, who was playing on his estate. The kid was attracted to the dogs; he wanted to play with them, and in so doing, accidentally he hurt the paw of the dog, he hurt the paw of one of these hunting dogs of which the landowner was so proud. And so the landowner decided the punishment would be that he would give the kid a head start and then set the dogs upon him. And before the eyes of the mother, the dogs would tear the child apart. And the mother was forced to view that, was forced to view the hideous tearing apart of her own child by hunting dogs.

He said, "What should be done to such a man?" And Alyosha said, "He should be punished; he should be whipped." "Oh," he says, "there's a devil in you too, brother, eh?" Ivan says, "Look, it's not that I reject the idea of paradise, it's not that I reject the idea of God, but I respectfully return my tickets to paradise rather than go there at the price of even one drop of innocent blood. Who could forgive such a person who did what I just described?" And Alyosha says, "Wait, wait; there is one person, there is one figure in history who could forgive even that." And Ivan says, "Oh, I was waiting for that. I was wondering how long it was going to be before you would talk about Him," of course the figure of Christ. He said, "You know, I made up a little story about this and I'd like you to hear it; it's called, "The Tale of the Grand Inquisitor," the part of this novel, of course, that is most often quoted and most often thought about by the readers of this novel.

And then Ivan proceeds to tell this terrible tale. As a matter of fact, when Dostoevsky was writing this, he was at the height of his passion and he was dictating to his wife. You remember that, as a very young woman, she was able to take dictation. Sometimes he would dictate whole scenes to her. He dictated this whole thing to her in the height of passion, and at the end he said, "Anna, Anna, what do you think of it?" She said, "Marvelous"; she said, "Marvelous." He said, "No, look, I don't want to hear that; I want to hear your real opinion." And she said, "Well, to tell you the truth, I didn't understand it." He said, "What do you mean you didn't understand it?" He began to explain it. And she says in her memoirs, "The more he explained it, the less I understood."

And, of course, when you read it, you can well understand why she had trouble in understanding it. It's a very tricky and a very difficult thing to understand. It's the height of Dostoevsky's, in some ways, very nasty and very sadistic, dialectics but, at the same time, something that goes very deeply to the heart of the human soul, the human heart.

The scene takes place in 15th-century Seville where the sidewalks are warm and you can feel the warmth under your feet, very unlike Russia of course. It's a time after an *auto-da-fé*, when many people had been tortured and killed by the Inquisition of the church because they were heretics; although this was, of course, done *ad maiorem gloriam Dei*, "for the greater glory of God." And as the people are waiting in suspense, after the whole thing has been over—people have been hanged, people have been burned and quartered, the horrible tortures of the inquisition—you notice suddenly, on the Square, there is lying a very neat little coffin. And in this coffin is lying a dead young girl, perhaps 12 or 13 years old, beautiful even in death. It looks as if she might just be sleeping.

Here she is in the coffin and the family is grieving terribly; you can imagine what it means to lose a young child like that. There are virtually no words to describe their grief and, of course, it ties in with the sufferings taken before. And as this is going on, suddenly He appears, and people immediately recognize him. They immediately recognize it's Jesus. This is an epiphany; he has come and he has come to visit them. And they beg him, "Please, please, Lord, resurrect this child." And Jesus goes to the coffin and he says, "*Talifa kumi*," "Young maiden, arise." And miraculously, suddenly, the girl who had been dead sits up in the coffin, wipes the tears from her eyes, wipes the sleep from her eyes, and the parents are overwhelmed with joy. The Savior has come back and, once again he has caused a resurrection, once again he has caused a miracle. This is magnificent and, of course, they go to worship him and to hail him and to do everything that a good Christian would think would be done at the appearance of the Lord.

In the midst of all this joy, suddenly an old man appears, perhaps in his eighties, the Grand Inquisitor, who has just been coming from the torture and the murder of the so-called heretics of the church. He looks at this; he frowns, and suddenly he says, "Arrest that man." You understand he's an officer of the church; he's something like a bishop in the church. But, nevertheless, to Jesus, he says, "Arrest that man." And, of course, Ivan Karamazov says, such was his authority that nobody dared oppose him, and Jesus Christ himself they took away under arrest. You can imagine the effect this has on any believing Christian at that particular time in Russia.

And, of course, then we see the Grand Inquisitor in the cell, in the holding cell, where he confronts Jesus with a curious accusation. He says, "That you, the Savior, you, Jesus, who founded this church"—well, of course, Jesus didn't really found the church—it was Paul—but nevertheless Jesus' ideas were the foundation of the church—"you have been obstructing the work of the church." Now how could it be that Jesus Christ himself would be a stumbling block to Christians? It's, of course, an argument that atheists are very happy to use. They often say, "Well, you call yourself a Christian, but if Jesus were alive today he would sympathize with us and not with you, who call yourself Christians but act in very cruel and very wrong ways." Jesus is totally silent. Now why was it that the Grand Inquisitor considered Jesus to be an obstacle to the church, not the one who gave the ideas to the church, but rather an obstacle? Well, because, you see, Jesus wanted people to come to him freely. Jesus just wanted people to come to himself—to Jesus—to Christianity, freely, out of love, not by guilt, not by miracle, but out of love. And, of course, it takes a very, very strong person to come to belief and to religion simply out of love.

The Grand Inquisitor says:

> Because your religion is fine for a few strong people throughout history. Oh, yes, perhaps one or two percent of the people are strong enough to maintain a belief from a basis which you want. But we appeal to the masses of people who are weak, who are slaves, who want people to dominate them. They want bread. They bring their bread to us and then we give it to them, and they're grateful for the fact that we

give it to them. They don't want freedom; they don't want the kind of strength that you bring to them. They want rather the slavery, the security that we give them.

Of course, begin to think about this and think about some of the problems of the 20th—and let's hope not also—the 21st century. Dostoevsky is probing something here very close to what we know, not only in religion but in politics and aesthetics and many other things as well.

"You want strong people; we appeal to weak people. I have sacrificed the salvation of my own soul." He says:

> Look, I know what's going to happen when I die and come to the afterworld. Your people are going to send me to hell; but even as they're sending me to hell for the good of the people, for the good of the masses of people who are weak, who want to be slaves, I am taking care of them. You appeal only to the strong people. That's why you're stopping the work of the church, and I will block what you're doing. I will see to it that you stay under arrest. I will not let you interfere with our work.

Jesus says not a word. And then, of course, the Grand Inquisitor goes to a very famous part of the New Testament. You remember that Jesus goes out into the wilderness for fasting and for contemplation. And while he's in the wilderness of course—this being a Dostoevsky novel, and, of course, Dostoevsky having read the Gospel—who was he approached by? He was approached by the devil. And the devil is out to get Jesus, to make him understand the strength of the devil, and so he brings to the fore very powerful ways in which to get Jesus. First of all he says to Jesus, "Look, I understand that you are the Son of God. I understand that you have magical powers. Throw yourself down from that tower. You know that if you do it, your father will immediately save you. People will see it; they'll see the miracle and they'll believe."

Excuse me, I have skipped a step. Of course, in the beginning he says, "Look, you see those stones." He said, "Turn those stones to bread. People want bread; people need bread. Give it to them and you'll give them sustenance and they'll follow you." And of course, Jesus gives the very famous answer. He says, "Not by bread alone does man exist." "*Ne khlebom odnim zhivet chelovek,*" "not by bread alone." "All right," says the devil, "in that case, put yourself up on a tower. Go to the very top of that tower and throw yourself from the tower. Of course, God your Father will save you. Of course, angels will come down to hold you and prevent your fatal fall. People will see that miracle and will believe. They will believe because of that miracle." Jesus says, "Tempt not the Lord thy God." In short: "Don't tempt me with power. Power is not something that I want." "All right," he said, "these are the cities of the world. I put them before you. Take power over those cities." And Jesus says, "Get thee behind me, Satan." Having said this, the Grand Inquisitor says, "You made a mistake. You should have listened to what he said." And suddenly Jesus gets up, kisses him on the lips, and wordlessly walks out of the cell.

Well, Alyosha says, "I don't understand it. What's going—what do you mean? What are you trying to say? You're saying to me, on one side you're for the atheists; on the other side you're for the church. Is this against the Roman Catholic Church? What's going on?" And Ivan says, "Huh, has your imagination been so ruined by realism you can't take fantasy?" And Alyosha suddenly gets inspiration; he kisses Ivan wordlessly on the lips and walks out. And Ivan says, "Plagiarism"! Anyone who thinks Dostoevsky does not have humor in addition to death is quite wrong.

Lecture Fifteen
The Novelistic Presence of Christ and Satan

Scope:

Dostoevsky replies to the problems posed by the Grand Inquisitor with the teachings of the elder, Father Zosima. Alyosha tries to follow these precepts and ends up close to a loss of faith, saved by Grushen'ka, the one who is supposed to be an infernal woman. Ivan has his famous interview with an ironic devil who deals all too succinctly with the intellectual's problems. The whole affair is interrupted and then completed with Dmitrii's trial, where the wrong person is convicted for a murder whose real culprit we readers have met through Ivan's interviews with Smerdiakov. The final statement of the novel comes through Alyosha's sermon at the gravestone of a young boy who has died. He leaves us at the edge of a hint about the reality of Christian resurrection, while the author leaves us a virtually unmatched literary masterpiece.

Outline

I. At the time of writing *The Brothers Karamazov* in the late 1870s, Dostoevsky was well known and respected in the court of Tsar Aleksandr II, Russia's most liberal tsar, whose regime had liberated the overwhelming majority of his subjects from serfdom.

   A. In the court was a very conservative high-church official and thinker named Pobedonostsev. Dostoevsky would sometimes send him copies of unfinished manuscripts.

   B. When Pobedonostsev read "The Tale of the Grand Inquisitor," he interpreted it as an argument for atheism and accused Dostoevsky of betraying his own pro-religious convictions.

   C. Dostoevsky replied that he had only wanted to show the Russian atheists that he could make a better argument with his writing finger than they could with their whole heads put together. But he told his critic at court not to worry, because the rest of the novel would be a refutation of the argument.

D. Clearly, Dostoevsky intended to accomplish this refutation through the character and teachings of Father Zosima. As we read this section, we realize that Dostoevsky is creating a new gospel for the 19th century, the 20th century, and, perhaps, the 21st century as well.

  1. Dostoevsky's "gospel" is about the life and teaching of Zosima, showing that he was one of those saints who sinned his way to monkdom.

  2. Zosima urged his fellow monks to respond to people's suffering with love. For Zosima, hell is where it is impossible to receive love.

E. We also learn that Father Zosima instructed Alyosha to go out into the world. He cannot escape responsibility for his brothers. He must give a positive answer to the Bible's greatest question, posed by Cain in Genesis: "Am I my brother's keeper?"

F. Alyosha sets great store by his elder's instruction, and he is sure his mentor will die in sanctity, meaning that his dead body will emanate fragrance, rather than stench.

  1. This being a Dostoevsky novel, full of smells, as personified by Smerdiakov and his mother, one can almost predict the next step.

  2. The elder's corpse not only smells in the normal way, but the smell arises more quickly and more intensely than usual.

G. Alyosha is so devastated that he thinks he is losing his faith; he leaves the monastery. In so doing, ironically, he is still following the instructions of his deceased elder. Dostoevsky always proceeds by paradox.

II. Alyosha manages to break some of his own monkish vows. He has drunk vodka, and he has eaten sausage.

A. Dostoevsky now puts us in proximity to one of the infernal women in the novel, perhaps his greatest female creation. Grushen'ka, who has seduced at least two members of the Karamazov family, now has her eyes greedily fixed on Alyosha, whom she sees as the little saint. She manages to get Alyosha to visit her.

B. Suddenly Grushen'ka sits on Alyosha's lap and starts to embrace him. He is a young man who has never been close to a woman before, and he thinks of such situations only with fear and trembling.

C. In the midst of this provocative situation, Grushen'ka suddenly learns of the elder's death. She is immediately overcome by remorse and guilt. She quickly gets up from Alyosha's lap and tries to face her own self-loathing and guilt.

D. She says that, for once in her life, she may have done right when she stopped abusing Alyosha.

E. It is in this context that Alyosha recovers the spiritual strength that he received from Father Zosima, and he is once more content with his faith.

III. For Alyosha's brother Dmitrii, the brush with women has not been as salutary. Having been deeply involved with Katerina Ivanovna, the daughter of his military commander, Dmitrii then feels strongly attracted to Grushen'ka, the object of his father's affections.

A. Once again, we are confronted with a murder scene in a Dostoevsky novel. Although Dmitrii is present at the time that his father is murdered, the circumstances are not immediately clear. Still, Dmitrii is suspected of having committed parricide. His dislike of his father was well known, and he had bloodstains on his clothes.

B. Meanwhile, he goes on a mad dash for Grushen'ka, only to learn that she has gone off to meet a former Polish lover. He splurges a great deal of money on a feast to take to her in the town to which she fled.

C. In a magnificent description of a Russian feast, Dostoevsky sets the scene for Dmitrii's successful wooing of Grushen'ka. Their blissful dreams are, however, interrupted by the arrival of the police and the chief investigator.

D. Dmitrii then has to go through the complete humiliation of a police interrogation, where every fact seems to increase the weight of evidence indicating parricide, which Dmitrii insists on denying.

E. The ultimate humiliation is the personal search, during which he must completely undress, exposing a misshapen toe that has always embarrassed him.

1. We get a replay here of the exposure of the unadorned self in Dostoevsky's *Poor Folk* and in Shakespeare's *King Lear*, when the old king comes out undressed in the storm.

2. Human nakedness is both a physical condition and a view into the exposed human soul.

F. It soon becomes clear that Dmitrii will be tried for his father's murder.

IV. Meanwhile, Ivan is beginning to feel a terrible sense of guilt for the murder of his father, because it is he who has preached to the world that there is no God and, therefore, that everything is allowed.

A. Ivan's half-brother Smerdiakov is strongly attracted to the idea that if there is no God, he can do anything he wants. It is interesting that Sigmund Freud considered *The Brothers Karamazov* one of the world's three greatest literary tragedies, along with Sophocles's *Oedipus* Rex and Shakespeare's *Hamlet.*

B. Ivan decides to visit Smerdiakov, who tells Ivan it was he who murdered their father.

C. Ivan becomes sick and almost insane.

D. Alyosha comes to announce that Smerdiakov has just hanged himself.

V. Dmitrii's trial takes place, and he is found guilty at a trial that exemplifies all the rules and procedures of the reformed Russian legal system.

A. The defense attorney actually believes that Dmitrii is guilty but, according to the rules of the reformed legal system, makes the cleverest arguments he can for his client.

B. We readers know that, contrary to his own beliefs, his arguments are correct. Dmitrii is innocent.

C. At the final moment, Katerina Ivanovna, jealous of Dmitrii's love for Grushen'ka, produces a letter that Dmitrii had written to her. In it, Dmitrii says that he hates his father, wishes him dead, and will plan his father's murder.

D. The balance is tipped, and Dmitrii is convicted. The whole question of guilt and punishment is a much more complicated matter than a human legal system can grasp, or so argues Dostoevsky.

VI. The final statement of the novel comes with Alyosha's sermon at the gravestone of a young boy who has just died; he was part of a group of children whom Alyosha is mentoring toward a better future in Russia.

    A. Dostoevsky lets slip one phrase: No smell comes from the coffin of the young boy. This information, of course, resounds immediately with the memory of Zosima's coffin and the smell that emanated from it.

    B. Many natural reasons can explain the contrast: age versus youth, death in summer versus death in winter, and so on. Yet the fact remains that fragrance and freshness are possible, even in death, and salvation and immortality lie within reach, if not within certainty.

VII. Dostoevsky leaves us on the edge, just a few months before his own death in 1881. His is a literary legacy that will not soon be forgotten.

Suggested Reading:

Robert Belknap, *The Genesis of the Brothers Karamazov*.

Joseph Frank, *Dostoevsky— The Mantle of the Prophet, 1871–81*, vol. 5.

Questions to Consider:

1. When Ivan makes contact with the world around him, through Smerdiakov, the result is a murderous disaster. What evidence does Dostoevsky give to show that Alyosha's going out into the world will produce better results?

2. Dmitrii is convicted for a crime that we know he did not commit. Is this conviction a commentary on the legal reforms in Russia, or is it a statement about Dmitrii's moral need for suffering?

Lecture Fifteen—Transcript
The Novelistic Presence of Christ and Satan

In relating to the "Tale of the Grand Inquisitor," it is important to know that Dostoevsky, by this time, had become a very strong supporter of the tsarist regime, so strong, as a matter of fact, that there were many people in the regime who became very much interested in him, most especially one man by the name—for most Americans, unpronounceable—Pobedonostsev. Pobedonostsev was a very clever conservative, if not reactionary, who realized well the talent of Dostoevsky and was very much interested in helping him where he could, even arranged an interview with the tsar himself, between Dostoevsky and the tsar himself. Dostoevsky was in the habit of sometimes giving him copies of the manuscripts of his novel that he was working on. When Pobedonostsev received the manuscript of the "Tale of the Grand Inquisitor," he became very worried. He said, "Look, I thought you were on our side. This seems to be an argument for atheism. Have you gone over to the other side? Do you really think that what you've written here helps the regime and helps the cause of conservatism, which you, yourself, seem to want to support?" And Dostoevsky replied this way. He said, "Look, I wanted to show those so-called atheists"—talking about his critics and about many of the intellectuals of his day—"I wanted to show those so-called atheists that with my little finger I could make a better argument for atheism than they could do with their entire head." And, of course, this seems to indicate that the thing is, indeed, an argument for atheism, although one might argue about that. "But," he said, "the whole rest of the novel is a reply to this. The whole rest of the novel is an attempt, not only an attempt, to show but will show that these problems can be solved, that, as a matter of fact, there is an answer, and this answer is to be found in the kind of salvation that I consider Christianity to be."

And, of course, Dostoevsky follows this up clearly with the section in the novel that has to do with Father Zosima, the teachings of Father Zosima. And as we read this section, we begin to realize that what Dostoevsky is doing is creating a new gospel for, of course, in his case, the 19th century, but clearly the 20th century and perhaps the 21st century as well. The gospel, of course, is an account of the life and teachings of Christ. This particular section is an account of the life and teaching of Zosima. It seems that Zosima, when he was a young man, was a very different kind of a person than he was now. He was one of those saints who sinned his way to Christ, so to speak. He engaged in all kinds of—he was a member of the military; he engaged in duels—he engaged in all kinds of things, but then he realized that this was not the way to live and instead became a monk.

And as a monk, he urged the monks to somehow become aware of how the people felt, to become aware of the sufferings that people were going through, and to respond to that in ways that they could really understand. And, of course, the only solution for this was the whole question of love, the ability, through Christ, coming to the kind of freedom that people wanted with a combination of love. Hell, as he put it, is the place where it's impossible to express or to receive love. These are the teachings of Zosima. And, of course, as he does it, he uses many different parts of the Bible in a very lively way, in a way that is very, very close to people's experience. It's clear that Zosima, just as the elder whom Dostoevsky had talked to earlier—we talked about in the last lecture—knew very well how to appeal to the psychology of people and he wanted the monks to be able to do this.

Furthermore, he tells Alyosha, "Look, Alyosha" he said, "you cannot remain in a monastery." Alyosha tries to object to this, "No, no, I want to stay here. This is a place where I am happy. This is a place where I really want to be." He says:

> No, you have to go out into the world. You have to make it clear to people in the world that a Christian life, a decent life, a moral life is a way that they can live and, at the same time, achieve both happiness and love and all of those things. As a matter of fact, you have to give an answer to that great unanswered question of the Bible.

As you may remember, at the very beginning of the Bible, when Cain, who has, of course, murdered his brother, is asked by God, "Where is your brother?" Cain replies, "How should I know? I can't constantly keep track of my brother. Am I my brother's keeper?" And, of course, that question, "Am I my brother's keeper?"—Am I responsible for the sanctity and for the happiness and for the morality and many other things of my brother?—is one that goes all the way through the Bible. It's always a question. There's never a final answer to this, although Dostoevsky surely thought that the final answer was in Christ.

Alyosha has to go out and try to solve that question: Am I really responsible for my brother? Am I really responsible for other people in the world? Is there an imperative for me to help the life of other people? Have we been put in this world, as the Old Testament and Mohammed says, to help one another? Have human beings been put here so that we can help one another or have we been put here for other reasons? That's the question to which Alyosha is assigned to give a positive answer by going out into the world.

Of course, Alyosha is deeply attached to his elder. He sets great store by his teachings, he sets great store by his life and, above all, he believes that the elder will prove to everyone that he was indeed a holy man by dying in what was called sanctity; that is to say, he was—perhaps a legend, perhaps a story in the Russian Orthodox Church, that when a saint died, his body didn't smell the way other bodies did, but rather gave forth a fragrance. Furthermore, there was great political opposition to the elder in the monastery. There were people led by a character named Father Ferapont, who thought that Zosima was a terrible man, a man to be opposed, and, of course, a man whose position caused great jealousy not only in Ferapont but in the people who followed Ferapont.

Well, Zosima dies and, of course, to Alyosha's deep and total consternation, not only does the body not only not give off fragrance but it starts to smell much earlier than most bodies normally smell, and within a few hours the room is almost overpowered with the smell, to the extent they even have to open the window. Alyosha is devastated and, of course, Ferapont and his people are exulted. They said, "You see, we told you he wasn't really a holy man. We're the ones to be followed, not Zosima." Alyosha is deeply hurt; he takes this as a kind of an insult. And, of course, you understand the business of stench in Dostoevsky is a very, very important thing. Remember stinking Lizaveta, remember Smerdiakov; the fact that there were certain parts of the house of Fedor Pavlovich that always smelled of the cooking of cabbage. And if you ever smelled that, you know it smells very much like the disintegration of a human corpse.

Alyosha is so overwhelmed by this that, as a matter of fact, he decides he'll have to leave the monastery. He could no longer believe in something. He was so looking forward to the sanctity of the death and it didn't turn out to be sanctity at all; on the contrary, it seemed only to give ammunition to those who opposed Zosima. And so he went out into the world and, of course, ironically, it was the stench of Father Zosima that forced him to follow, that gave the effect that made him follow the advice that Zosima had given him, namely: "You must leave the monastery; you must go out into the world." Dostoevsky always proceeds by paradox and by contradiction. And so Alyosha leaves the monastery. His old friend Rakitin, the skeptic, is all too ready, "Well, I see at long last your eyes have been opened. Our little saint is no longer a little saint. Listen, have some vodka." And to his amazement—you understand a monk was not supposed to drink vodka—to Rakitin's amazement, Alyosha says, "Yes, give it to me. I'll drink the vodka." And he says to him, "Here, have some sausage." A monk wasn't ordinarily supposed to eat sausage; he was supposed to be kind of semi-fasting. Rakitin is amazed. He said, "Well, our little saint has certainly fallen very quickly and very far." And Rakitin remembers that Grushen'ka, the infernal woman, has promised him a certain amount of money if he can bring Alyosha to her because she wants to seduce not only the old man who, of course, by that time has been murdered, and not only Dmitrii but also all members of the Karamazov family. She has now set her cap to seduce Alyosha.

Well, Rakitin says, "Well, in that case, I know there is somebody who would like to see you." He said, "Lead on; I'll go to the woman." And so Rakitin brings Alyosha to Grushen'ka's place, to the place where Grushen'ka lives. Well, she is ready to devour him whole. Of course, she sets herself forth in front of him in the most seductive fashion. And no sooner does he sit down than she sits on his lap and starts to embrace him. Alyosha, of course, has never before in his life been close to a woman. His body sets to trembling; he is terribly upset. He doesn't know what to do. And Grushen'ka uses all the tricks of an experienced seductress in embracing him and kissing him and trying to somehow arouse him. And as she is doing this—and, of course, Alyosha is in terrible fear and trembling; he doesn't know what to do—all of a sudden she hears from Rakitin that our little saint, his elder, has died. She says, "Ah." She hears that Zosima has died, and all of a sudden something gets to her very, very deeply. She jumps off his lap; she jumps off Alyosha's lap. She says, "Good heavens, forgive me. I understand what this means to you. I'm deeply sorry. I deeply apologize for what I have just done." And you realize that Grushen'ka too is suffering from a very deep sense of guilt and, you might say, almost self-loathing.

She begins to think in what way can she appeal to Alyosha—as a sister to a brother, rather than as a would-be seducer. And she recalls that once she heard a legend that there was a woman once who, the one decent thing this woman had done in her lifetime was to give an onion to somebody who was almost starved. And when this particular woman who had given the onion died and tried to get to paradise, they said, "Well, there's only one thing you've done in your life that would enable you to get to paradise: that was the onion." They said, "Here is an onion." It's hanging from the entranceway to paradise, to heaven. "Grab that onion, and if you can hold on to the onion, we'll pull you into paradise." And so she grabs the onion and they begin to pull her and, of course, when other sinners see that, they try to hold on there because they too want to be dragged into paradise. And pretty soon she has a whole string of people and she fears the onion will break. She says, "No, get off of me. It's my onion." And she tries to kick them off, and as soon as she tries to kick them off, the onion breaks and, of course, she doesn't get to paradise. And Grushen'ka says, "Once in my life perhaps, I have given that onion. Once in my life perhaps, I understand that you don't push off other people when they try to share your good fortune," obviously referring to what she has just done to Alyosha.

And Alyosha understands; this appeals to Alyosha in a very deep way. He then returns to the monastery and hears the protagonists, the people who were on the side of Zosima, reading the gospel. And as he hears this, he falls into a slumber and he has a dream, this time a very good dream, a very sweet dream, about the famous story of Christ at Cana, where Christ performs the miracle of turning the water into wine in time for the wedding celebration. And as Alyosha visualizes this, thanks to the decency of Grushen'ka who, in a certain sense, has given him that onion, sees this beautiful dream, as he sees the dream, he seems to hear both the voice of Christ and the voice of Zosima and he somehow recovers his faith. I suppose some people might see this as an overly sweet, a sort of a saccharinely sweet scene. I see it as something that goes very deeply into the feelings of Alyosha and undoubtedly into the feelings of Dostoevsky.

Now, of course, for Alyosha's brother, Dmitrii, the relations with women have been far from salutary. There is not only the infernal woman whom I've already mentioned, Grushen'ka; there is also Katerina Ivanovna—obviously a name that Dostoevsky liked because he uses it again in this novel—whom he has insulted in a very bad way after helping her by covering the debts of her father. Her father had made off with certain money from the military and Mitia took the money, which he had got from his father as his inheritance, to her so she could pay it back to her father. In the beginning, of course, he had been very good to Katerina Ivanovna and she had kind of fallen for him; her passions were directed in his direction. And while she was doing this, instead he veered towards Grushen'ka. So, of course there were very jealous feelings between her and Grushen'ka, and Dostoevsky shows this in the novel in a very, very strong way.

Dmitrii is tremendously eager to get Grushen'ka to come with him. And, finally, after the murder of his father, where, as a matter of fact, he has been very close to the actual murder at the time, although when we see the murder going on we never quite see who actually did it, circumstances are such that all the people around the town believe that it is Dmitrii who has killed his father, that Dmitrii is a parasite. The fact that all of a sudden he seems to have money, the fact that there was a certain amount of blood on his clothes, the way it was done, the fact that the old man had been waiting for Grushen'ka and thought that Grushen'ka was there, all these circumstances added up to people believing that Dmitrii had really killed him and, of course, the way it's described, we don't know whether Dmitrii has actually killed him or not; although Dmitrii was at the place where the murder took place.

Now, of course, he is trying to get Grushen'ka to fall in love with him. He is trying to get Grushen'ka to marry him, and you learn that she, as a matter of fact, is waiting for a former Polish lover who has come to take her back. And, of course, there is a scene where Dostoevsky, like a Russian of that particular time, makes rather nasty fun of the fellow who is the Polish lover. You get some nuance, some reflection, of the dislike that existed at that time between the Russians on one side and the Poles on the other. And as this is going on, Dmitrii comes into the room, and somehow he gets the Poles to go away because he gives them money to go away. He then orders a tremendous amount of food and drink and they get together to have a real Russian banquet in the countryside. And Dostoevsky goes to town in describing what a real Russian *debauch*, what a real Russian banquet is, with gypsy dancers, with sweets, with all kinds of wines, with vodka, with the finest kind of food. Dmitrii seems to spend his last kopek in order to bring off this tremendous banquet and impress Grushen'ka. And just as Grushen'ka, in the scene with Alyosha, Grushen'ka turned from a rather nasty seducer into a very understanding person who understands what love is, so with Dmitrii in this scene she begins to understand that she has made a big mistake in going for this Polish lover, that Dmitrii Karamazov, the Russian, is a person of deep feeling, of deep understanding, that she could be together with him in a very good way. And she gets the idea that she will eventually become the wife of Dmitrii. As a matter of fact, at one point, he wants to sleep together with her. She says, "No, no, no. Let's wait, let's do it in the right way. Let's wait until we get married." And as they sort of doze off in the room, they hear the sounds of the banquet, they hear the celebrations going on next door, and through the sleep and the dreams of Dmitrii, you suddenly hear bells. Dmitrii is dreaming of bells that are going on. And, of course, he suddenly wakes up to realize that, as a matter of fact, there are real bells. A police *troika*, a police carriage, has come to investigate him and, of course, there were bells on any good *troika* in those days.

And suddenly, from having experienced the warmth and the wonder of being with Grushen'ka, Dmitrii is plunged into the hell of a police interrogation because the prosecutor, Ippolit Kirillovich, who doesn't like Dmitrii anyway, is deeply convinced that Dmitrii has murdered his own father. And as they go through that investigation, you realize that circumstances are piling up in a way that people really are going to believe—there is really going to be very, very good proof—that Dmitrii did commit that murder because the question is, Where did he get that money? The money, of course, had been waiting with the old man for Grushen'ka to come, and whoever murdered him obviously took the money. This goes on and on, through many, many different circumstances. They remember that Dmitrii had threatened once upon a time that he would kill the old man, that he had beaten the old man, beaten him to the extent that the old fellow was bloody. It looked very bad for Dmitrii. And, at a certain point, they said, "Now you have to undress." He said, "Look, why do I have to undress?" They said, "That's part of the investigation. We have to see you completely without clothes on." And, of course, Dmitrii has a toe of which he is somewhat ashamed; it's a somewhat misshapen toe, and that toe is exposed, and suddenly we get a replay here of the exposure of the unadorned self that I talked about earlier in *Poor Folk*. And you also, here, get something of a reprise of a play that Dostoevsky really admired, *King Lear*. You remember where King Lear suddenly strips to the bone, strips so that he has no clothes on in the heat in the middle of a terrible storm, the idea being that only when one is completely unprotected by clothes does one get to the real person, and Dmitrii is now subjected to that terribly painful test.

Well, it's clear that they have reason to arrest Dmitrii. He is forced to go with them, and it soon becomes clear to all the townspeople that there is going to be a trial, that it's going to try Dmitrii for the murder of his own father. Meanwhile, we then go back to the other brother, that is, Ivan, the intellectual brother. Now Ivan is beginning to feel a terrible sense of guilt for the murder of his father because, of course, it is he who has preached to the world that there is no God. And if there is no God, then everything is allowed. And, of course, this has been particularly picked up by his half-brother, Smerdiakov, who is most strongly attracted to this kind of teaching, that, "Well, if there is no God, then I'm free to do anything that I want to in this world." Ivan is beginning to feel more and more that he, too, is guilty of the murder of his father even though obviously he didn't commit the actual murder. And, of course, it is rather interesting that Sigmund Freud, in his development of the idea of the Oedipus complex, wrote an essay where he said there are three great examples in history, in the history of literature, of parricide. He talks about *Oedipus* of Sophocles, he talks about *Hamlet* of Shakespeare, and he talks about *The Brothers Karamazov* of Dostoevsky, putting them all in this category. I'm not trying to make an argument here for Freud's theory, but it is interesting that a superior intellect like that of Freud would see these three works of literature as somehow connected with each other thematically and, of course, obviously connected with this whole idea of the Oedipus complex, where the son has both love and hatred towards the father and sometimes is capable even of the killing of the father.

Ivan is going through this. While he is going through this he decides to go to see Smerdiakov, his half-brother. Smerdiakov, who had earlier been a tremendous admirer of Ivan, now looks at him with a certain considerable distaste, almost a kind of intellectual condescension. "Yes, it was you who got me to this state and look where I am. Look at the kind of fix I'm in. I'm sick and nobody wants to have anything to do with me." As a matter of fact, in three interviews with Smerdiakov, in one of these interviews Smerdiakov tells you that it was he that murdered the old man. He even shows him the rubles that he took from the time when he committed the murder. Ivan understands that his brother, Dmitrii, is being unrightfully accused of a murder. The result is that he's going to try and help his brother. But as he has these interviews with Smerdiakov, he feels more and more badly about what he's done. He gets an increasingly sick, almost insane state of mind. As he goes back to his room, planning what he's going to do, suddenly another presence is in the room. When he looks more carefully—now you remember that scene with Svidrigailov in *Crime and Punishment*—here he sees somebody dressed as a Russian gentleman, very well dressed.

As this person begins to talk with him more and more, he suddenly understands who this person is. It's the devil himself who has come to visit Ivan, who has come to torture Ivan. You get a marvelous half ironic, half comic, half horrible scene, three halves there, of an interview between Ivan and the devil. It's interesting, in this particular scene, the very first sputnik, that is, the very first artificial satellite in the world—in imagination, of course—is sent into the heavens. The devil talks about ethereal spaces, a place where it can be 150 degrees below zero, and tells Ivan of a game village girls play where they convince a peasant to put his tongue to an axe when it's very, very cold, only 30 degrees below zero, but still very, very cold. Of course, the tongue sticks to the axe; the peasant has to tear the axe off, it being very painful. Ivan says, "Well, what happens to the axe? Can there be an axe there?" Ivan is talking about the ethereal world, 150 degrees below zero. The devil says, "Well, it would begin flying around the earth like a satellite, like a sputnik. It rises and falls like an artificial satellite in the sky." So you can say it was Dostoevsky who launched the first cosmic satellite.

The devil also talks about the Russian atheist who denies the existence of God, who denies the existence of an afterlife and denies the existence of paradise. He suddenly dies and wakes up to find himself in paradise. He thinks it a terrible scandal; this place doesn't exist. He lies on the ground and pounds and pounds on the ground, "No, it can't be here. This place doesn't exist." He does this for several eons. Suddenly it hits him—there really is a paradise. He walks millions of miles in order to get to paradise and becomes such an enthusiastic preacher of God in paradise that the Russian atheist won't even let him shake hands with him. The devil said, "You Russians, you always go to extremes."

Then the devil brings up the Grand Inquisitor. He obviously knows what's on Ivan's mind. Ivan says, "Don't you dare bring up the "Tale of the Grand Inquisitor." The devil says, "Oh, no. That was quite a good story you told there." As the conversation goes on, Ivan picks up a glass and throws it at the devil. The devil jumps up. Ivan has obviously remembered Martin Luther, who threw an inkstand at the devil. Suddenly there is a knocking at the window; the devil disappears. Ivan finds that Alyosha has come to tell him that Smerdiakov has committed suicide. Smerdiakov has hanged himself. Ivan realizes it's up to him to save his brother, Dmitrii, from the false accusation of parricide.

Then, near the end of the novel, we have the scene of what Dostoevsky calls a judicial error. A trial that takes place with a verdict really is an error. It's the trial of Dmitrii. The curiosity of the whole town has been aroused. All the women of the town are tremendously on the side of Dmitrii; they find him a very attractive, romantic figure. All the men of the town are very jealous of Dmitrii and want to see him convicted. Dmitrii has a defender with a Polish name, an attorney from Petersburg who has come to defend him in this very prominent trial. He'll get a tremendous advantage from his name being known throughout the country. At that time there had been some legal reforms in Russia; a system they had been working on for 20 or 30 years was being put into effect. This was during the reign of Alexander II, one of the most liberal of all the tsars. The idea was to bring Russian law more connected with western ideas of jurisprudence, the Napoleonic code, the idea of the person was innocent until proven guilty, the idea there would be a defense lawyer who wouldn't have to believe in the innocence or guilt of his client but simply make the best argument he possibly could for the client. There would be a prosecuting attorney who would make the best argument he possibly could make. Then it would be up to a jury to sift out evidence and a judge who would see to it that things were done according to the law. Now this was a system that anyone living in America understands very well. This was something new in Russia and, of course, Dostoevsky is giving his own take on this reform and this new system in the course of the novel.

Now Fetiukovich, the defense attorney, is obviously convinced that Dmitrii really did kill the old man; he's quite cynical. And so what he does is to make an argument, make the very best argument for something which he believes is false; that is to say, he's trying to make the very best argument he can for Dmitrii's innocence, although he doesn't really believe in Dmitrii's innocence. And what he manages to do is to make an absolute monkey out of every witness that the prosecution calls. When the old servant who has been so kind to Dmitrii comes and is absolutely convinced that nevertheless Dmitrii did the murder, Fetiukovich asks him, "What year is this?" And, of course, the old man—he's a peasant, he's illiterate—he doesn't know. He says, "Your honor, he's wont to make fun of me." And of course everybody laughs. And he goes—this happens with witness after witness. Fetiukovich shows that what they say makes no sense whatsoever.

The prosecutor, Ippolit Kirillovich, hates Dmitrii and is deeply convinced that Dmitrii really is guilty and he argues passionately for what he believes is the truth to show that Dmitrii is guilty. But, of course, he's very frustrated by the skill of Fetiukovich, the defender, because Fetiukovich, he is making mincemeat out of every one of his witnesses. But at the final moment Katerina Ivanovna, one of the infernal women who is terribly angry at Dmitrii because she knows he wants to go off with Grushen'ka and has the jealousy of a woman scorned, suddenly gets up in the courtroom and produces a letter that Dmitrii has written to her, and in this letter he talks passionately about how he hates his father, wishes him dead, and will plan the murder of his father. And, of course, that tips the balance; that eventually causes the convicting of Dmitrii for a crime he didn't commit.

Now what's interesting is that Fetiukovich, who is absolutely cynical and who doesn't believe the arguments he is making, is actually arguing for what we, the readers, know is the truth. We know that Dmitrii did not murder the old man, that, as a matter of fact, it was

Smerdiakov. But here is Fetiukovich, the cynic, arguing for the truth, whereas Ippolit Kirillovich, who is deeply, sincerely convinced that Mitia is wrong, is guilty, is actually arguing for something that's false. The cynic is somehow leading to truth and the sincere man is actually leading to an unjust verdict. With this irony, I think, Dostoevsky is trying to give his own opinion about the notion of human justice, because, of course, what he believes is that human beings can't judge other human beings.

But the novel ends with a sermon by Alyosha at a stone at the grave of a young man who has died, Ilusha, a young man. And as Alyosha is preaching the sermon to young boys whom he obviously is going to bring up in a much better way than the Karamazovs have been brought up—part of the novel is about how young people are brought up—Dostoevsky says, the same Dostoevsky who has so many heavy things through the novel, very lightly, in one phrase thrown away that you can miss very easily when you read the book, he says, "Strange to say, the body of the young boy didn't smell." Remember the contrast, of course, was Zosima. Well, after all, it was natural. This was a young boy cut off like a young flower. Zosima was an old man cut off in the summertime. This is wintertime. There are all kinds of natural reasons why he would smell and, yet, he didn't smell. And, of course, the implication is that resurrection will, after all, have taken place, that that seed of wheat which was in the earth will give forth fruit if it dies. And, of course, the legacy that Dostoevsky left with this novel, and all the other novels, is a very, very powerful legacy.

Lecture Sixteen
Lev Nikolaevich Tolstoy, 1828–1910

Scope:

In the large novels by Tolstoy, the reader often feels as if he or she is entering an entire universe. Although this is undoubtedly an exaggeration, there is something God-like about the massiveness and the life-giving quality of Tolstoy's writing. His life spans almost the whole period of highest Russian literary creativity. His opinions cover a vast range of Russian and human affairs, yet he can also be concerned with the smallest and most banal details of everyday family life. This dichotomy is perhaps best summed up in the beginning of his second great novel, *Anna Karenina*: "All happy families resemble one another; each unhappy family is unhappy in its own way. All was confusion in the Oblonsky household." This literary giant lost his mother at an early age and his father not much later. He was thrown out of the University of Kazan', and he partook in the fighting of the Crimean War in 1854–1855. His first work was a remarkable account of childhood, adolescence, and youth; shortly thereafter, he published an account of the long and bloody battle for the city of Sevastopol', which controls the sea access to Crimea. A Siberian prisoner was deeply impressed by the writing of the young man. That prisoner's name was F. M. Dostoevsky.

Outline

I. Tolstoy was born into an aristocratic family, the owners of estates in the Russian countryside near the city of Tula, to the southeast of Moscow. His mother died when he was an infant, and his father died when he was a young boy; he was mostly brought up by aunts. He would eventually possess an inherited estate, Iasnaia Poliana ("Clear Glade"). The name of this country home and farm, near Tula, would later become world famous.

   A. As a young man, Tolstoy was sent off to the old and well-established University of Kazan'. His high intelligence, together with his wild addiction to gambling and the pursuit of women, did not escape the notice of university officials.

   B. The president of the university was a man by the name of Lobachevsky, one of the most famous names in the 19th-century history of mathematics. He tried to talk sense to the young man, urging him to use his remarkable talent and intellect for good purposes within the university and to behave himself in a more circumspect manner, appropriate—in Lobachecsky's opinion—to a person bearing the title belonging to a member of the Tolstoy family.

C. Tolstoy, even as a young man, had a very different idea of what was appropriate behavior for a Russian aristocrat. He did not change his ways and soon, in 1847, found himself excluded from the university. In no way reformed by his experience or the good advice of Lobachevsky, Tolstoy continued his dissolute life in Moscow and in St. Petersburg.

II. In 1854, he wrote the first of a three-part story. The later parts were called *Adolescence* and *Youth*. He sent *Childhood* to Nekrasov, the same editor who had discovered and encouraged the young Dostoevsky in 1845; the editor was obviously a man who recognized genuine talent when he saw it.

A. *Childhood* is not autobiographical, but Tolstoy's childhood had much to do with the many psychological insights in the story.

B. Nekrasov's judgment was fully confirmed by the reactions from readers. Praise flew in from all sides, including from Dostoevsky, although there were some readers who were shocked by a young man picturing his parents and elders with the objective eye of the literary observer, rather than presenting them exclusively with filial devotion.

C. Tolstoy was remarkably adroit in beginning his novels. In *Childhood*, he begins with the waking up of the 10-year-old Nikolen'ka. The boy's tutor, a German who has been hired by the family to look after the youngster and educate him, has been swatting flies over his bed.

    1. Nikolen'ka reacts with annoyance and despair, thinking the German is trying to torture him because he is the youngest in the family.

    2. Just a few moments later, Nikolen'ka is deeply ashamed of himself for having made up a bad dream about the death of his mother to explain to Karl Ivanovich his bad mood. He realizes that the tutor is deeply attached to him and wishes him well.

D. The highly sensitive nature of the 10-year-old boy, his introspective nature and tendency to constantly analyze his own exaggerated sensitivity and change his judgments about people—these are traits that are representative of the mature Tolstoy.

E. As a contrast to Karl Ivanovich, Tolstoy presents a Frenchman, St. Jerome. His cold vanity comes as a complete contrast to the warmth of Karl Ivanovich. The French phrases constantly thrown about by the new tutor serve only to irritate Nikolen'ka and deepen his distaste for the Frenchman, with his petty vanities and self-righteous code of conventional good behavior.

F. All through the tales, the expression *comme il faut* ("as one should behave in good society") takes on a pejorative meaning, both for Nikolen'ka and for the author of the tales. For Tolstoy, *comme il faut* is always a nasty contrast to genuine and natural feeling.

III. Nikolen'ka takes considerable pains to show us what real feelings are, as opposed to the surface reactions often presented in society. Verbal expression for Tolstoy was far less important than body language.

    A. This importance becomes clear when Nikolen'ka goes into his father's study and witnesses a conversation between the aristocratic owner of the estate and his chief steward, a serf.

        1. When the master spoke, the steward listened with a respectful look on his face. Yet his fingers, clasped behind his back, began to move quickly and in different patterns.

        2. It was as if his fingers told his secret thoughts, by no means respectful to the master's opinions, as opposed to the words and gestures of respect that the master could see.

    B. We see this contrast between real emotion and surface convention even more strongly when Nikolen'ka analyzes his own reactions to his mother's death. Although Tolstoy's own mother died when he was 2 years old, Nikolen'ka is more than 10 years old when his mother dies. Nikolen'ka cannot cry, although he knows he is supposed to. It is only much later that he can express his grief.

C. This scene has a remarkable psychological resemblance to Stendhal's lightly fictionalized autobiography, *The Life of Henry Brulard.*

  1. Stendhal talks about his inability to cry at his mother's funeral, precisely because he felt the loss so acutely. People around him could not understand and considered him hard-hearted and unfeeling.

  2. Tolstoy greatly admired Stendhal at a time when the French writer was not widely popular.

  3. Yet he could not have read the autobiography, because it was not published until long after Tolstoy's tales.

  4. This similarity shows how deeply the psychology and the writing of the two men ran parallel, despite their national and ideological differences.

IV. Tolstoy also has a great deal to say about education in these tales. For example, by listening to St. Jerome, Nikolen'ka was able to pass the university entrance examination, but at the same time, he totally rejected everything St. Jerome did, because he considered him a person of terrible vanity.

V. The narrator of these tales does have one statement that reverberates through Tolstoy and through literature.

  A. *"Schastlivaia, schastlivaia, nevozvratimaia pora detstva! Kak ne liubit', ne leleiat' vospominanii o nei? Vospominaniia eti osvezhaiut, vozvyshaiut moiu dushu..."* ("O happy, happy, irretrievable time of childhood! How is it possible not to love, not to cuddle its memories? These memories refresh me and raise up my soul...")

  B. Something in the essence of childhood is deeply moving to Tolstoy. The quality of childishness is very important to understanding the psychology and characters of the mature author.

VI. During the time that he was writing about the life of Nikolen'ka and at least partly about his own upbringing, Tolstoy was also serving as an officer in the Russian army during its disastrous campaigns in the Crimean War (1854–1855). He described military life and the terrible destruction of war in a way that gripped the imaginations of many readers.

A. The stories were all entitled *Sevastopol'*, the fortified city on the south of the Crimean peninsula, which juts out below Russia into the Black Sea. It was besieged by the British, French, and Turkish allies and defended heroically—but in the end unsuccessfully—by the Russian troops described by Tolstoy.

B. In the beginning, inspired by the kind of patriotism common at the beginning of a war, Tolstoy described events in a way that gained great favor from the Russian government.

C. In the second and third installments, Tolstoy gave a realistic picture of the horrors and some of the confusion on the Russian side. This picture was received less favorably by the Russian government, and Tolstoy was denied advancement in the military. He later said that he could not be a general in the army, so he would be a general in literature.

D. He had a lot to say about the nature of true courage and steadfastness, as opposed to the phony kind, often touted in military rhetoric. The collection of stories shows his thinking about the realities of wartime and the famous military valor of the Russian army. One can easily see how Tolstoy put this thinking together with the accounts he had read in Stendhal's novel *The Charterhouse of Parma.*

E. In Stendhal's novel, the protagonist, Fabrizio, who worships Napoleon, moves heaven and earth to fight with Napoleon's forces. Fabrizio is at the Battle of Waterloo, which we see not through the strategy of the generals and military analysis, but through the eyes of a drunken man. Yet he exhibited courage beyond what was officially touted as courage.

F. For Tolstoy, genuine courage was found in the common soldiers who held their ground through great suffering yet were often totally ignored by the government.

VII.   It is equally important to remember Tolstoy's famous statement near the end of the second fragment called *Sevastopol'*. In answer to his readers' questions, "Where is your expression of evil... where is kindness...? Who is the villain, who is the hero?" Tolstoy says: "The hero of my tale, whom I love with all my soul's powers, whom I have tried to evoke in all his beauty, and who always was, is, and will be magnificent, is the truth." There could not be a better place to begin our consideration of *War and Peace.*

    A. Tolstoy's experience of the Crimean War taught him a great deal about war and the military, whereas his understanding of peace encompassed a great deal of what people call the banality of everyday family life and relationships.

    B. Family life, for Tolstoy, is also discernible in war. Thus, his *Tales of Sevastopol'* is the workbook for his grand novels, in which no two individuals or animals are alike.

Suggested Reading:

Lev Tolstoy, *Tales of Army Life*, translated by Louise and Aylmer Maude.

Lev Tolstoy, *Childhood, Boyhood, and Youth*, translated and with an introduction by Michael Scammell.

T. G. S. Cain, *Tolstoy.*

Questions to Consider:

1. Is the notion of *comme il faut*—the ordinary conventions of polite society—as bad as Tolstoy presents it? What would the author reply to a person who defended the necessity of day-to-day conventions and politeness in a civil society?

2. In seeking the truth, which Tolstoy calls the real hero of his Sevastopol' tales, how does he arrive at his notion of military bravery, shorn of its official governmental exaggerations?

Lecture Sixteen—Transcript
Lev Nikolaevich Tolstoy, 1828–1910

When we talk about the art of Dostoevsky and the tremendous impression that he made on people's imagination, in the context of Russian literature, the name that almost immediately comes to mind is Tolstoy, Lev Nikolaevich Tolstoy, who, of course, to a very great extent lived almost at the same time as Dostoevsky. They were born eight years apart; of course, Tolstoy outlived Dostoevsky by several decades. They were very, very different kinds of people, very different kinds of writers and men. And yet, somehow, their two writings together seemed to define a whole epic of literature—in the case of Tolstoy, one might almost say a whole world, a whole universe of literature. When you read one of the great novels of Tolstoy, you feel as if you are kind of drawn into a universe; there is something godlike about his creation of these novels. He is a fascinating individual and, of course, a great writer, and he began his life on an estate, very much unlike Dostoevsky, on a large estate in the Russian countryside near the city of Tula, which is something like a five- or six-hour drive to the southeast of Moscow, a drive, of course, in the modern sense of the automobile. In Tolstoy's day it took quite a long time to get there by horse and carriage.

Tolstoy's mother died when he was about two years old—this is the actual truth of his biography—and he was brought up largely by several aunts, although his father lived until he was somewhat older into his childhood. He never really knew what it meant to have a personal, close mother, although the aunts did their very best to raise him as best they could. He obviously grew up as a man with considerable resources and a man who stood to inherit considerable resources, together with an estate that these days has become world famous. It's called Iasnaia Poliana, which in Russian means "Clear Glade" or "Clear Field," something like that. And, of course, he had, you might say, the security, the stability to realize that he could always fall back on that. Perhaps, at least, partly because of that, certainly partly because of his own very strange temperament, his early years were marked by a tremendous kind of debauchery, a tremendous kind of absence of discipline in his personal life, which meant that when he went to the university—he actually went to the University of Kazan, a city roughly four to five hundred miles to the east of Moscow, a city which, as a matter of fact, you may remember had been the center of Tatar power near the existence of the old Kiev—he didn't behave himself very well. There was a tremendous amount of gambling, a tremendous amount of drinking, not to mention activities with women that we might not entirely approve of these days and perhaps in those days as well.

Eventually he was called into the office of the man who was the president of Kazan University in those days, a very famous name from 19th -century mathematics. His name was Lobachevsky, about whom, if you know anything about mathematics, you have certainly heard, a man who was very famous also in certain satires that later on were sung about Russia in those days. Lobachevsky tried to talk to the young Tolstoy, man to man, you might say. He said, "Look here, you are a person with considerable intelligence, considerable talent." Lobachevsky was no fool; he recognized talent when he saw it. "Why are you behaving this way? Why don't you use that intelligence, why don't you use that sensitivity, to get yourself to behave the way an aristocrat really should behave? the way a man who bears the name of Tolstoy should behave? You shouldn't be doing this. You shouldn't be involved in this kind of debauchery." Well, Tolstoy, I'm not quite sure what he said. My inclination is that he told him to go to hell. And very soon Tolstoy found himself thrown out of the university. They didn't want to have anything to do with a person who behaved in this way.

So Tolstoy went back to Moscow and partly to Petersburg, where he continued to behave himself in just exactly the way I've described above, a tremendous dissolution, an enormous amount of gambling. He piled up terrible debts which he really couldn't pay at that time. Of course, relationships with women were temporary and were simply the matter of attractions at the moment. In short, this was a very different kind of Tolstoy from what we know from the later works and certainly what we know from the man who became a preacher, which Tolstoy became at the end of his life.

In any case, in the middle of the 19th century, in the 1850s, Tolstoy had some contact with writers in Petersburg. He began to get some idea of what literature was all about and he got the impression that he, too, would like to participate in literature. And then, in 1854, he wrote the first of three collections of stories, the first called *Childhood*, the second called *Adolescence*, the third called *Youth*— that is, *Detstvo*, *Otrochestvo*, and *Iunost'*. And he submitted the first part of the stories, that is, *Childhood*, to an editor whose name you have already heard, Nekrasov—you remember, the one to whom Dostoevsky first sent his works, something like 12 or 13 years before then. Nekrasov was obviously a good judge of literary talent and he decided to publish the work, *Childhood*, by Tolstoy. Many people took it as Tolstoy's own autobiography; of course, that's not true. To a very great extent it is fiction, but obviously the childhood experience of Tolstoy had much to do with the psychological insights that Tolstoy puts into this novella, this so-called autobiography. As a matter of fact, when it was published, praise came in from all directions. By the way, it was not published under his name, under his last name; it was published under the initials L.N., which obviously stand for Lev Nikolaevich, his first name and patronymic.

Nobody knew exactly who it was, but, as I said, praise flew in from all directions, including, by the way, a man who was already in exile in Siberia, a man by the name of Fedor Mikhailovich Dostoevsky. Dostoevsky, having no idea who it was, said, "This is a talent which is going to brighten the Russian firmament in literature." Dostoevsky recognized immediately that here was a real talent although, again, he had no idea who it was. The sole criticisms that came in were those who said, "Here is a young man who has the nerve to criticize his own parents." And they thought that somehow this was immoral, this wasn't right, so *Childhood* did come in for some criticism—by the way, not only in Russia but also in England, where people were shocked at the idea that a young man would have critical remarks about his parents.

But, in any case, this story establishes, begins his reputation as a beginning writer of considerable promise. Like much of Tolstoy's work, the beginning of this novel is very adroit. It deals with a young man named Nikolenka. Of course, Nikolenka is connected with the name Nikolai. Tolstoy is Lev Nikolaevich, so he might well have had his own father somewhat in mind with this name. And it begins with the gradual awakening from sleep of a young man who has a German tutor by the name of Karl Ivanovich. And at this particular point he doesn't want to get up and he's quite annoyed that Karl Ivanovich is waking him up. And, as a matter of fact, Karl Ivanovich wakes him up by swatting flies over his head. And of course, he hears the noise of that flyswatter slapping against some solid surface and it annoys him tremendously. He gets up all out of sorts. Karl Ivanovich is

©2006 The Teaching Company Limited Partnership

really a kindly sort of man, although at this particular point Nikolenka is annoyed with this terrible Karl Ivanovich. "He's always bothering me; he's making me do it. He's a nasty man; he just wants to see me suffer." Karl Ivanovich, of course, is sensitive enough to realize the young man is out of sorts. He says, "What's the matter? Did you have a bad dream?" And Nikolenka gives in to a terrible impulse to answer. He says, "Yes, I dreamt that my mother died." And he no sooner says this than he feels deeply guilty about the fact that here in his own dream he has managed to kill his own mother. And, of course, he feels equally badly that he has lied to dear old Karl Ivanovich. Just a few seconds before he'd said, "That nasty Karl Ivanovich, he always wants to make me unhappy," and all of a sudden he realizes Karl Ivanovich is a very decent man. Why, oh why, is he doing this sort of thing to him?

This kind of introspection, this looking into the inner psychology of a person, which is quite different from what a person shows on the outside, of course, is very representative of what Tolstoy will grow into as a mature writer. He is constantly showing different sides of the characters. At one point, Karl Ivanovich is this terrible man; the next thing, oh, it's "dear old Karl Ivanovich." And, of course, it becomes dear old Karl Ivanovich even more powerfully when the German is replaced by a French tutor by the name of St. Jerome. As down to earth, as sympathetic, as sensitive was Karl Ivanovich, so petty, vain, and proud is the Frenchman. As a matter of fact, when Karl Ivanovich realizes that he is about to lose his job, he dictates in German to his young ward, that is, to Nikolenka, "The worst vice that exists in human existence is *Undankbarkeit*, ingratitude." And he tells him how to spell that in German. He has to write that *Undankbarkeit*. And, of course, this idea of ingratitude that poor old Karl Ivanovich is suffering from, this is something that affects the young man very, very deeply.

But now he has to deal with St. Jerome and, of course, St. Jerome wants him to grow up like a young man who knows French culture, who will fit into aristocratic Russian society; so what he is always supposed to be is summed up by a French expression, which for all of Tolstoy's life stands for something very negative in his way of thinking, *comme il faut*, that is, "as it is done" by the rules of conventional behavior, as one should behave in good society. And, of course, as far as Nikolenka is concerned, as one should behave in so-called good society or high society, *comme il faut* is exactly the opposite of how one really should behave if one has any sense of genuine human feeling and human morality; that is, the conventions of society are, as far as Tolstoy is concerned, totally at war with the feelings of people and how people really feel and think. The contrast between *comme il faut* and genuine feeling is something that Tolstoy will examine all through the rest of his career.

People's real feelings are not what you see on the surface and, of course, not what are expressed in words. The expression of words, for Tolstoy as an author, is far less important than the expression of the body. If you examine a person's body carefully when you are talking to him, you will see that the body is reacting as the person really feels; the words are totally deceptive. You see this very clearly where the young Nikolenka bursts in on a session that his father is having with the chief steward at his estate. You understand that the Russian aristocrats did not run their estates directly but had someone who probably had been born as a serf, who had some talent as an administrator, to run the estate; this is a steward. And so, of course, the steward is talking to the father in a very respectful way, and if you look at his face and if you listen to his words, it's deep respect to the master's opinion. But, says Nikolenka—of course, obviously Tolstoy—if you look behind him, his hands are held behind him, are clasped together, and by the motion of the fingers you can tell that everything he is saying to the master is exactly opposite to the way he genuinely feels inside. And if you would look at the movement of those fingers, which the father can't see, but which, of course, the man is unconsciously doing, then you would understand genuinely what the soul of that man was.

There was a famous critic by the name of Merezhkovsky who wrote a famous essay called "Tolstoy and Dostoevsky" in which he posited the notion that Tolstoy was the poet of the human body, Dostoevsky was the poet of the human soul. Now I would be reluctant to go quite that far. Merezhkovsky, of course, loved these contradictions, these opposites in his writing, and made a great deal of them. Obviously Tolstoy, in describing the physical aspect of a person, had a lot to say about that person's soul. And Dostoevsky was not solely the poet of the human soul, although, as a matter of fact, you will notice some of his characters are nowhere nearly described so well physically as they are described spiritually, by their words and by their arguments. The body in Tolstoy's hands, the flesh in Tolstoy's hands, became something tremendously living and tremendously insightful in human life.

What's very interesting to me, from a literary point of view, is the way that Tolstoy has Nikolenka describe his reactions to his mother's death. Now you understand that Tolstoy's own mother died when he was two years old, obviously long before he had a way of expressing it. In Nikolenka's case, he is 10 years old when the mother dies. And what he finds so difficult is he can't cry. He knows he's supposed to cry because when people gather around the dead body, when people gather for the funeral, of course it is *comme il faut*—it's the way society tells you to act—and when somebody dies, you should cry. But, somehow, he can't muster the tears, and people look at him and say, "What a terrible young man that is. He can't even cry at the funeral of his own mother?" That is, tears, as a conventional way of expression, mean nothing. It's only the deep feelings that a person has, that have nothing to do with the conventional way you show tears at the time of death, that are what really describe genuine grief and genuine missing of the mother. And it's only much, much later, when Nikolenka is by himself, that he can cry.

It's interesting that a writer who had a very strong influence on Tolstoy, a French writer by the name of Stendhal—as you probably know, that's a pseudonym; his real name was Marie-Henri Beyle—Stendhal, when he wrote a really famous autobiography called *La Vie de Henry Brulard*, that is to say, *The Life of Henry the Burning*—*Brulard* is "burning" in French—Stendhal obviously wrote this in the 1840s. Since he died, he obviously couldn't write it after 1848, when he died. It's curious that Stendhal expresses almost exactly the same thing, that at the death of his mother he was unable to cry, and, of course, when he was unable to cry, people around him thought that he was a terrible youngster and so on and so on. Now what I find especially interesting about this is that Stendhal's autobiography, *La Vie de Henry Brulard*, was not published until the 1880s, that is to say, 40 years after the death of the writer. Tolstoy wrote his autobiography, of course—what he called his autobiography—in the 1850s. So there is absolutely no chance that Tolstoy could have read this in Stendhal. In short, Tolstoy did absolutely in a parallel way what Stendhal did, in no way knowing that Stendhal did this. This seems to me to indicate that in the temperament of the two men there was something very, very parallel that had nothing to do with direct influence.

Now, of course, this is all the more interesting when you realize that in many ways they were opposite characters. Stendhal was a worshiper of Napoleon; Tolstoy had great contempt for Napoleon. Stendhal was very much interested in *comme il faut*; Tolstoy hated *comme il faut*. To be sure, Stendhal was very much interested in the Russians, but, of course, he knew nothing about Tolstoy—that is, in spite of the fact that in many ways they were opposites, nevertheless there was something in their temperament that was very, very parallel, and there is something both paradoxical and, it seems to me, explanatory in the way that the influence went. Although it was not direct influence, it was parallelism.

Tolstoy, of course, was very much interested in education, how you brought up young people, how somehow young people were formed to become the adults that they became. And St. Jerome worked very, very hard to get him properly prepared for the university. In those days, of course, the aristocrats were trained by their tutors and not by public schools in how to get into university, so they had to bone up very, very carefully on the entrance exam. By listening to St. Jerome, Nikolenka was able to pass the entrance examinations to get into the University of Kazan, while at the very same time he was totally rejecting everything that St. Jerome did because he considered him a person of terrible vanity.

In any case, the young fellow comes into the university, very proud of his abilities, proud of the fact that he could look into the human heart and so on, and then he came to the Latin examination. He saw that the young fellow next to him was very much worried about the Latin examination, while he, himself, had no worries; he knew Latin very, very well. He could handle anything that was tossed at him. And so he began to tutor the young fellow, how he should react to the Latin examination when he got it, and the professor noticed that he was condescending to this young man next to him. As a matter of fact, he even tried, secretly tried to coach him. The professor said, "Never mind. Wait till it's your turn. We'll see how well you know Latin." Well, of course, the young man that Nikolenka tried to help got through and Nikolenka's vanity received its comeuppance when the professor presents him a passage from the Latin poet, Horace. But, he says, "Not only could I not translate but nobody could have translated this piece." It was so difficult and so complicated that no human being could possibly translate this piece. Well, I think anybody who has ever taken a Latin exam or, for that matter, anybody who has ever taken an examination knows very well how that feels. So his vanity got its comeuppance in a very, very effective way.

There is a famous quote from this novel that, of course, is very, very touching in relation to Tolstoy. He says:

> *Schastlivaia, schastlivaia, nevozvratimaia pora detstva! Kak ne liubit', ne leleiat' vospominanii o nei? Vospominaniia eti osvezhaiut, vozvyshaiut moiu dushu...*

> Oh happy, deeply happy, irretrievable time of childhood! How was it possible not to love, not to cuddle, not to bring to one's bosom his memories? These memories refresh me and they raise up my soul.

There is something in the essence of childhood, the naiveté, the innocence, the deep belief in what one does that is deeply moving to the mature Tolstoy. And as Tolstoy goes about the writing of his novels, clearly he tries very, very hard to get back to those deeply moving, those deeply direct sentiments that one has as a child. The quality of childishness is very, very important toward understanding the psychology and the characters of the mature Tolstoy. And here you have this statement in this beautiful early sense of Tolstoy stating this.

Turning to a different work, *Tales of Sevastopol'* was an outgrowth of what Tolstoy saw and experienced when in 1854-55 Russia got involved in a disastrous war, the so-called Crimean War. Tolstoy was a second lieutenant and saw action in the war. As a matter of fact, their results in the Crimea were so bad for the Russians that Nicholas I, himself—remember our old friend who gave Pushkin such a hard time and exiled and almost executed Dostoevsky?—in a sense then got his own comeuppance because that army to which he had given so much attention, so many resources, and so much love was defeated by the combined forces of the British, the French, and the Turks down in the Crimea. Turkey wanted to rule certain territories of that place, and the Russians had made demands on them, which the British and French did not want to see happen because they were very much worried about the balance of power in

Europe. They were worried that the Russians would become too powerful and it would be impossible to maintain the balance of power in Europe, so they allied themselves with the Turks and tried to help them against the Russians. The result was a hideously bloody war, at least hideously bloody by 19th-century standards, where there was a siege in the city of Sevastopol, which is down on the peninsula that juts out into the Black Sea in the southern part of Russia. The Russian troops defended the city absolutely heroically, but in spite of all their heroism, the British, French, and Turkish allies inexorably moved in on them and, furthermore, the supplies for the Russian army and the strategies of the Russian generals were very badly handled. The strategies and the supplies on the British, French and Turkish side were much more sophisticated, so that gradually they managed to grind the Russians down and push them back towards Sevastopol.

In the beginning, Tolstoy had great enthusiasm for what he considered to be the heroism and the national destiny of Russia. And he believed that the government was engaged in the campaign that was tremendously important for Russia. He went all out as an enthusiastic Russian patriot. Then his eyes began to open up; he began to realize that, as a matter of fact, what this was really exposing was the backwardness, the corruption, the bad organization of this empire which, on the surface, had been so rigorously and well organized by Nicholas I. And so then he began to turn critical. Obviously the Russian government was not very happy about the criticism that he aimed at the war movement. They saw him as someone who was on the other side, someone who was making them feel ashamed of themselves, and so they saw to it that he got no advancement in the army. And Tolstoy later on said, "Well, I wanted to become a general in the army, and that was closed off to me, so instead" he said, "I became a general in literature"—Tolstoy, the general in the field of literature, the general in the army of writers. This is something that he talks about later on in his life.

Of course, what Tolstoy was very much interested in was the nature of true courage and steadfastness as opposed to the phony kind often touted in military rhetoric. The work shows how his mind is thinking about the realities of wartime and the famous military valor of the Russian Army. One can easily see how he put this together with the accounts that he had read in Stendhal's novel, *The Charterhouse of Parma*, where the protagonist of Stendhal, a man named Fabrizio del

Dongo, who worships Napoleon—now you understand Tolstoy did not worship Napoleon—and yet, this protagonist of Stendhal worships Napoleon and moves heaven and earth in order to go and fight with Napoleon's forces, although, as a matter of fact, his family is very much against Napoleon, very much against what Napoleon is doing in bringing revolutionary ideas not only to France but also to northern Italy where the family lived.

And so Fabrizio gets himself involved in the army of Napoleon at the battle of Waterloo. And suddenly we see the battle of Waterloo through the eyes of a drunken man, the most famous battle in European history in the 19th century, seen not through the point of view of strategy of the generals, not through some careful analysis of what happened militarily, but rather through the eyes of a drunken man. And yet, this drunken man exhibited, perhaps unconsciously, a kind of courage that was far beyond that of what was officially touted as courage. As far as Tolstoy was concerned, the official notions of courage, the official rewarding of courage were all wrong. Genuine courage was that of the common soldier who, through thick and thin, through the suffering in the battlefield, through insufficient supplies, sometimes through hunger and thirst and many other ways, nevertheless held his ground. And this was very often the kind of people, directly the kind of people who were ignored totally by the government.

There is a very famous statement by Tolstoy near the end of the story that tells a lot about his art and what is going to become of the art. He says something like this:

> The hero of my tale, whom I love with all my soul's power, whom I have tried to evoke in all his beauty, who always was, always will be, who always is and always will be, is not some hero or villain, is the truth. There is only one thing that I glorify in my tales, and that is the truth. And there is no such thing as a human being who is either entirely heroic or entirely evil, entirely good or entirely bad. All human beings are tremendous mixtures of various moral qualities, and I will catch these various moral qualities and put them together in people whom you really believe. And that is the hero of my tale; that is the truth; that is the one I will always be faithful to.

Of course, there could not be a better place to begin the consideration of the famous novel, *War and Peace*, than this particular statement because, of course, in *War and Peace* you get the picture of people who are tremendously mixed. You get a statement of the question, "What do we mean by war? What do we mean by peace?" Now remember that Tolstoy had seen war down in the Crimea. He had seen war at its most terrible point and, of course, the point that led to a terrible and seemingly disgraceful Russian defeat. This is what is the meaning, the genuine meaning of war. As far as peace was concerned, where could you understand peace? Well, of course, you understood peace in family life. You understood peace in the relationships of brothers and sisters, of cousins and uncles and aunts, of that everyday life that we all know that, of course, many critics considered to be banal. My goodness, who doesn't know relations between fathers and sons? Who doesn't know the relations between brothers and sisters? Who doesn't know family life? "Tolstoy" they said, "is the artist of the banal." As a matter of fact, there is a great deal of truth in that.

Tolstoy sees the banal, Tolstoy sees the relationships of family life, but, he says, "The banal is not just banality; the banal is the essence of life." And, as a matter of fact, this is shown not only in peace but also in war. These human qualities that we see in family life carry themselves out in the relationship between soldiers, the relationship on the battlefield, the relationship of politics. Everything in the world, in a certain sense, can be reduced to family life. So that you don't just examine war on the field of battle, you don't just examine politics in the words of statesmen, you don't just examine military strategy in the words of generals, no, you get down to the life of the individual, the life which is totally unpredictable. You get together thousands and thousands of people the way you do in an army, it's impossible to predict what they're going to do because the fate of every human being is individual and it's connected with that human being. You must examine the individual human being. In examining the individual human being, you are examining one of those thousands and millions of fates that make up the entire fate of the entire world. That's what war and peace is genuinely about and, of course, the young Tolstoy, who is beginning to examine this in ways that would lead to the kind of literature that he was doing.

So, in a certain sense, the presentation of Sevastopol, as he called it, his description of the Crimean War called *Tales of Sevastopol'*, these descriptions are, in many ways, the workbook, just as *Diary of a Writer* was the workbook for Dostoevsky on how he constructed *The Brothers Karamazov*. So this book, this early piece of his, *Tales of Sevastopol'*, is the workbook on how he will develop his grand and enormous novels, which seem to encompass an entire universe where no two individuals are exactly the same. As a matter of fact, not only are no two individuals exactly the same, no two animals are exactly the same—no two horses have the same character in his works. This is what we get out of the early works of Tolstoy. This is what's going to develop in his establishment of family life, the very famous family of Tolstoy that produced—well, his wife gave birth to 13 children, seven of whom grew to maturity. This is what Tolstoy is going to present in those great novels which we'll examine in the following lectures.

Lecture Seventeen
Tale of Two Cities and a Country Home

Scope:

After the young Tolstoy settled down to domestic life, at the famous estate at Iasnaia Poliana, he used his military experience, his reading of Stendhal, and his wife, Sofiia Andreevna née Bers, to great purpose. Between 1865 and 1869, he wrote and rewrote a 1,500-page novel about warfare and its effect on family life. His wife recopied the manuscript seven times! Starting out to write about the Decembrist Uprising of 1825, he pushed back to the events of 1801 and 1802, then went forward to the great Napoleonic invasion of 1812. The magnificent St. Petersburg, so elevated by Pushkin and Dostoevsky, was now presented as the cold city of bureaucrats and power-seekers, enlivened only by a young man, Pierre Bezukhov, who clashed with the norms of aristocratic society. We then see the contrasting city of Moscow, the home of the marvelously warm Rostov family, followed by the Bolkonsky estate out in the Russian countryside. The Bolkonsky family shows the order coming out of the 18th-century French Enlightenment, leavened by the true Christianity and luminous eyes of Princess Mariia Bolkonskaia.

Outline

I. The middle of the 1850s and the end of the Crimean War saw the death of Tsar Nikolai I and the ascent to the throne of a new tsar, Aleksandr II, the man whose regime would put an end to serfdom for tens of millions of Russian peasants.

  A. A new spirit of political and social reform swept over Russia, which included the return from Siberian exile of the Decembrist rebels of 1825. Their return aroused a new and widespread interest in that period.

  B. Tolstoy decided to investigate the nature of events that caused the uprising, and he realized that he would have to go back in history before 1825. In truth, he would have to think about the nature of history itself. This led him to a consideration of Napoleon's invasion of Russia in 1812 and of the whole nature of war and peace.

II. His novel *War and Peace* begins brilliantly with the exclamation of a highly placed aristocratic woman in St. Petersburg of the very early 19th century. She is greeting a guest to her salon in a manner modeled directly on the 18th-century French custom, and she speaks almost completely in French, with but a few Russian words thrown in:

> Eh bien, mon prince, Gènes et Lucques ne sont plus que des apanages, des pomest'ia de la famille Bonaparte. Non, je vous previens que si vous me ne dites pas que nous avons la guerre, si vous vous permettez encore de pallier toutes les infamies, toutes les atrocités de cet Antichrist... je ne vous connais plus, vous n'êtes plus mon ami, vous n'êtes plus moi vernyi rab, comme vous dîtes. Nu zdravstvuite, zdravstvuite. Je vois que je vous fais peur, sadites' i rasskazyvaite.

> Well, my prince, Genoa and Lucca are no more than family places for the Bonapartes. No, I warn you that if you don't tell me that we shall have war, if you still permit yourself to ignore all the infamies, all the atrocities of this Antichrist...I shall recognize you no longer, you are no longer my friend, you are no longer my obedient servant, as you call yourself. Well, greetings, greetings. I see that I've frightened you. Sit down, and tell me about what is happening.

A. At one and the same time, Tolstoy catches the aristocratic Russian superpatriot, raging against the upstart Bonaparte, and the woman who has been brought up to communicate in French, the language of aristocracy and civilization. She runs her salon with the mastery of a factory owner running his machines. Hers is what Tolstoy calls a conversation machine.

B. In the first scene, we meet the Kuragin family, with its father, Prince Vasilii. The Kuragin family personifies Tolstoy's attitude toward the capital city of St. Petersburg. It is a place of cold and scheming bureaucracy, and it tends to stifle the expression of genuine human emotion. This city is quite different from the one we have seen in Pushkin, Gogol', and Dostoevsky.

C. Prince Vasilii has an incredibly beautiful daughter, called La Belle Helène, and two sons: Anatolii, a wastrel and scoundrel, and Hippolyte, an idiot.

D. The atmosphere is somewhat lightened by the presence of two young friends who will convey many of Tolstoy's ideas throughout the novel.

    1. We meet Pierre Bezukhov, a young man educated in revolutionary France, who holds opinions that scandalize the hostess of the salon. He is also a bastard son of the rich Count Bezukhov, a fact that links him even more to nature rather than to the artifices of society.

    2. He is joined by his friend Andrei Bolkonsky, scion of one of Russia's most prominent families and a person determined to be his own man.

III. One of the greatest elements of Tolstoy's art is that his characters develop as in real life.

A. Pierre goes to Andrei's house and meets Andrei's beautiful wife. She is treated badly by Andrei, who sees her as totally empty. Pierre is upset when he witnesses this abuse.

B. We move to Moscow, a very different city from St. Petersburg at that time. Here, we enter into the house of the Rostov family. The father, Count Rostov, represents one of Tolstoy's favorite depictions of human nature. The old man does almost everything wrong.

    1. He squanders the considerable amount of money he received from his wife's dowry, and he will leave his family in difficult material circumstances.

    2. He has only the vaguest ideas, or interests, in child rearing; he refuses to think seriously about their problems.

    3. He falls victim to the cheapest form of patriotism.

    4. Yet we cannot help but love him, as do all the people around him. And he produces two of the most adorable children in the world.

C. Natasha Rostova, the third child by birth order, is the all-time darling of Russian readers. Together with Pushkin's Tatiana Larina, from *Eugene Onegin*, she is the Russian dream of femininity: quick to understand and react, extraordinarily responsive and sensitive to other people's feelings, unconquerable in her decent sense of morality.

1. She serves as a compass to all of our feelings of integrity and selfless love.
2. She is quite capable of stumbling over her weaknesses, and she knows what suffering is, but she is always able to transcend the low sides of human feelings and come up with the best.

D. Nikolai Rostov, the second child in birth order, is the person you would always want to have on your side in a fight. He stubbornly sticks to his principles and to his friends. He makes no pretense of cleverness or high intellect, yet his feelings are always true and admirable, even when they conflict with the rules and conventions around him.

E. Vera Rostova is the very picture of an oldest child trying to hold her own against a younger brother and sister who are tremendously attractive. She manages to irritate them and many others around her with her petty notions of morality. Yet we sympathize with her because we know her situation so well.

F. The youngest brother, Petya, will play a tremendous role later in the novel when he goes to war, for which he pays a terrible penalty.

G. It is almost incredible how much life and warmth Tolstoy creates in these characters. Tolstoy's domestic scenes in Moscow are the very essence of family life. And he presents them with the simplest of words and phrases.

IV. Tolstoy then takes us to what has traditionally been considered the heart of Russia—the old aristocratic estates of the Russian countryside.

A. Here, we will meet the members of Andrei Bolkonsky's family, headed by Prince Nikolai Andreevich Bolkonsky, the super-rational product of the 18th-century French Enlightenment as it was perceived in Russia. He appears to be a cold man, but behind this façade is a warm, thinking, and admirable person.

B. His daughter, Princess Mariia, seems physically ugly at a superficial glance. Even her father, in the presence of company at the dinner table, calls her ugly.

C. But, typically for Tolstoy, we see into her character through another physical characteristic, her deep and luminous eyes. They give evidence of a deeply religious spirit, in the best spiritual sense of that word.

   1. She is determined to live her life to bring comfort and understanding to the people around her.

   2. This determination most especially includes her father, who treats her badly. She understands that he cannot live without her.

D. In the unforgettable scene in which he tries to teach her geometry, Mariia can only sense the smell of his cigar and can make neither head nor tail of the primly logical postulates of mathematically defined space. Yet, in spite of this, Tolstoy makes the love between them come through to us.

E. Mariia reserves her understanding for a group of poor wanderers, "God's folk," whom she receives and comforts in her parts of the house, much to her father's distaste.

F. She does have a correspondent friend from St. Petersburg society, Julie Karagina, who tries to fill her in on the latest gossip. Mariia replies with admonitions to live as Christ lived. Her father is as much disgusted by the correspondence as by the group of God's folk, yet he grumblingly allows his daughter to live as she sees fit.

G. Prince Vasilii is trying to make a match between Mariia and his son Anatolii, because he needs Prince Bolkonsky's money. Bolkonsky views with distaste the prospect of his daughter's marriage to Anatolii.

H. When Bolkonsky's servants clear the snow in preparation for Prince Vasilii's visit, Bolkonsky demands that they put it all back! This scene illustrates the perversity and power of Bolkonsky.

Suggested Reading:

Gary Saul Morson, *Hidden in Plain View: Narrative and Creative Potentials in "War and Peace."*

Lev Tolstoy, *War and Peace*.

Questions to Consider:

1. How does the fact that the early-19th-century Russian aristocracy spoke mostly in the French language, and even thought in French, affect their society at a time when Russia would soon face the threat of Napoleonic invasion?

2. What contrasts do you see between the warm, fun-loving Rostov family life in Moscow and the highly disciplined, tightly organized Bolkonsky family life in their Russian country estate? What do these contrasts do for the shape of the novel?

Lecture Seventeen—Transcript
Tale of Two Cities and a Country Home

In the next two lectures we are going to be talking about one of the most famous novels in the entire world, *War and Peace*, which for me, is a very special novel, and I hope you'll pardon me if I just inject a short personal note. When I started the study of the Russian language, the very first thing I read in Russian was *War and Peace*. I sat down one summer and got through it from beginning to end and, of course, for me, it took on a very, very special aura—you might even say patina. I was amazed because here was a novel made up of totally, well, not totally—that's not entirely true—but to a very great extent, of aristocrats, of people who were counts and princes and all the titles that European nobility carried. And to my amazement, I felt that I knew these people in some cases better than the people I knew in everyday life. Tolstoy was such an incredible magician, a man with extraordinary magical powers that made these people come to life in a very, very special, a very animated, a very lively way, and to this day I feel I know these people in some ways better than people with real flesh and blood although, as a matter of fact, in actual reality they're only ink spots on a page. It's incredible; he is a real— in Russian it's called the *koldun*, a magician, a wizard who manages to bring these things to life.

In any case, we're talking about the middle of the 1850s and the end of the Crimean War and, of course, the death of Nicholas I, who was so terribly disappointed at what happened to the Russian Army in that war. There was a new tsar on the throne, Aleksandr II, probably the most liberal tsar who ever ruled in Russia. It was his regime that would put an end to serfdom and slavery for tens of millions—as a matter of fact, well over 100 million—Russian peasants. And a new spirit and political and social reform swept over Russia. It became a very different Russia. I'm sure that some of you remember the word that was in the American press when Gorbachev ended the Soviet Union, the last few years of the Soviet Union. The word was *glasnost'*, which literally means "giving voice," or you might even say "voication" would be a literal translation. And, of course, what it meant was a kind of freedom of speech, a freedom of expression in contrast to the repression that had taken place before. That word *glasnost'* was taken directly from the reign of Aleksandr II. It was interesting that Gorbachev, who considered himself a Bolshevik leader, would grab onto a slogan that was conceived and used by a tsar—of course, a very liberal tsar.

Among other things that happened in these reforms was the pardoning of those Siberian exiles of the Decembrist rebels from 1825 that we talked about earlier. Those who were still alive were allowed to return to Russia and, of course, their return aroused a new and widespread interest in that period. People were tremendously curious to see who these people were, what they did that produced these ideas that were still so much alive in the Russian imagination, particularly in the imagination of Russian liberals.

Tolstoy noticed this, of course, and, as a matter of fact, took part in it. And he thought it would be interesting to think about this. What were those things that produced that Decembrist revolution? What implications did it have for the future of Russia? And in order to investigate that, he soon realized he had to go back in history, before 1825, and actually this led him to a consideration of Napoleon's invasion of Russia in 1812 and then, of course, of the whole nature of war and peace. And, of course, in order to understand this, he felt he had to go back even further to the beginning of the 19th century. So we have the brilliant opening of this novel in the salon of a highly placed aristocratic woman in Petersburg of the early 19th century. She is greeting guests to her salon, which of course is modeled directly on the French custom, and just like the habit of the aristocrats of those days, she is speaking almost completely in French, as Tolstoy later says, a few paragraphs later he says, "In that artificial, stilted French in which our grandfathers spoke." You remember he's writing this novel in the 1860s and, of course, he's looking back to the beginning of the 19th century. With this strange, I would say, rather effecting mixture of French and Russian, she is greeting one of her guests, Prince Vasilii, she says:

Eh bien, mon prince, Gènes et Lucques ne sont plus que des apanages, des pomest'ia de la famille Bonaparte. Non, je vous previens que si vous me ne dites pas que nous avons la guerre, si vous vous permettez encore de pallier toutes les infamies, toutes les atrocités de cet Antichrist... je ne vous connais plus, vous n'êtes plus mon ami, vous n'êtes plus moi vernyi rab, comme vous dîtes. Nu zdravstvuite, zdravstvuite. Je vois que je vous fais peur, sadites' i rasskazyvaite.

Well, my Prince, Genoa and Lucca are no more than appendages of the Bonaparte family. [And she says, "Bonaparte," emphasizing that he's Italian, not even French.] No, I'm warning you if you're not going to tell me that we're going to have war with this monster, if you allow yourself still to make pale all the infamies, all the atrocities of this Antichrist... [That's the way she deals with Napoleon.] I no longer will know you, you are no longer my friend, [Then again she slips into Russian] you are no longer my obedient servant, as you say. [And then she slips completely into Russian] Well, greetings, greetings. I see that I am making you afraid, sit down and tell me all about it.

There is something comic about this and Tolstoy knows that very well. Here she's blasting the French; here she's speaking as a Russian patriot—as a matter of fact, you might say Russian super-patriot, raging against the upstart, Bonaparte, and she has been brought up to communicate in French, the language of aristocracy and civilization. The contrast between the use of French and the anti-French feelings, of course, makes it seem, in many ways, ridiculous. She runs her salon with the mastery of a factory owner running his machines. Hers is what Tolstoy calls *razgovornaia mashina*, a conversation machine.

You would think that conversation would be real human communication, that people would get together to talk about what they think about, what they feel, but, of course, in her salon, what she wants to make it is again what Tolstoy would call *comme il faut*—remember we talked about that the last time—everything being done according with conventions of the society, and if the conventions don't match the human feelings, then so much the worse for the human feelings.

We meet the Kuragin family. The father, Prince Vasilii, is the one that Anna Pavlovna has been talking to. Now you understand, Anna Pavlovna is a *freilina*, that is, a lady-in-waiting in the court and also *priblizhennaia imperatritse*, a close associate of the empress. She is a woman of real power because, of course, a word from her in the empress's ear can have great implications for Russian politics. Prince Vasilii is a powerful man; he's a man with real connections in the Russian Empire. It's not accidentally that he's been brought to this evening party and, of course, it's not accidentally that he—of course, one person uses the other and, of course, one allows oneself to be used in order in turn to be able to use the other person. Tolstoy catches this very well, and, for him, Petersburg is a city that is made up of those kind of so-called human relations, which are not human at all but rather parts of a so-called *razgovornaia mashina*, a conversation machine.

The Kuragin family personifies Tolstoy's attitude towards the people in St. Petersburg. Prince Vasilii, who says, as a matter of fact, "I don't have the bump," the idea was you had certain bumps on your head that showed you what sort of a person you were. As he said, he didn't have the bump of paternity and, of course, this picture of Petersburg is quite different from the way we've seen it in Pushkin and Gogol'. You remember I quoted you those lines from Pushkin, *Liubliu tebia, Petra tvoren'e*, "I love you, oh creation of Peter." For Pushkin, for Gogol, for Dostoevsky, Petersburg was extraordinarily enticing; for Tolstoy, Petersburg was a city of cold bureaucrats. And here you have a family of this Prince Vasilii. His daughter, Helène, she is called in French La Belle Helène, the beautiful Helen and, of course, obviously referring back to Homer's poem, the Helen who entranced a whole army, the Helen who entranced, first of all, a whole city to abduct her to Troy and then a whole army from Greece to come save her. You remember the phrase, "The face that launched a thousand ships"; this is La Belle Helène.

And then she has two brothers, honestly, one worse than the other. There is Anatolii Kuragin, who is a scoundrel and, in some ways, almost a monster. And then we have his brother, Hippolyte, who is a total idiot and who, as the father says, "They both cost me over 40,000 rubles a year." He can't stand them. And, of course, they fit in perfectly in this aristocratic salon, where everything is done by the book. There are, furthermore, some French émigrés whom Anna

Pavlovna serves up—these émigrés, of course, are from the old French aristocracy, who detest Napoleon almost as much as Anna Pavlovna does. She presents them to her salon with great pride: "Here are real French aristocrats that I brought for your delectation." And Tolstoy makes the marvelous remark, which is so typical for his imagery; he says, "She served up the French aristocrat like a beautiful hunk of roast beef which, when you see it on the plate on the table, looks tremendously appetizing. But" he said, "if you saw that roast beef in the kitchen, you wouldn't touch it"—again, the difference between the appearance and the physical reality that we talked about last time.

Of course, the conversation goes about Napoleon, about how crystal pure the Russian tsar is, how wonderful Russia is and how terrible Napoleon, this terrible revolutionary regime of Napoleon, is, the terrible crimes of Napoleon. We hear all about this and then, all of a sudden, a young man bounds into the room who is going to break up this *comme il faut*; he's going to break up this society. His name is Pierre Bezukhov. He's a natural-born son of the rich Count Bezukhov, which makes him even more natural in Tolstoy's eyes, and he says at one point, blushing, he says, *Je suis un bâtard*, "I am a bastard son." But this bastard son, of course, is somewhat outside the rules of society, having had a natural birth. He has been brought up in revolutionary France and he comes back bearing the latest revolutionary ideology from France. You can imagine his coming into this drawing room, this salon, where Napoleon is the chief enemy and suddenly praising Napoleon. You can understand how he upsets the conversation machine. Poor old Anna Pavlovna does her best to try somehow to repair it, but this young man, this bear, as she calls him, comes in. She said, "Won't somebody help me civilize this bear?" At first, of course, the people are terribly shocked, but then we begin to understand this is really a very good-natured young man; he is nowhere nearly so bad as his words make him seem, and pretty soon a real conversation ensues, again, much to the anguish of Anna Pavlovna who has no idea where the conversation is going to go.

And then we meet a second character in the other side of this novel, a young man named Andrei Bolkonsky. He's the scion of one of Russia's most prominent families and a person determined to be his own man, think his own thoughts. As friendly and open and would-be sociable as is Pierre, that tight and self-defensive and almost something like a fortress to be approached is Andrei Bolkonsky. He is a man who knows his own worth and is determined that everybody around him will recognize his own worth and, furthermore, that everybody around him will not use any kind of fakery in relation to him.

Interestingly, there is a very close relationship, a very close friendship that has already grown up between Andrei and Pierre and, of course, this will develop through the novel as both of them grow. Again, one of the great things about Tolstoy is the characters grow; they don't stay the same. They begin as young men, and as they grow they become older and more mature people, exactly the way people grow in life. It's remarkable the way they do it.

After the salon is over, Pierre goes to Andrei's home and meets—gets to know a little bit better—the very beautiful young woman, the little princess—*malen'kaia kniaginia* in Russian—whom Andrei has married, one of the most beautiful women in Petersburg. But to his dismay, Pierre discovers that their family life is not only bad but actually terrible. Andrei treats his wife in a way that it seems is really unforgivable. I realize, of course, that this is in a very different time; you can't judge that time by the rules of our present time. But even so, there is something really awful in the way he relates to his wife. He seems almost to reduce her to an animal. He refuses to listen to anything that she says. Evidently she has irritated him to the last degree. He has perhaps married her because she was very, very beautiful, but he sees her as totally empty, and when she tries to appeal to him, "Andrei, after all, our marriage is presumably based on love," Andrei will have nothing of it." Pierre, of course, is really hurt by this relationship and reacts with considerable hurt. And in order to try to distract him, he begins to talk about the war. He says, "Look, I couldn't possibly fight in this war against Napoleon." He said, "I'm ready to go to war like any man, but I certainly wouldn't go to a war in which I totally disbelieved," to which Andrei replies, "Well, if people only fought in wars in which they believed, we'd never have any wars." And Pierre says, "That would be marvelous, *prikrasna*, that would be wonderful." The paradox of the just war and the not so just war, how can there be justice in this mass killing of people" It's something, of course, that makes us think.

This is the view we get of Petersburg. And then Tolstoy takes us to another place, a very different kind of a city. He takes us to Moscow. Moscow, of course, is a very different city or, I should say, Moscow was, and perhaps still is, but at least for the purposes of the novel was, the beginning of the 19th century, a very different city. Petersburg was the example of European civilization brought to Russia, the creation of Peter the Great. As you may remember, we talked about that earlier. Moscow is that old-fashioned city where heavy merchants take heavy candles to church and speak very slowly and talk about the ancient traditions of a very old and a very non-European Russia. And in Moscow, we enter into the house of a genuine family, the Rostov family, which is perhaps the paragon of all families ever caught, not only in Russian literature but, I would say, in world literature.

The father, Count Rostov—*Graf* means count in Russian—Graf Rostov, represents one of Tolstoy's favorite ideas. This man does everything wrong. He squanders the really quite large dowry that his wife brought, so eventually the family is going to be penniless. He thinks that he knows how to bring up children. He obviously doesn't know the first thing about bringing up children, and yet, in spite of that, the children turn out to be very good. He falls victim to the cheapest kind of patriotism, towards which, of course, Tolstoy has great contempt. He believes in everything around him. He desperately wants to be one with the crowd around him and he pours out resources in order to bring people to enormous parties, where the money just flows out as if it were water flowing over a dam or something like that. He is a man who morally, psychologically, philosophically does everything wrong and yet you can't help but love him. There is a warmth about the man, there is an attraction about the man that immediately draws you in. And, of course, it's this warmth, this attraction which is carried over to his children.

First of all, of course, we see Natasha, the absolute paragon of femininity in Russian eyes and in Russian literature. She, together with Tatiana Larina, whom we talked about earlier in *Eugene Onegin*, are the two great feminine characters of the 19th century, the Russian dream of femininity, quick to understand and react, extraordinarily sensitive and responsive to other people's feelings, unconquerable in a decent sense of morality. She serves as a compass to all of our feelings of integrity and selfless love. She is capable of stumbling over weaknesses, and we see that in the novel. But she is always able to transcend the low sides of human feelings and come up with the best. Natasha—it's impossible not to love Natasha. If you don't love Natasha, don't talk to me.

Then, of course, there's her brother, Nikolai Rostov. He's a person you would always want to have on your side if you had a fight. He stubbornly sticks to his principles and his friends. He makes no pretense of cleverness or high intellect. "Ours is not to think," he says; "ours is to act." Yet his feelings are always true and admirable, even when—or I should say perhaps especially when—they conflict with the rules and the conventions around him. Tolstoy sees him, of course, as someone who punches through this *comme il faut.*

Then there is a character, I must admit, I have tremendous sympathy for although it doesn't apply to my own personal situation. She is the oldest; she is the first-born child. And imagine trying to compete with a sister like Natasha. Everyone immediately, of course, is drawn to Natasha. Think of the jealousy, think of the anguish, that this must cause the older sister. And so she manages to react to it with a certain kind of primness, with a certain kind of self-righteousness. According to her, everything that she does is perfectly right and everything that they do is totally wrong. And, of course, she irritates the devil out of her younger brothers and sisters and they react by, "Madame Jolie, Madame Jolie." They call her a name which is a prissy woman who has no—so she said, "Well, you may call me Madame Jolie, but I know that I'm beautiful and I know that I'm much more moral than you are." She is someone for whom morality is something that she knows and no one else knows.

And then, of course, there is the youngest brother, Petya, whom we see somewhat less in these early scenes and yet eventually in the novel he plays a tremendous role when he desperately wants to go to war and, of course, he goes to war and pays a terrible penalty of war. People get killed in wars and, of course, you can imagine the feelings of his mother when this happens.

It's a scene of incredible warmth and a scene, of course, where Pierre, Pierre Bezukhov, the one who cracked the conventions in Petersburg, is obviously going to play a very important role. Tolstoy's domestic scenes are the very essence of family life. He presents them with the simplest of words and the simplest of phrases. It's incredible the way he manages to get this and, of course, one of his later novels is called, *Semeinoe Schast'e, Family Happiness.* Family is a very, very important thing to Tolstoy and he is the last person in the world who would talk about that hideous phrase, "family values," that political hypocrites use when they make public speeches. He understands the genuineness of family values, but he would never use such a word. Instead, we see the deep emotional feelings of a family that to a very great extent, at least in the Rostov family, are positive, but sometimes are negative. He understands the antagonisms as well as the love that exists in the family. In short, you really feel family life in this novel.

There is a wonderful scene in the Rostov household where they hear what Pierre has done to get himself thrown out of Petersburg. He has tied the chief of police to a bear and pushed both of them into the canal. And, of course, this is a horrible thing. I mean, imagine being tied to a bear and being dumped in the canal. And yet, the way they tell it, it sounds enormously funny. The people in the Rostov household of course, are terribly shocked, but the old man immediately laughs. He has the genuine attitude towards this horrible and yet very comic scene. Well, of course, when Pierre did that, he wasn't going to stay very long in Petersburg, at least not at that particular time.

So now we've seen two different places in Russia, of course, places that are very, very important in the novel. And then Tolstoy takes us to a third place and, of course, this third place is tremendously important as the anchor of this triangle, of these three different places. It's the heart of Russia; it's an estate called Bald Hills, *Lysaya Gora*. It brings to mind an epigraph in Pushkin, where he makes a pun. The Latin poet, Horace, talks of the countryside. He says, "*Oh rus*," and, of course, the Latin word, *rus*, connected with the English word, "rustic," talks about the countryside. Of course, Pushkin has these letters in Latin characters because it's from a Latin poet. And then in Cyrillic characters, in Russian characters, he says, *Oh Rus'*, referring, of course, to the old Russia that we talked about in our very first lectures. In other words, the countryside and Russia are two things very, very close together, and the heart of Russia is in its countryside, in those grand estates, in the slaves who work on the estates and so on and so on.

And, of course, on this estate is the father of Andrei Bolkonsky, the man I talked about before. His name is Nikolai Andreevich Bolkonsky. So of course, his son is Andrei Nikolaevich. It obviously works that way in the aristocratic families. This is a man, as Tolstoy says, genuinely of the 18th century. He represents a kind of rationalism. He represents a man who works on a lathe everyday. He represents a man who schedules his life and the life of his daughter, who lives with him, in exact ways, going about it at particular hours, doing exactly the same thing every day. At a certain hour he works on the lathe, a certain hour he listens to his daughter playing on the clavier, a certain hour he tries to teach his daughter geometry and so on and so on. At first glance, he seems to be a tremendously cold, a tremendously severe man. And yet you understand very well that behind this façade—again, Tolstoy, the surface and the reality— behind this façade is a very warm, a very thinking and a highly admirable person. The way Tolstoy gets this across, again, is something that I don't think any other writer could achieve.

Now he has a daughter by the name of Mariia; her name, of course, is Mariia Nikolaeva Bolkonskaia. Tolstoy describes her and, of course, clearly, if you would see her at first glance, she would seem physically ugly. Her features are irregular' her complexion is mottled. It certainly doesn't help when her French companion, Mademoiselle Bourienne, insists on dressing her very, very stylishly even though the style not only does nothing to help Mariia but makes her look something like a trained monkey. And the insult is compounded when she comes to the table and her father actually, in front of other people, calls her ugly. When I think of something like that, I think, "My God, how can a father do something like that?" But that was the nature of this father.

But Tolstoy allows us to look into her character through another, again, physical characteristic, her deep and luminous eyes which give evidence of a deeply religious spirit in the best spiritual sense of that word. She is determined to live her life to bring comfort and understanding to other people, not to herself but to other people, like Christ. She is ready to sacrifice herself for the benefit of those—I hesitate to use the word "humanity" because that's an abstraction. It's not humanity; it's people, it's individual people. Remember, Dostoevsky's character used to say, "I love humanity, but I can't stand people." We know such people. Mariia is not like that. She tries to bring comfort and beauty to everyone around her; it makes no difference what their class is, what their background is. And even her father, her father who is so difficult for her to handle, who does what, in my eyes, as a father of the 20th and perhaps the 21st century, does everything wrong, treats her as no human being should treat any human being. And yet she understands that behind this is a genuine attraction to her. As a matter of fact, he can't live without her. There's a love that exists between them that's very hard to make out in the beginning and, yet, as the novel goes on, it goes deeper and deeper and deeper, not into words but into the heart, into the feeling. This is an incredible achievement in this novel.

Well, he is determined that Mariia is going to learn geometry because geometry is pure logic. Geometry is where you learn to think, where you don't make one step until you're absolutely sure that it's completely covered and predicted and defined by the previous step. And he is going to teach this to his daughter, Mariia. And, of course, as he comes in, he is smoking a cigar and, of course, she can make neither head nor tail of the primly logical postulates of mathematically defined space, of volume, of angles, of proof, of A being B and B being C, and the speed of one leading to the speed of the other; this makes no sense to her. All she feels is the smell of the cigar of her father. And, of course, he understands that he mustn't yell at her. He tries hard to hold himself back, not to be unkind to her, to make her want to study geometry, but he can't stand it that she can't see the logical steps that he takes. "Idiot", *durak*, "You fool, what's the matter with you?" "Look, I'm sorry; I shouldn't do it that way." But, of course, what she feels is only his growing irritation with her absolute inability to grasp the postulates of geometry.

It's everyone's nightmare, of course, that somehow you couldn't fathom, somehow you couldn't get through, or the personality of the teacher, which is absolutely opposite to your own personality, and which can't get it across. And yet, in spite of this, you feel the love, the relationship, the connection that exists between them. It's incredible the way Tolstoy makes this come across. Mariia, of course, has an antidote to this, God's folk, poor people and religious people whom she receives and comforts in her parts of the house, much to her father's distaste. He wants nothing to do with these God's people who know nothing about rationality, who know nothing about what he believes in. She also has a correspondence with her friend from Petersburg society, Julie Karagina, who tries to fill her in on the latest gossip. And, of course, Julie is giving her gossip, which perhaps Mariia is receiving in spite of her words, but she says, "You mustn't think about gossip. You must think about Christ's teaching." And, of course, the old man looks at this correspondence and helplessly saying, "What have I brought into the world?" It's exactly the opposite of the way that she feels.

Well, the old Prince Vasilii is trying to make a match between his son Anatolii and Mariia because he wants, of course, to get the money of the old man. And Prince Bolkonsky doesn't want him to come, so he awaits, with some distaste, the possibility of his daughter marrying this fool in the family. And the servants, meanwhile, go out and shovel the snow so there'll be a clear path for Vasilii to come. When he hears this, he says, "Who told you to clear that snow? Put that snow back." And the scene, in a certain sense, closes when the servants are going to the enormous effort of putting back all the snow that they shoveled off. It shows the force of the old prince and the perversity of the old prince in this magnificent family on the estate of Bald Hill.

Lecture Eighteen
Family Life Meets Military Life

Scope:

What happens when good family people with rich domestic experience meet the hideous bloodshed of a massive war, the most massive one Europe had known up to the year 1812? How did Napoleon's Grande Armée affect the nation with the largest land mass in the world? Tolstoy shows us how through his extraordinary characters. Nikolai Rostov, the young man filled with sincere patriotism, seeks glorious death for the sake of the tsar and the fatherland. But when the French soldiers shoot at him, he wonders why anyone would want to kill such a nice person as himself. Andrei Bolkonsky discovers the nature of true courage and fortitude, plus the blue sky over the Battle of Austerlitz. This discovery is intensified at the Battle of Borodino, paradigm of all modern mass battles, from Gettysburg to Stalingrad. And a great deal of this experience is seen through the eyes of the loveliest feminine creature in 19th-century literature, whom no one can resist loving: Natasha Rostova.

Outline

I. After the well-organized routines that we observed in the families living in tsarist Russia, we see the equally regularized life of the Russian army in peacetime. Of course, the soldiers are all aware of the looming threat of the fight with the army of Napoleon, but in the beginning, that is far away. What Nikolai Rostov and his companions face are the day-to-day operations and problems of army life.

   A. Because of his social standing as a count, Nikolai enters the army as an officer, with his own servant, equipment, and horse. He is prepared to behave himself as he always does: with generosity, an open heart, and feelings that are crystal clear to all. He has been completely taken in by the ideology of patriotism. He wants his fellow officers to accept him as one of them and to know that he is a decent fellow.

   B. To his dismay, he soon discovers that a fellow officer has covertly taken some money from another officer. With impulsive anger, he confronts the man and publicly accuses him of thievery and nasty behavior.

C. To Nikolai's surprise, he soon discovers that the villain of the piece is himself, not the thief. Nikolai is guilty because he has publicly questioned the honor of another man in his regiment, and this reflects badly on the reputation of the entire unit. The more senior officers pressure him to apologize to the thief, thereby defending the collective honor of the group.

D. This expectation of Nikolai goes so strongly against the young man's open and honest nature that he finds it well nigh impossible. And he suddenly finds himself in a completely unexpected position: the man who acts against his own military unit, which he adored with all the fervor of young, sincere Russian patriotism.

E. This lesson is Nikolai's first in the special nature of honor as conceived by people who by no means share the Rostov family characteristic of openness and honesty.

F. The next lesson comes directly through Nikolai's own reactions, when at long last, he enters Austria (a Russian ally), where the regiment has traveled. An inspection is to occur. Marshall Kutuzov demands that his troops wear their old, worn uniforms, because he does not want the Austrians to think that they are ready for battle. The ruse does not work.

G. Suddenly, Nikolai sees French uniforms and realizes, with a start, that the soldiers wearing them are shooting at him, Nikolai Rostov, whom everybody loves! How is this possible? What could they possibly have against him? He turns to flee and, luckily, ends up among Russian troops once more, unhurt. He begins to understand the reality behind all the stories of military courage and valor.

H. Tolstoy does not depict Nikolai as a coward; he is as brave as a Russian officer should be. But he begins to understand that true valor is not something one boasts about on parade. It is, rather, a determination to hold one's ground; it comes from experience and a certain kind of maturity.

I. Nikolai becomes skeptical of those who boast about their courage. Tolstoy shows us another scene in which an artillery officer is in mid-battle and facing enormous odds.

    1. His troops hold their ground until there are only one or two guns left, and many men have been killed. The officer is criticized for not returning with the last gun. Andrei Bolkonsky defends the officer.

    2. With these scenes, we begin to understand the complications of war and that such complications can parallel family life and its values.

II. A wonderful interlude serves as a kind of intermezzo in the course of the novel.

    A. Nikolai returns from the army at the behest of his mother, who is worried about the financial ruin facing the family as a result of the irresponsible fiscal behavior of the old Count Rostov.

    B. Nikolai inspects the monetary records and immediately threatens the steward, who has been cooking the books. The old count listens to the excuses of the steward and defends him, whereupon Nikolai gives up completely on any attempt to control the situation.

    C. Instead, they take advantage of the glorious weather for hunting. We find ourselves embarked on a traditional Russian hunt, the beloved diversion of the Russian aristocracy.

    D. In contrast to the old count, who only manages to make himself a pest on the field of the hunt, Nikolai rides with both passion and skill. Suddenly, nothing seems so important to him as catching the wolf.

        1. When we finally catch sight of the hunted animal, it actually speaks good Russian!

        2. It is hard to believe, but Tolstoy makes the reader believe that the animal is talking! Once again, the wizard is at work.

    E. The master of the hunt is actually a serf, but when he sees the old count bungling his hunter's duties, the serf shouts at him as if their social roles were reversed.

1. The atmosphere of the hunt was so special that it even overruled the rigid caste system of early-19th-century Russia.
2. The hunt was its own universe within the more general universe of the country at that time.

F. Nikolai meets a character called Uncle, who invites Nikolai and Natasha to his home, where everything is in the order required by the traditional Russian countryside.
   1. Nothing seems quite so delicious as the food and drink, and Uncle brings out his guitar and plays Russian songs.
   2. Natasha, who has been educated in the French manner, suddenly throws off her shawl and starts to dance like a true Russian girl. Tolstoy says:

   > Gde, kak, kogda vsosala v sebia iz togo russkogo [voz]dukha, kotorym ona dyshala, - eta grafinechka, vospitannaia emigrantkoi frantsuzhenkoi, - etot dukh...?

   > ("Where, how, and when, out of the Russian air that she breathed, did she absorb this into herself, this little countess, educated by an émigré Frenchwoman, this spirit...?")

   > Where did Natasha get this spirit, from where did she get those movements, which the *pas de châle* should have wiped out a long time ago? But the spirit and movements were exactly those inimitable, unstudied Russian ones that her dear uncle was expecting from her.

G. Once again, Tolstoy is arguing for a direct expression of human feeling, coming from deep inside the individual soul, unlearned and inimitable, the basis of all genuine human relations. It occurs in the intermezzo, but it applies to the entire novel, in scenes of both peace and war. One could almost say that this is not a novel about War and Peace, with capital letters, but rather, about the wars and peaces, with small letters, of the human soul.

III. After the intermezzo, Tolstoy takes us back once again into the maelstrom of war, attempting to catch the greatest movements of troops in Europe known at that time.

    A. Napoleon moved a huge army, put together from many different nationalities, across Europe and into the vast spaces of Russia. He was met by an equally large army of Russians, most of them peasants, trying to stem the thrust of the most famous military tactician at that time.

    B. In opposition to the figure of Napoleon, Tolstoy gives us the Russian Marshall Kutuzov: heavy, half-blind, deeply skeptical of all brilliant military strategy, and determined to defeat the enemy by relying on patience and the nature of the Russian fighting man.

    C. When his brilliant generals, many of them German and French military men of international fame, propound their complex battle plans, Kutuzov goes to sleep. He knows a good night's sleep is the most important preparation for battle.

    D. Following the example of Stendhal in *The Charterhouse of Parma*, Tolstoy shows us the huge Battle of Borodino through the eyes of a man who knows very little about it. Stendhal uses a drunken Fabrizio del Dongo; Tolstoy, a naïve, civilian-clothed Pierre Bezukhov. Both of them make us see the reality more clearly than we would through the eyes of a seasoned expert.

    E. Andrei Bolkonsky, who will be mortally wounded on the battlefield, had been betrothed to Natasha. But he had left for a year, and during his absence, Natasha received a proposal of marriage from Prince Vasilii's son, Anatolii, who did not tell Natasha that he was already married! When Bolkonsky returned, he called off the marriage to Natasha and was determined to find Anatolii.

    F. When Andrei is wounded on the Borodino battlefield, he is taken to a ghastly military hospital, where he indeed finds Anatolii, a coincidence that most novelists would not have dared to employ. Yet Tolstoy succeeds.

    G. The coincidence corresponds to the point that Tolstoy has been making throughout the novel: Human plans, however brilliant and complicated, cannot grasp or control human reality, which goes far beyond the scope of any possible rational plan. Mere coincidence is far more powerful and convincing, at least to the author of *War and Peace*, than the cleverest of human plans and designs.

H. How does this novel end? Natasha, now married to Pierre, rushes to him, holding a dirty diaper and says, "Look! It's brown. It's no longer green. The child is no longer sick!" And, thus, the novel ends with a dirty diaper—something that only Tolstoy could bring off.

Suggested Reading:

John Bayley, *Tolstoy and the Novel*.

Questions to Consider:

1. Nikolai Rostov, the oldest Rostov child in Moscow, goes through extensive military experience and makes a successful marriage with Mariia Bolkonskaia, the religious daughter whose luminous eyes proclaim her great soul. How do both of these experiences teach Nikolai the true meaning of human valor?

2. Natasha Rostova, the darling of almost all Russian readers, experiences closeness both with Andrei Bolkonsky, the doomed cerebral character, and Pierre Bezukhov, the man with a Tolstoyan heart. How does she influence these men, and what does her experience with them do to her as a human being?

Lecture Eighteen—Transcript
Family Life Meets Military Life

In talking about the novel up to this point, we have been talking to a great extent about family life. It's tremendously important in Tolstoy. His wife, Sofiia Andreevna, played an extremely active part in his activities. Not only did she recopy the full manuscript of *War and Peace* seven times by hand, no less, but she also bore him 13 children, of whom seven survived early childhood. But, remember, this novel is entitled *War and Peace, Voina i Mir*; you would think at least, that the family life is part of peace and is part of the place away from the war.

Then Tolstoy takes us to the army, and naturally we're in the military part of the novel. We first see it through the eyes of Nikolai Rostov, the son. He's from an aristocratic family; like his father, he's a Count—or in Russia you would say Graf Rostov—so, naturally, he's an officer in the Russian Army. He brings his own horse. His mother, in particular, doesn't even want him to go to war, but he's eager to sacrifice himself for Russia. He would like nothing better than to lay down his life for the Tsar and he talks about it in dramatic terms. He's been taken in completely by the ideology of patriotism and the idea that, for Russia, he will give all; it will be glorious to die on the field of battle. Nikolai feels this, and he feels it very sincerely. He expresses it strongly, not in the words of an intellectual, as somebody who knows how to use words well, but rather in a somewhat clumsy fashion. But the more clumsily he says it, the more deeply we know that he feels it and it's genuinely true.

So finally he gets his wish, against his mother's will. And we see him bringing his horse to the regiment where he's stationed. He enters with tremendous openness, almost, you might say, with cheerfulness. He wants to become a part of the group; he wants them to receive him as a comrade. He wants them to know that he, Nikolai, is a very decent fellow. And he knows he really is a decent fellow. He wants them to understand what kind of a really regular person he is. Then he's in for a shock, because it turns out that he learns through a friend of his that one of his fellow officers has stolen some money from his other friend in a place right near where Nikolai lives. He's terribly upset that a comrade would steal from a comrade. It's something absolutely unallowable and the full force of his anger and feelings come to the surface and we know that Nikolai is capable of great feeling.

He demands to be taken to where this fellow lives. He sees the man eating in the mess hall. Nikolai goes up to him; the man is in a very friendly way, having no idea what's happened. Nikolai accosts him, he says, "How could you possibly do something like this? This is a terrible thing to do. You've got to make amends." You can imagine the shock of feeling this, particularly from a person who is not only of Nikolai's high aristocratic standing but also his tremendous emotional force. The man is terrified; remember, he is of a much lower rank than Nikolai. He says, "Please, please, your Excellency, don't do this to me. Don't put me in a situation where my entire reputation is ruined by the regiment." Nikolai is determined this must not go on and he brings it to the Commander. To Nikolai's enormous surprise—remember, he is a very naïve young man—the villain of the piece turns out to be not the thief but he, Nikolai. This is because Nikolai has publicly questioned another man in the regiment and then this reflects badly on the reputation of the entire unit. If this gets out, the unit will have a horrible reputation. If you challenged him to a duel or something like that privately, that would have been different. But to make a public accusation like this, what's going to happen to the regiment? They pressed Nikolai to apologize, not that they don't press the man who stole to apologize, but Nikolai.

Tolstoy here is making a very strong comment about the military conventional notion of honor. What is honor? What is courage? What are genuinely comradely relationships? This goes so strongly against Nikolai's open and honest nature he finds it impossible to do. He finds himself in a completely unexpected position as the man who acts against his whole military unit, which he, himself, had adored with all the fervor of young and sincere Russian patriotism. It's quite a lesson for the man who came from the kind of family the Rostovs represent, with the characteristics of openness and honesty. This is a very difficult thing for Nikolai to do. That's the peacetime army.

Now the army is being moved from Russia to Austria because Austria is their ally, that is, the Russian's ally. And they hope, the Russians, that is, hope by fighting Napoleon in Austria they won't have to fight him at home in Russia. They are soon disabused of this notion, of course, when they find out what happens. But we see—we, the readers, see—what it means to get into a battle. First of all, the unit is marched a long and hard way, all the way from Russia to Austria. Their shoes and uniforms are in terrible shape. All of a sudden, there is going to be an inspection by the Austrian General's staff, so the men immediately shine up their shoes and try to patch up their uniforms as best they can. They rub up the metal so it shines and they get themselves into regular lines and files and they make a good military impression when they're inspected.

We get our first view of a very important character in the novel from Tolstoy, Marshal Kutuzov, who, as many of you probably know, is a great hero of the war of 1812 and the victor over Napoleon. Kutuzov looks at this and is highly displeased. They say, "What, why, didn't we do it right? Didn't we shine enough?" "No" he says, "I want you to put on those worn-out uniforms, those worn-out shoes, and stop that shine on the metal." "But, your Excellency, we want to make a good impression." "Don't you understand? I want the Austrians to realize what shape we're in; we're not ready for a battle. They want us to attack immediately; we have to delay." Then Tolstoy shows you the marvelous scene of arms and legs flinging in all directions as they fling off good uniforms, put on worn-out uniforms, scuffing up the shoes, and fixing up the metal so it doesn't shine so much anymore. In short, they do everything the opposite to what they just did.

Remember the scene where they cleared the snow and had to put the snow back, earlier in the novel? Exactly the same thing is happening here. This is Tolstoy's commentary on what it means to expect the regularity of society, that somehow you can control things by conventional or abstract rules. And, of course, Tolstoy knows this is impossible. So Kutuzov is very happy when the Austrians go by and see just how tired and ragged his troops really are. Of course, that doesn't carry much weight with the Austrians. All they know is they want to stop Napoleon and they want to stop him now. The Russians have to get into battle almost immediately. So Nikolai understands that pretty soon he'll have a chance to fulfill those words about sacrificing himself for the Tsar and for the good of Russia. He is going to get into an actual battle, and this is very exciting for him.

Tolstoy magnificently handles the transition to battle. You see the two armies opposite each other. You see two riders going on patrol, going in a circular way, around the front, where the front exists between the two armies. Of course, it's very quiet. The campfires are flickering and surprisingly peaceful for two forces that are about to go at each other with a desire to kill as many of the other people as they possibly can. Then, as Nikolai is on reconnaissance, riding with his horse, suddenly the action begins; the motion happens and you feel it as closely as if you were actually there. Somehow he manages to put it on paper. Nikolai rushes with enthusiasm into the battle; the horses are galloping; there are bullets everywhere; there is noise everywhere. Suddenly the horse stumbles and he falls. And here he is, on the field of battle, without any kind of fast transportation. To make matters even worse, those people opposite him in French uniforms are approaching him and he can hardly believe his eyes—they're shooting at him. He says, "But wait a minute, this makes no sense. I'm such a nice fellow. Why would anyone want to shoot me? I know the rustle of my mother's dress. My mother loves me. I'm a decent brother to my brothers and sisters; everyone loves me. Why on earth would anyone want to kill me, such a nice guy?" That obviously doesn't cut much ice with the French troops, and suddenly he realizes he had better get out of there if he wants to stay alive. He turns and he runs and flees as fast as he can, luckily making it back to his own lines. The irony and humor in this scene is absolutely unmatchable.

Now you understand Nikolai is no coward. We've seen him running away, but he's not a coward. He's as brave as a Russian officer should be. And if you know anything about the Russian Army, you'll know that bravery in that army is not something that's rare. But he's beginning to understand that genuine valor has nothing to do with those dramatic words he used about sacrificing oneself for the Tsar. It's rather a determination to hold one's ground, come what may. It comes from experience and a certain kind of maturity. This is a lesson that really sinks in to Nikolai and he begins to grow out of the youngster that Nikolai Rostov once was. He becomes rather skeptical of those who use brave words, the very same words, by the way, that he once used behind the lines, brave words such as, "What I did in this battle and what I did in that battle."

It turns out that the Austrians, who were so eager to stop Napoleon, all of a sudden surrender Vienna, their capital city, without even a fight. Napoleon's officers tricked them in a very superficial way into not fighting. And now, all of a sudden, the Russians are alone. They, highly outnumbered, will have to face the brunt of Napoleon's army.

Now Tolstoy shows us another scene that, in a certain sense, is a kind of a contrast to what I just talked about. He shows us a scene of an artillery officer who really was in the middle of the battle, who really was, and exhibited the kind of bravery that we come to expect. His men are facing impossible odds. They have to pull up the cannons with manpower; they don't even have the horsepower to pull them up, and they're heavy guns. The enemy shells are landing all around them and they're facing this terrible battle. They hold their ground, no matter what. The enemy balls come in and they kill one man and then another man. And they put one man out of action and now another man out of action. But in spite of all these things, they hold their position; they defend it until there are practically only one or two guns left. They try very hard to bring those one or two guns out and back to the lines, but it proves to be impossible and, with the loss of a large number of men, the officer comes back to the army lines.

He has just carried out something that we see, through Tolstoy, as incredibly brave. He exhibits what the Russians would call *stoikost'*, that is, the ability to stand fast, no matter what. To our dismay and surprise, the superior officers criticize him. They say, "Look, you left seven guns. You didn't bring back the one that was left. What's the matter with you? Are you a coward?" The officer who is the head of this artillery group is a simple man; he's not an aristocrat. Words don't come easily to him. He is not the kind of officer who can argue with a superior commander, nor does he even want to argue. He simply stands there and takes it like a good Russian. We think, "Good heavens, here's a man who has really shown genuine valor being given exactly the wrong kind of response from his own army." And who steps in for him but Andrei Bolkonsky.

You remember Andrei, this rather rigorous, stern fellow who defends his own honor but at the same time doesn't take trickery or falsehood from anyone else. He steps in and says, "No, you don't understand. This man has been the most valiant man on the field. Understand what he did, understand how he was doing it, under enemy fire in a way that was very difficult. Don't give him a hard time. Understand, this man is a genuine hero." It's Andrei Bolkonsky that Tolstoy gives an understanding that he, Tolstoy, has about military life.

Remember, Tolstoy was a part of the army in the Crimean War. He's no stranger to this kind of situation. Between the scene with Nikolai Rostov and the scene with the artillery officer, you begin to understand the complications of war. You also begin to understand that some of those human relations that we saw in family life in peacetime also take place in wartime. Human relations are seen in a patriarchal relation to the men under you and their feelings of the men under you. In a certain sense, they're the children of the army. Perhaps there isn't quite that difference between war and peace that you might expect, given this type of story and given how it's organized. Perhaps the values of family life also take place on the field of battle. It's something we have to think about.

In any case, we have an interruption here. Nikolai comes home at the behest of his mother, who is terribly worried about the financial ruin facing the family. The father is such a profligate spendthrift, the money goes out here, the money goes out there. You understand this; this is really her money, although it's the money in the dowry that was given to him. And, of course, given the rules of that day, it is he who controls it. But as long as he's alive, the creditors are not going to press the family for his debts. But what happens when he dies and the family is left with no money and the creditors move in? what then? She says to Nikolai, "Look, you've got to come home. You've got to defend, if not me, at least the whole family in the interest of your brothers and sisters as well as your mother." Nikolai does as he's told; he's a decent young man. He does have a sense of responsibility and honor towards his family.

He comes home to inspect the monetary records of the family and he soon finds out that the steward has been a total crook. He's dipped his hand in the till quite a bit. Nikolai gets very angry and yells and screams at the steward, who gets enormously frightened. He even runs out of the house and takes refuge behind a bush where they would normally hide. His father comes and says, "Look, look, you don't understand the double entry bookkeeping. What you thought was his having his hand in the till was actually continued on the next page." Nikolai throws his hands up and says, "Huh, what do I understand?" He simply throws over the whole mess and instead decides to go out. There's glorious weather for hunting and we suddenly find ourselves embarked on a traditional Russian hunt, the beloved diversion of the Russian aristocracy.

I'd like to call this an intermezzo in the novel, suddenly this tremendous warmth and mutual understanding. Here these people are out in the field of the hunt. We see many members of the Rastov family, including the old Count himself, in their riding costumes and on horseback, a position as ordinary for them as it would be for us to sit in an automobile. We also see, in a certain sense, this analogy being made between the field of the hunt and the field of battle. Nikolai is bound and determined to catch that wolf. Suddenly nothing seems so important to him as catching that wolf. Lo and behold, when we finally catch sight of the hunted animal, believe it or not, the animal actually talks good Russian. You wouldn't believe this, but the first several times I read this book, I actually believed that the wolf was talking. So you said, "Now, hold on, wait a minute. Wolves don't talk. They don't talk English; they don't talk Russian or any human language that we'd recognize. What is this?" Tolstoy actually animates the wolf to a point where he has the character entirely equivalent to any of the characters in the story, any of the human characters. There are not two wolves, two foxes, two rabbits or two horses that have the same character in this novel, any more than there are two human beings that have the same character.

Tolstoy, as I said before, is a wizard and manages to make this world come to life. There is something Godlike in what Tolstoy does. He is creating a universe, in a certain sense, this way, the way that God creates the universe in the Bible. And that says Tolstoy is almost comparable to some kind of god. The scene is a remarkable scene and all the more remarkable because the old Count Rostov is bungling his hunter's duties. Of course, he's had a bit to drink and eat to fortify himself before he goes out. He goes out in the field and he's supposed to watch for the fox, but he doesn't know how to watch for the fox and so he bungles it. And the man who's a serf, Danilov, actually screams at the Count, giving it to him the way you would think the Count would give it to one of his own serfs. Obviously, in the context of the hunt, the whole social situation is reversed. Who is in charge of the whole situation? It's the serf and, of course, both of them are quite embarrassed at what happens at this turn in social relations.

Meanwhile, Nikolai rides out on his side of the hunt and manages to run across some people against whom the Rostov family has a lawsuit; they are arguing about who is the owner of certain lands that lie between their two estates. To Nikolai's amazement, he is expecting to really give it to this fellow. You are ready for Nikolai's well-known temper to explode again against the guy, and the man he meets turns out to be a very courteous gentleman. Nikolai immediately picks up the decency of this guy's feeling. Instead of the anger you expect to find, you suddenly find two men who understand the decency of each other—instead, of course, they talk about the dogs, and Nikolai is tremendously eager for his own dogs to do a better job than the dogs of his neighbor.

At this time he also meets a character called Uncle, who invites Nikolai and also Natasha, Nikolai's sister, who has insisted that she be allowed to come on the hunt, despite the fact they don't want a woman. But Natasha is strong enough; nobody can resist Natasha. So she too is on the hunt, and she and Nikolai are invited by Uncle to visit his house, and you enter a genuine Russian house in the countryside. It's a house with a housekeeper and, of course, one might have some questions about what the actual relations are between the so-called housekeeper and Uncle, who has no other woman in the house. The housekeeper gives them the most delicious food. You wouldn't believe how good it tastes as it does in the countryside right here. There are meat pies, liquors and liqueur; there is absolutely everything to absolutely satisfy the palate, not to mention, of course, good solid Russian bread that bites back when you eat it. Oh, it's magnificent.

Then the Uncle takes hold of his guitar and starts to play Russian songs. When Natasha hears this, she suddenly jumps up, drapes her shawl around her shoulders in the way of a traditional Russian dancer, and starts to dance in a Russian way. It's not the way she's been taught to dance by these French Western teachers but like a true Russian girl; it's a very famous scene. As a matter of fact, it's the basis of a book that's been recently published in this country called *Natasha's Dance*. Tolstoy says:

> *Gde, kak, kogda vsosala v sebia iz togo russkogo [voz]dukha, kotorym ona dyshala, - eta grafinechka, vospitannaia emigrantkoi frantsuzhenkoi, - etot dukh...?*

> Where, how and when did she suck in this into herself from that Russian soul, by means of which she breathes; this little Countess who is brought up by an émigré French teacher,—where did Natasha get this spirit...?

She wasn't trained to it, she wasn't educated to it, and yet, this being Natasha, she exhibits the most beautiful part of the Russian spirit. Those movements were the *pas de châle*, the *step of the shawl*, which should have been wiped out a long time ago. But the spirit and movements were exactly those inimitable and studied Russian ones which her dear Uncle was expecting of her, the exact expression of feeling. Once again Tolstoy is arguing for human feeling coming from deeply inside the individual soul, unlearned, inimitable, the basis of all genuine human relations. It occurs in this intermezzo, but it also applies to the entire novel, both in the scenes of war and of peace. One could almost say this is not a novel about War, with a capital W and Peace with a capital P, *Voina i Mir,* but rather about the wars and peaces, with small letters, of the human soul. When you examine the genuine nature of the human soul you realize there isn't that difference between war and peace that the overview of history tempts us to make.

So the intermezzo ends with some beautiful scenes and we're taken back to the maelstrom of war, attempting to catch the greatest movements and troops in Europe known at that time. Napoleon has put together, from many different nationalities, a huge army. These are not simply Frenchmen, by the way. Some of the bravest soldiers were Poles, who were fighting to get the independence of Poland from Russia, an independence which Napoleon had promised. These soldiers came from all the way across Europe and into the vast spaces of Russia. Here they were met by an equally large, or perhaps an even larger army, of Russians, most of them peasants. Russian soldiers were often called "peasants in overcoats," trying to stem the thrust of the most famous military tactician at that time.

So here we have Napoleon, brilliant, dashing, verbal, a man who knows how to stand before an army. Remember his remarks in Egypt, "Centuries looking down upon us." He says, "The pyramids of Egypt see you." Remember Napoleon there; he knows exactly how to talk to his troops and inspire Frenchmen to achieve the valor of which a Frenchman is capable. On the other side, much to the disgust of many of the Russian aristocrats, and even perhaps of the tsar himself, Marshal Kutuzov, heavy, half blind because he lost an eye in an earlier battle against the Turks, clumsy on a horse, deeply skeptical of all brilliant military strategy, and determined to defeat the enemy by relying on the patience and the nature of the Russian fighting man. Why was it that the tsar was forced, almost against his will, perhaps against his will—at least according to Tolstoy—to put Kutuzov at the head of the army instead of one of those dashing brilliant military strategists, whether a foreign general or one of the Russian aristocracy in the tsar's own family. This was done clearly because they understood that Kutuzov knew the Russian soldier. He understood a good night's sleep is the most important preparation for battle.

We have the generals talking about how they're planning a brilliant battle which is sure to defeat Napoleon, and it is done entirely either in French or in German; "*Die erste Kolonne marschiert... die zweite Kolonne marschiert... die dritte Kolonne marschiert*"—the first column shoots here, the second column follows there, and the third column comes behind. Of course, they couldn't possibly predict where those columns were going to actually end up in the real battlefield, covered with smoke. Nobody knows where he's going, particularly because of this smoke from the artillery; you can't see much further than your own arm and your own nose. It was impossible to predict, and yet these generals were doing brilliant military strategy which they were sure would defeat the enemy. Of course, Napoleon himself was well known as an extraordinarily brilliant strategist. And what did Kutuzov do, the Russian commander? As I said before, when they talk about strategy in the night before the battle, he falls asleep, because a good night's sleep is what you really need before a battle.

One of the most famous parts of the book is Tolstoy's description of the Battle of Borodino, which the French call *La bataille de Moscou*, the Battle of Moscow. Borodino is a city not too far to the west of Moscow where huge numbers of Russians were facing huge numbers of French. Remember, I told you before, in Stendhal's novel, *The Charterhouse of Parma*, he has his protagonist, Fabrizio del Dongo, on the field of battle, seeing the battle through the eyes of a drunk man. He had gotten pretty drunk when the battle started. In short, you see the battle from the point of view of a man who knows nothing about military strategy; you see it through the eyes of a completely naïve person who really doesn't understand what he's seeing and, according to Tolstoy, that's really the way to see a battle. You see a battle not the way you think it should be but the way it really is. Pierre, at the Battle of Borodino, is dressed in civilian clothes with a big feather on top of his hat, which makes it even more dangerous, and, of course, he is totally ignorant.

In this scene, Pierre Bezukhov is what Fabrizio del Dongo was for Stendhal at the Battle of Waterloo. We also see Andrei Bolkonsky, who is going to be mortally wounded on the field of battle; he is going to get a wound which will cause his death in the later course of the novel.

You understand that Bolkonsky had been betrothed to Natasha, but he had left for a year, making Natasha suffer a great deal. In the course of that year, Anatolii Kuragin, one of the sons of Prince Vasilii—and this Anatolii was as close to a scoundrel as a Tolstoy character ever gets—he has seen Natasha, he has been attracted to her, and he feels lust, so he proposes marriage to her. He proposes that she run away from her family and marry him. Of course, what he doesn't tell her is that he is already married—he is already married and can't marry her—but this will get her to run away and have physical relations with him. Luckily for Natasha, the family has alerted a cousin named Sonya to the fact that something strange is happening. When Anatolii comes into the house, Sonya notifies the people who are defending the house and they have to flee. But, of course, Natasha is in total disgrace; it becomes clear that she, a betrothed woman, has, all of a sudden, without any warning, decided to run off with another man. When she learns the truth from Pierre that Anatolii was actually already married, Natasha falls into a terrible sickness, which has a profound effect on her personality and plays a significant role in her maturation from a young girl into a mature person.

When Bolkonsky comes back, he doesn't blame Natasha; he blames Anatolii. And then, of course, he calls off the marriage. He's determined that he will find that Anatolii, come what may; you don't do this to Andrei Bolkonsky and get away with it lightly. And with all the resources of the Bolkonsky family, one of the richest in Russia at that time, he looks for Anatolii high and low, east and west, north and south. It's as if Anatolii has been swallowed up by the earth; nobody can find him. Now Andrei has been mortally wounded on the battlefield of Borodino. Tolstoy shows us a military hospital, and it's terrible, a doctor with a bloody finger, holding a cigar with just the tips of his finger where there is no blood. And Andrei is lying there in the dispensary, and next to him an amputation is taking place, and we feel the saw as it goes back and forth over the human bone, and the character is crying in pain. He gives out a cry, "Oh, oh, oh," and we hear that cry through the whole place. The doctor holds up the leg, which he has just amputated; it's just horrible. And we suddenly realize that that young man whose leg has just been cut off is Anatolii Kuragin.

Now how can a writer get away with a coincidence like this? If this were any other writer, the critics would be screaming this is an unbelievable coincidence. Yet Tolstoy makes it happen. It seems to me that he makes it happen because it deals with the deepest philosophy of the novel, namely, that you cannot predict human behavior. Human behavior is so complicated in so many different variations that mere coincidence is more convincing than any ideology, any strategy, or any idea. You end up with Tolstoy's view of history.

How does this novel actually end, this novel of *War and Peace* and its huge armies going back and forth? Natasha, later on, is married. She is the mother of a child; she is married to Pierre Bezukhov, whose earlier unhappy marriage ended with the death of his wife and now he's the husband. And Natasha comes running in with a diaper in her hand. Of course it's, "Look, look. It's brown; it's no longer green. The child is no longer sick." And anybody who has changed diapers, of course, as I have many times, knows what this means. This magnificent novel ends with a pair of dirty diapers. The armies, Napoleon, Kutuzov, the Russian aristocracy, the families, the Tsar, it all ends up with a pair of dirty diapers. Only Tolstoy could pull off something like this; only Tolstoy can make the magnificence of everything I've just described end up with a pair of dirty diapers.

Lecture Nineteen
Vengeance Is Mine, Saith the Lord

Scope:

After the publication of *War and Peace*, with fame and controversy raging over his head, Tolstoy turned to the creation of another manuscript, written between 1873 and 1877. It deals, in a way, with the opposite of healthy family life, the theme of adultery. First, in the case of the Oblonsky household, Tolstoy deals with it lightly, ironically, using the title protagonist, Anna Karenina, to bring the family back together. Then, Anna's own adultery, with Count Vronsky, brings a more savage tone, appropriate to the biblical reference (Epistle to the Romans, 12:19) quoted in part as the title of this lecture: "Vengeance is mine, saith the Lord, and I shall requite." Tolstoy pulls off something few writers can achieve. He writes a comic parody that makes fun of his own tragic center of the novel: Steve Oblonsky's comically related adultery in contrast to the tragedy of Anna Karenina's. He also manages to present a woman as seen through the eyes of *other women*: Kitty and Dolly, both of the Shcherbatsky family. I know of no other male writer who ever successfully managed that psychological leap.

Outline

I. Tolstoy tried, throughout the huge canvas of *War and Peace*, which Henry James compared to an elephant hitched not to a carriage but to a coach house, to show his view of history. Many critics castigated him for what they considered banality, because he makes such large issues of everyday feelings and events. Yet, in so doing, he manages to bring to life deeply felt emotions of family life and human struggle that we all know and experience.

II. Not long before he began to write *Anna Karenina*, Tolstoy had served as a police witness to the disfigured corpse of a woman who had thrown herself under a train. She had been the mistress of a local landowner who then abandoned her. This experience gave a jolt to Tolstoy's imagination, and he started to write about an immoral woman and the inevitable punishment that would result from her behavior.

A. The epigraph to the novel is a cruel quotation from the Bible, even stronger in its Church Slavonic wording than the English translation: *"Mne otomshchenie, i az vozdam"* ("Vengeance is mine and I shall requite," Epistle to the Romans, 12:19).

B. When Tolstoy began his novel—it went through six or seven drafts, as most of Tolstoy's novels did—he pictured the female protagonist in a very unsympathetic way, whereas her husband was treated as a fine gentleman. But Tolstoy realized that the novel would not be balanced if he developed it that way. He gradually elevated the moral character of the woman (Anna) and diminished the morality of her husband. Thus, Anna engages a tremendous amount of sympathy from the reader, whereas her husband turns into an empty, shortsighted person.

C. The beginning of the book has become one of the world's most oft-repeated literary phrases: *"Vse schastlivye sem'i pokhozhi drug na druga, kazhdaia neschastlivaia sem'ia neschastliva po-svoemu"* ("All happy families resemble one another; each unhappy family is unhappy in its own particular way").

D. Yet the paragraphs that follow the opening lines convey a different mood and flavor: Everything was upset in the Oblonsky household, because Oblonsky's wife had found out that her husband was carrying on a love affair with the children's French governess. We are introduced to Steve Oblonsky, one of Tolstoy's most endearing characters.

E. Like the old Count Rostov whom we saw in *War and Peace*, carelessly going through his wife's substantial dowry so the family would be left penniless, Steve Oblonsky enjoys his pleasures without careful thought for his wife or his children. What these characters do is wrong, yet Tolstoy makes us love them. Tolstoy is no friend of conventional morality, although he is no stranger to human suffering.

F. And then, in an almost satiric vein, if one considers the theme of the novel, the one who brings Steve Oblonsky back together with his long- suffering wife, Dolly, is none other than Steve's sister, Anna Karenina.

1. Anna makes Dolly understand that she must forgive Steve—a family is at stake, and, in Anna's opinion, what Steve has done is relatively mild.

2. Tolstoy makes all these developments come across in a somewhat comic fashion.

G. At still another early point in the novel, Tolstoy shows his unusual understanding of women. Dolly's sister, Kitty, has been through a terrible trauma. She was enticed by the admiration of Count Vronsky, who then changed course and sought the affections of Anna Karenina.

H. Dolly comes in to console her sister, who has fallen into a deep depression. Kitty realizes that her sister has come to offer consolation, and this only infuriates her.

1. She then presses Dolly on her sorest point: Kitty tells her that she would never go back to a man who had betrayed her; Dolly might, but she, Kitty, couldn't.

2. For a moment, both sisters realize the strength of the insult and the cruelty. And, suddenly, they both break into tears, "as if they were the necessary lubricant without which the machine of mutual communication between the sisters could not work."

I. At this point, it seems to me, Tolstoy does something very unusual, perhaps even unique, for a male writer. He sees the world through feminine eyes, rather than through the eyes of a male observing women from the outside. Even Dostoevsky, with all of his colossal psychological insight, observes his women through male eyes.

III. The affair that has developed between Vronsky and Anna Karenina could lead to serious problems. Anna's husband, Aleksei Karenin, a highly placed bureaucrat, seems a cold person, but he loves Anna and is deeply hurt by her infidelity.

A. The infliction of physical pain on Karenin is made even more powerful by the famous scene of the officers' steeplechase race.

1. Vronsky is riding a beautiful, sensitive mare named Frou-Frou. He has sense enough to let her take the course, and she jumps at her own will, as Vronsky refrains from giving directions or pressure with the reins.

But, at the very last minute, he makes the unpardonable mistake of pulling up her head.

    2. Because of Vronsky's clumsiness, the magnificent mare falls with a broken back, and the attendants have to shoot her. Vronsky shouts out in grief and in guilt. The death of the horse is a foreboding of the tragedy to follow.

B. Anna, who has been watching the race, thinks that Vronsky has been hurt, and when her husband sees her reaction, he realizes how very attached to Vronsky she has become. He warns her that if she continues her affair with Vronsky, she will lose both him and her son. But Anna knows she cannot give up Vronsky.

C. The physical consummation of Anna and Vronsky's desires affords little pleasure. After the event, she drops her dishonored head, and Vronsky feels what a murderer must feel.

    1. Tolstoy talks of Anna's spiritual nakedness and compares Vronsky's attempts to cover her with kisses to a murderer hacking his victim's body to pieces, which he will try to hide.

    2. Tolstoy does not spare the reader's sensibility when he describes horror.

IV. But perhaps the most painful moral direction in the novel is given by Anna's nine-year-old son, Serezha.

A. We see Serezha later, when he is already in the sole custody of his father. Clearly, the father has not the slightest idea of how to approach a nine-year-old boy, even his own son. Tolstoy is unsparing when it comes to the world of the St. Petersburg bureaucrats. In the author's view, they are completely divorced from reality.

B. Tolstoy contrasts this coldness to the love and warmth the boy receives from the simple servants in the house, who teach him how to make windmills. Tolstoy had definite ideas about the education of children: One can open their hearts only with the key of love.

C. Anna sees in Serezha's innocence a moral compass that unerringly shows the right and wrong directions for her own life's actions. With great pain, she realizes what her passion with Vronsky will inflict on those around her, most especially her own son.

D. This realization sets the context for one of the most moving and painful scenes in the novel. Anna has been forbidden to see her son, who has been told that his mother is either dead or a bad person. She is determined to see him on his birthday. Boldly she arrives at the door, and the servants let her into the house.

E. For agonizing moments, mother and son stare at each other, bathed in their mutual tears. He indicates that he never believed that she was dead. But she cannot stay for long; the servants have to get her out of the way before Aleksei Karenin returns.

F. This scene is almost impossible to read straight through. Tolstoy grasps the feelings of mother and son so powerfully and so simply that one's whole sensibility rises up against the context.

G. The cruelty of this scene is reminiscent of an episode in Tolstoy's life. Once a month, Tolstoy would hold a "consultation" with the surrounding community.

   1. On one of these occasions, one of his daughters came to him with a rabbit that had a broken foot. Tolstoy took the rabbit and broke its neck in front of his daughter.

   2. This story seems consonant with Tolstoy's personality. Underneath the wide-flowing love lay a quality of remorselessness, which perhaps explains why he was able to capture the mixed qualities of human beings—both the attractiveness and the cruelty—in his novels.

V. Anna and Vronsky go to Italy to avoid the condemnation of St. Petersburg society.

A. After Anna has her portrait painted by a professional artist, Vronsky tries his own hand at a portrait.

B. But Vronsky is an amateur artist, just as he is an amateur in human relations. His appreciation of Anna is less than that of a true companion in life.

VI. When they return from Italy, Anna finds herself ostracized by St. Petersburg society.

- **A.** Vronsky, as a man, is free to go anywhere he wants. Anna feels their growing estrangement. Because she is not free to socialize, she becomes upset at Vronsky's absences. She starts taking drugs, and Vronsky becomes more reluctant to return to her.

- **B.** Anna's situation is aggravated by the legal machinations of her husband, who is trying to keep order in his life. But even he comes to realize that not all of life can be forced to his will.

- **C.** When Dolly visits Anna, she realizes how lucky she is to have a family, even with all its cares.

VII. Anna decides to end her life. She is at the railroad. She hears the train approaching and puts her head on the rails. In Tolstoy's words:

> Muzhichok, prigovarivaia chto-to, rabotal nad zhelezom. I svecha, pri kotoroi ona chitala ispolnennuiu trevog...knigu, vspykhnula bolee iarkim chem. kogda-nibud' svetom ... stala merknut' i navsegda potukhla.

> A small peasant was working on the rails, while muttering to himself. And the candle, by which she had read the book filled with anxieties, deceits, suffering, and evil, sputtered up more brightly than ever before, lit up for her what had previously been dark, threw off wax, grew dim, and forever went dark.

- **A.** The novel's epilogue leaves Vronsky with a toothache that gnaws terribly inside of him as he volunteers to go off to the Balkan Wars in the midst of a Russian patriotic upsurge, which Tolstoy treats with utter skepticism.

- **B.** Vronsky's toothache represents the pain of the adulterous affair and its terrible end.

Suggested Reading:

Lev Tolstoy, *Anna Karenina*, translated by Louise and Aylmer Maude, with an introduction by W. Gareth Jones.

Edward Wasiolek, *Tolstoy's Major Fiction*.

Questions to Consider:

1. The French theater developed a form called *bedroom farce*; it became so popular that the two words almost came together. Tolstoy has constructed a novel, part of which is a tragedy of the bedroom. In what way can the bedroom farce turn into a bedroom tragedy?

2. Nabokov calls *Anna Karenina* a novel about a horse race, obviously referring to Vronsky's ride on the mare named Frou-Frou. To what extent is the critic justified in making that disastrous race a central theme in the novel?

Lecture Nineteen—Transcript
Vengeance Is Mine, Saith the Lord

In this lecture I am planning to make some remarks about *Anna Karenina*, the second of Tolstoy's great novels, written something like 10 to 15 years after he wrote *War and Peace*. Both these novels are enormous pieces of work. *War and Peace* was more than 1,000 pages and *Anna Karenina* was close to 1,000 pages. When people looked at them, they were virtually overwhelmed simply by their size, not to mention by the power of the novels themselves. In Western eyes in particular, at least in those days, it seemed strange the novel would be so immense and so enormous. You may have heard the phrase, "The loose and baggy monster." The American-born writer, Henry James, who wrote mostly in England, made a remark that became famous when he compared a novel by Tolstoy to a monster harnessed to his great subject, human life, as an elephant might be harnessed for purposes of traction, not to a carriage but to a coach house. His own case is prodigious, but his example for others, dire. "Disciples not elephantine he can only mislead and betray." Those are the words of Henry James. To James, it seemed incongruous to have a form of the novel previously so carefully circumscribed, and you know this, particularly if you read some novels by Henry James, dealt with in such length and power by a man like Tolstoy, whose force and talent James compares to the traction power of an elephant hitched to a coach house, no less. Naturally, a writer with a fine and delicate precision of Henry James sees a dangerous precedent in the broad and sweeping genius of the elephant-like Tolstoy. James, through Marcus, set off the imaginations of many critics when they think about the work of the great Russian novelist.

In any case, I'm sure that everybody knows *Anna Karenina* is a novel that has to do with adultery. As a matter of fact, one might almost call this a tragedy of adultery. And that leads to a certain problem in literature. The traditional dealing with the idea of adultery had been almost entirely comic, in the form of a French bedroom farce. It was quite conventional in those days—as a matter of fact, in these days—to talk about a bedroom farce. But to talk about a tragedy of a bedroom, tragedy and bedroom somehow didn't seem to go together. The bedroom somehow wasn't the place for tragedy, it seems. It was the skill of Tolstoy that turned this into a possibility, a possibility, of course, that made a very, very different form of literature. In Tolstoy's own life, he had once been called by the police to be a witness to the corpse of a woman who had committed suicide, who had thrown herself under a train. The woman had been the lover and mistress of one of Tolstoy's neighbors and the police needed a witness for the inquest that came afterwards. It seems to have been this incident that jolted his imagination to the idea of treating the whole matter of adultery. You can get some of that horrible reaction in seeing a corpse in the epigraph of the novel, which is very heavy in Russian; as a matter of fact, it's not even Russian, it's Old Church Slavic. *Mne otomshchenie, i az vozdam*, "Vengeance is mine," saith the Lord, "and I will requite." That was taken from the Epistle to the Romans, Chapter 12, Verse 19. Clearly Tolstoy is making some kind of judgment here about the terrible action Anna took, and what sort of a person that she turned into that she would receive vengeance from the Lord God himself.

As a matter of fact, when Tolstoy started writing the novel, he had gone through six or seven drafts, as most of his works do. The female character—actually under a different name, Tatiana—was pictured in a way that it would be difficult to have any kind of sympathy with her whereas her husband, Aleksei Karenin, was treated as a very noble and fine gentleman. But once the author did this—and obviously this showed something of Tolstoy's attitude toward the event that came from his imagination—he soon realized the novel simply wouldn't make sense that way; it wouldn't have any balance. You couldn't write a novel like this and make it seem realistic if you portrayed the woman so badly and the man so well. So step by step, the character of the woman whose name turned into Anna, went higher and higher in a moral sense and the character of her husband went lower and lower. So in the actual novel, Anna is somebody I think virtually every reader engages a tremendous amount of sympathy for, at least partly from Tolstoy himself, whereas her husband turns into a bureaucratic, empty, unfeeling, shortsighted kind of person that you really wouldn't want to have much to do with. I would call him a windbag, but perhaps that's a bit strong.

The novel begins, oddly enough, with a satire on the tragedy that's going to take place. The beginning sentence of this novel is probably the most famous beginning sentence in all of literature: *"Vse schastlivye sem'i pokhozhi drug na druga, kazhdaia, neschastlivaia sem'ia neschastliva po-svoemu*," "All happy families resemble one another—each unhappy family is unhappy in its own particular way." This is the beginning of the novel. It's followed by everything being in confusion in the Oblonsky household because it turned out that the master had been in sexual relations with the woman who was acting as a caretaker for one of the children. The wife, whose Russian name is Daria, but everyone calls her Dolly—notice that here English names, it's a style to turn Russian names into English, unlike what we saw before in an earlier time when they turned them into French—Dolly is terribly upset. She wants nothing more to do with her husband. She wants to completely reject him. How could he possibly do this? Here she had worked very hard and raised a large family of children and here he was off having what he considered to be happy relations with the governess of the children, for God's sake.

In the opening part of the novel we see Stepan Oblonsky—but they call him Steve or, in Russian, Stiva—who is sleeping on the couch rather than in his bed because his wife has tossed him out of the bedroom. The novel opens, and that is that scene, opens with one of his dreams. Again, we see the position of dreams in Russian literature. He is terribly upset and doesn't know what to do. He realizes he has done something terribly wrong and yet, somehow, he can't quite bring himself to condemn his own act; it seemed to be so natural. He is a man who likes to take pleasure where pleasure can be grabbed. What's the matter with that? Of course, it's easy enough for him to say it. Imagine what it looks like to the wife. What we have here is another variant on the character we saw in *War and Peace*. That character was the old Count Rostov, who always did everything wrong and yet somehow you ended up loving him, not knowing exactly why, but there is something attractive about him. Oblonsky is exactly the same kind of character. Of course, the actions are not quite the same. But everything that Oblonsky does is wrong and brings judgment from his fellow characters and most especially from the character named Levin. This major character in the novel is a deeply thinking and feeling person whose behavior will form a strong contrast to that of Oblonsky. As I said, like with Count Rostov, everything Oblonsky does is morally wrong and we know it, even he knows it. But somehow you can't help liking the guy. There is something tremendously attractive about him. And again, it's

Tolstoy's commentary about that old notion of *comme il faut*, the idea of conventional morality, of doing everything the way society decides it should be done.

Well, the title character, Anna Karenina, is actually the married sister of Stiva Oblonsky. Of course, her maiden name was Oblonskaia. She gets the news of Stiva's affair and she decides she'll come back and try to set things straight for their family. Obviously, it's rather ironic that Anna, of all people, should solve the problems of adultery, which is going to produce a terrible tragedy later in her life. In this part of the novel the adultery is really taken, from the point of view of the author, rather lightly, although it wasn't taken lightly by Dolly who is a member of the Shcherbatsky family, or by any other of the women in the story. And Tolstoy also understands that. Anna comes and she tries very hard to somehow reconcile Dolly with her husband Oblonsky, who is, of course, Anna's brother. She manages to talk to Dolly in a way that Dolly understands. Well then, after all, there has to be a kind of forgiveness. A family is at stake. A life is at stake. Stiva isn't really as bad as she thought he was and the shock of the realization of the adultery—I wouldn't want you to think that I take adultery lightly—I certainly don't—but somehow Tolstoy makes this come across in a somewhat comic fashion, that very same adultery which is going to be tragic later in the novel.

Now there's a young woman in the novel, Kitty Shcherbatskaia, who is quite entranced by Anna. Kitty is much younger, of course, than Anna is. She sees in Anna a very beautiful, attractive, stylish woman whom, in many ways, she, Kitty, would like to emulate. Now Kitty is being wooed by a man named Count Aleksei Vronsky. Vronsky is supposed to take her to a ball and she is very much looking forward to the ball, to which Anna, as a visitor, is also invited. To Kitty's horror, when Vronsky sees Anna, he has eyes for nobody but Anna, and he simply ignores Kitty. In short, Kitty is jilted by the very man she was counting on to get a proposal from and become his wife. As you might imagine, this is terribly upsetting to be jilted by Vronsky, who makes it even worse by entering into an affair with Anna. Kitty goes into almost a kind of mourning. She is Dolly's sister, so Dolly comes in to console Kitty, who has fallen into a deep depression, as I talked about before. Kitty realizes that her sister has come to offer her consolation, and wouldn't you think that she might be pleased by this sort of—her sister cares about her—but, instead, her reaction is one of being infuriated because she thinks that Dolly is looking down on her and making fun of her. This is only an excuse to come in and show how superior she, Dolly, was to her sister, Kitty. Kitty tells her that she would never come back to a man who had betrayed her. Dolly might, but she, Kitty couldn't. And for a moment both sisters realize the strength of the insult and the cruelty, a terrible thing to say to your sister. A terrible mutual feeling breaks out between them. There is no fight quite so bitter and quite so hot as a family quarrel. As the two sisters are there, ready to tear each other apart, suddenly they both break into tears as if this was a necessary lubricant without which the machine of mutual communication between the sisters could not work.

It seems to me, now my view—you could argue about this, I'm sure—but it seems to me that Tolstoy does something very unusual, perhaps even unique, for a male writer. He manages to see the world through feminine eyes. It's as if he gets himself into the head of a woman and sees the world the way a woman would see it rather than through the eyes of a male observing women from the outside. Even Dostoevsky, with all his colossal psychological insight, observes as a woman through male eyes, which, after all, is perfectly natural. He is, after all, a man. How Tolstoy pulls this off, I don't quite know, but he manages to do it. Now I have to add here that this could very well bring a certain amount of argument among women. I once tried to argue this in a class of mine at Northwestern University and one of my very bright and articulate female students said to me, with emotion, in fact, I will never forget, "Professor Weil, what do you know about women?" Well, I had to admit the obvious fact that I'm not a woman, that's for sure. But I said, "Look, after all, I have a mother, I have a wife, I have a daughter. These days at least, I have a granddaughter; I know something about women." She said, "Nah, you know nothing at all." So I'm not sure I could convince someone like that of my argument, but I still remain convinced that Tolstoy did have this uncanny knack of getting inside others in spite of the fact that they were very, very far from his own experience. He did this to the extent that he could actually even get inside the head of a woman. And I must say, I don't know if any other male writer, at least that I've encountered, was able to do this.

Now the affair between Vronsky and Anna, which started after they met again at the ball, could lead to some very serious problems. The Karenin family was, after all, a very highly placed family in

Petersburg, the capital in those days. Karenin was a high placed bureaucrat and this was something he was not about to take lightly, although one thing we also have to understand is Karenin seems to have a very cold and repulsive kind of character in many parts of the novel. Yet, in spite of all that coldness, one thing is unmistakable, and we see the original portrait that Tolstoy had in mind of Karenin; he deeply loved Anna. He feels deeply hurt by the fact that Anna has betrayed him. He is hurt that Anna has turned her affections towards another man in spite of the fact that she did this obviously in part because of the characteristics of her husband she couldn't stand. He cracked his fingers, he had long ears, that kind of thing. As a matter of fact, one might go so far as to say that Aleksei Karenin couldn't live in a normal fashion without Anna.

So the beginning of the realization from Aleksei Karenin that Anna really is going away from him is a very painful thing for him to take and, of course, in turn, for society to take. This is represented by Tolstoy in a rather unusual way in this novel. As a matter of fact, Nabokov, the famous critic and writer, has gone so far as to call *Anna Karenina* a novel about a horse race. Vronsky, who, of course, is going to be a lover of Anna, had a very fine horse that he loved by the name of Frou-Frou, a French name he gave to the horse. He was going to ride this horse in a steeplechase race. The horse was obviously very sensitive, very high strung. It had to be handled with a very light hand because, even if you made the slightest wrong move, you could ruin the horse and yourself. Clearly a certain analogy is being drawn between the relationships between Vronsky and the horse and Vronsky and Anna. So the race takes place and Anna and her husband are in the aristocratic crowd watching the steeplechase. And somehow Vronsky manages to get Frou-Frou over the first hurdle. Tolstoy describes the race in considerable detail. Then he manages to—that is to say, Vronsky—manages to get Frou-Frou over the second hurdle, then the third and the fourth. These things are very difficult to manage. You have to have a very fine kind of horsemanship in order to manage it. But at the very last hurdle, Vronsky, who seems to lose concentration for just a second, a fraction of a second, makes one very tiny wrong move and everything is lost. The horse's foot is caught in the obstacle because he didn't move it right on time. The horse falls. Vronsky is thrown from the horse. It is clear that not only has the horse broken several limbs but the animal has to be killed. The killing of this horse is obviously a foreboding of the tragedy that is going to happen in this novel.

Vronsky grabs his head in his hands and is subject to despair, the likes of which no human being could normally experience or know. He is plunged in the most hideous, black, awful kind of despair. Anna, as the other people watching the race, is terribly upset, first, because she thinks Vronsky is hurt. Her husband, Aleksei Karenin, when he sees this, realizes she is really very closely attached to Vronsky. And, of course, people see it and he is worried what people are going to see. As a matter of fact, he thinks more about what people will see than what he feels. In the carriage on the way home, he tells her what's going to happen if this continues, in a very pedantic way. He can't stand for something like this in the house. If she continues in this way, she is going to lose both him and her son, Serezha. Anna is overcome with grief but, at the same time, she can't lightly give up the love of Vronsky. This is something that she simply has to go through with.

In an almost unforgettable scene between Anna and Vronsky, we see the consummation of their physical relationship. Tolstoy expresses it with a series of dots. When these dots are over, Anna is lying on the floor, in Tolstoy's words, "Almost like a hacked, murdered body." Vronsky attempts to cover her with kisses, as a murderer might hack a body to pieces—a rather strange analogy—which he won't try to hide. Tolstoy doesn't spare the reader's sensibility when the author describes the horror of what's happened. This physical consummation is something that's very important and which causes Anna to agree to go away from her family and to leave her son with the father, and we know what this means from what Aleksei Karenin has threatened.

Now Aleksei Karenin has no conception of how you educate a young man. All he knows are the formal rules about teaching, trying to teach people. The more he tries to teach his son, the colder he gets; the colder he gets, the less the son learns, because, according to Tolstoy, the only way a person learns, the only way it's possible to impart knowledge to somebody, is with the presence of love. If love is gone, then no learning takes place. Believe me, this is a deep insight and might well be a good lesson for any teacher. I think Tolstoy knew what he was talking about when he was talking about education. When the servants, on the other hand, teach Serezha, the child, how to build windmills, then he learns. He has a wonderful time and he learns perfectly; but when the father talks to him, it goes in one ear and out the other.

At the same time, as Tolstoy says, the innocent child is a kind of a moral compass which shows both parents unerringly, just as a compass does, the right and the wrong directions of life's actions. Of course, Anna realizes through the reactions of her son the terrible things she is doing, but she can't help herself. In any case, when Anna leaves the house, Karenin tells the son that his mother has died. Then we come to a scene which I must admit, to this day, I cannot read straight through because it's so painful. The pain goes so deeply that even after many, many readings I still can't bring myself to read straight through it. Anna decides that she simply cannot live without seeing her son; so one night—her son is asleep at that point, of course—she comes into the house she has been forbidden, you remember, to come into, and with the help of the servants, who remember her from the old days and like her. Even though it's forbidden, they allow her into the house and she goes into the bedroom of her sleeping son and wakes him up. Of course, he thinks that she's gone—that's what he been told. And for several agonizing moments the son sees the mother and each one of them lives through this awful, deeply grinding pain, a separation between mother and son. At first, it seems to him that she is part of a dream but eventually he comes enough to wakefulness to realize this is his real mother in front of him; it's a scene of unbearable cruelty. Then, as the servants hear that Aleksei is coming into the house, they have to rush her away, and Serezha is, once again, bereft of his mother.

Tolstoy is known as a writer with a flowing kind of love and understanding. But when he lifts the lid of that understanding just a little bit, what you see underneath is a very cruel, almost sadistic way of looking at the universe, which, of course, is part of the talent of a writer. I must admit that I personally find his cruelty much more upsetting and much harder to take than that of Dostoevsky, which is virtually there on every page, because in the case of Dostoevsky it's open. You know exactly where the pathology is coming from; you know when to expect it, you know how to deal with it. In Tolstoy's case, it's hidden, and what's hidden is much more frightening in life. When it suddenly opens like that, oh, is it hard to take. In that sense, the surface of Tolstoy can be very deceiving in what he does.

Anna finds herself in a much more difficult situation. The cruelty here reminds me a little bit of the story a very famous and respected literary critic of the early century—his name is Shklovsky—told about. He told it about Tolstoy later on. Tolstoy, as you may know, had quite a large family. He was very much interested in his children and the education of his and other people's children. He wanted to help take part in the education, and so on. Once a week, he used to come out of his house to a place where people could come to for consultation. One time, according to Shklovsky, and I trust him as a reliable source, evidently one of Tolstoy's daughters came to him with a little rabbit, or a hare, and the hare had a broken foot. She said, *"Papa, Papa, zaichik, zaichik. Prosmetrit, Papa"*; "Look, the little hare, Papa, he's got a broken foot. Papa, please do something." According to the story, Tolstoy wordlessly took the hare into the hands of an experienced hunter and broke its neck in front of his daughter. Of course, this is a reported story. I don't have proof that it actually happened although, as I repeat, Shklovsky is a very reliable source. It seems to me that this is very consistent with the Tolstoy I have just been talking about. Underneath that wide-flowing love lay a remorseless and very stern view of humanity, and he saw humanity as it really was, humanity as it really is, a very great mixture of both good and bad qualities, and Tolstoy was able to catch both sides although, when you read his work, on the surface you think that what he caught was family happiness, as he once called it in later novels of his, with wonderful characters who are so tremendously attractive to the reader who comes into contact with them.

In any case, Anna finds herself in an increasingly difficult situation with Vronsky. They go off to Italy in order to get away from the condemnation of society around them. While they are in Italy, Anna has her portrait painted, first of all by a professional Russian émigré painter who is living in Italy, as was the case in those days for many people. Then Vronsky, as an amateur would-be painter, also tries to paint her portrait. Tolstoy gives us a sense of the difference between a portrait drawn by a professional painter and a portrait done by an amateur. Of course, that has something to do with Vronsky's appreciation of Anna; no doubt he probably had some talent as an artist, although he never put himself through the vigorous training that a genuine professional artist would have to do in order to produce a professional painting. So he knew something about painting, but he was an amateur. In the very same sense, he also knew something about Anna, and he had great feelings for Anna, although those feelings were as much of lust as they were genuine love and attachment. But somehow he couldn't quite overcome that; he couldn't get through that to really touch Anna's soul. There was a kind of companion a human being needs when you have a real conjugal relationship. The result was that what he saw in Anna was analogous to what he saw in art. Just as he was a kind of amateur in art, so he was an amateur in human relations. And, of course, amateurs pay a terrible price when they want to become professionals.

Eventually, of course, the two of them realized they couldn't live forever in Italy. They came back to St. Petersburg society. Then, as you might imagine, Anna is in a terrible situation because none of her former friends will have anything to do with her, at least publicly. They are afraid that if they associate with her, people will look at them the way they look at Anna. She can't go to any kind of social occasion; she's been completely ostracized by Petersburg society. Tolstoy obviously doesn't approve of this but, at the same time, it's the kind of punishment that society had at that time, at least for somebody who got involved in what they regarded as an illegitimate relationship. So Anna is confined to the countryside whereas Vronsky, as a man, is free. You might call this the famous double standard. Vronsky, as a man, is free to go anywhere he wants and interact with anyone he wants. He can continue to hobnob with his officers. As a matter of fact, Tolstoy points out in one particular point in this novel—it's one of the few places where he or, for that matter, anyone else in Russian literature talks about the issue of homosexuality. There are two officers in the company; there are two officers who come together all the time, wherever Vronsky goes, and these officers are very close to each other, and a few sarcastic remarks are made about the relationship. We don't often see that in a Russian novel. Tolstoy of course, catches all aspects of human behavior.

Then, of course, Vronsky comes back home and Anna is terribly worried, "Where have you been? I've missed you for so long. Ah, you're probably taking up with some other woman." She becomes really jealous and very hard to deal with. The relationship becomes a more and more difficult one, both for her and for Vronsky because she can't have the freedom of movement that she once had. She is much more unhappy. As a matter of fact, not only is she unhappy, and takes it out in words, but she begins to get on to morphine and other drugs that dull the senses and the kind of person she really was. Eventually, Vronsky finds he is almost reluctant to come back to Anna because she is always harping at him, always saying bad things to him, and she turns into a kind of a nag. The relationship really has devolved in a terrible way. Now Anna's situation has been aggravated by her husband's, that is, Karenin's, legal machinations which he instigates in the office of a Petersburg lawyer. Karenin is terribly annoyed when the lawyer clearly wants to laugh at the deceived husband and tries to cover up his laughter by simply clapping his hands noisily together, as if he's trying to catch moths. The incongruity of the scene well captures Karenin's desperate attempt to keep order in his life, which has lost all domestic order. Even Karenin has to realize that not all of life can be forced to comply with his rules. He, of course, knows the law as well—if not even better—than that lawyer, but somehow his knowledge of the law, his power as a bureaucrat, his power even to make laws leaves him absolutely helpless in this particular situation.

Stiva Oblonsky also discovers this when he tries to get a well-paid position in the new Russian railway companies, only to find that other people, not all of them aristocrats by birth, by the way, are far more clever than he when they pursue their own economic and mercantile interests. None of these machinations can help Anna's suffering situation in Russian society. Things obviously can't continue going that way for very long. Dolly comes to visit Anna; of course, in many ways, she envies Anna's freedom from the kind of child-raising that Dolly has had all too much of, she feels. But when Dolly sees the way Anna feels, she realizes just how lucky she is to have these children and the cares and worries of family life. Life looks very differently when you see it from another person's point of view.

When she leaves her, Dolly realizes that Anna is indeed in a terrible, terrible way. So Anna gets close to the inevitable end that we all know about in this novel. She decides there is nothing to do but to end her life. She ends it with the help—if that's the proper word—of perhaps one of the most powerful instruments in Russia at that time, with a railroad train. In an early scene of the novel, we saw Anna riding on a train. That's where she meets Vronsky, when she's riding on the train on the way to Petersburg; a very famous train ride that's described by Tolstoy. Now she sees a train and there's a peasant who is hammering on the rails. This is the memory she has on that trip that she took when she met Vronsky:

> *Muzhichok, prigovarivaia chto-to, rabotal nad zhelezom. I svecha, pri kotoroi ona chitala ispolnennuiu trevog...knigu, vspykhnula bolee iarkim chem. kogda-nibud' svetom ... stala merknut' i navsegda potukhla.*

> A small peasant was working on the rails, while muttering something to himself. [He was working with the iron; he was pounding with the hammer.] And the candle, within whose light she read the fulfilled anxieties of her life [the book of her life]. [This candle] sputtered up more brightly than ever before. It began to go out and forever went out.

She hears the sound of the train coming and Tolstoy makes us feel this in great detail. She put her head on the rails and something tremendously heavy, dark and awful comes; and that is the horrible end of her life.

The epilogue ends with Vronsky going off to join the volunteers in the Balkan wars. The Russians regarded the Slavic people as their *bratushki*, their own brothers and decided they had to liberate them. Tolstoy, of course, treats this patriotic upsurge with total skepticism and cynicism. Vronsky, in order to get away from the terrible guilt he goes through, volunteers to go to the wars. But, as Oblonsky comes to see him, all dressed in a uniform, he is suffering from a terrible toothache, and that terrible toothache represents the pain and the awfulness of this adulterous affair and its terrible, terrible ending.

Lecture Twenty
Family Life Makes a Comeback

Scope:

In contrast to the parody and tragedy of the Oblonskys and the Karenins, we see genuine and healthy conjugal life, with all of its attending stresses and joys, destined to last a lifetime. This destiny we observe as the result of the marriage of Kitty, née Shcherbatskaia, and Konstantin Levin, a character in many ways obviously related to his creator, Tolstoy. The novelist's first name is close to the character's family name; the proposal of marriage repeats verbatim the word game Tolstoy used in his own proposal to Sofiia Bers. Perhaps most important, Levin's final religious conversion, or epiphany, parallels Tolstoy's own—which we know will be as temporary; Tolstoy could never stop searching. As Isaiah Berlin put it brilliantly: Tolstoy was born to be a fox, an animal who runs far and wide over the fields; he desperately wanted to become a hedgehog, an animal that remains with one overwhelming insight and defense. *Anna Karenina* magnificently and profoundly shows this truth and this agony.

Outline

I. The publisher of *Anna Karenina* refused to print the skeptical epilogue, saying it was too long. Tolstoy wrote a sarcastic letter to the publisher, which he never sent, because it would have spoiled the image of the "all-loving" Tolstoy. His decision not to send the letter seems something of a paradox in view of his outward support of open expression.

II. In contrast to the dark and destructive relationship between Anna and Vronsky, the novel offers us the character and the family life of Konstantin Levin. Not only does his last name coincide with the first name of the author, but many details of his ordinary, daily life also bear a strong resemblance to those of Tolstoy.

   A. We first see Levin bursting into the office of Steve Oblonsky. Levin is tremendously eager to talk with Oblonsky about the possibility of proposing marriage to Oblonsky's sister-in-law, Kitty Shcherbatskaia.

1. Levin observes the "boring, useless" daily work of the bureaucrats, and he looks with disdain at the long and carefully tended fingernails of Grinevich, Oblonsky's bureaucratic colleague.

2. To Oblonsky's obvious amusement, Levin is repelled by the useless and ostentatious beauty of the fingernails, which would only get in the way of any work that Levin would consider seriously productive, that is, work on his agricultural estate.

B. Oblonsky encourages him to act fast with regard to Kitty, because it looks as if Vronsky is pursuing the same goal.

C. We then get the marvelous presentation of Levin and Kitty together for the first time. It occurs at an ice-skating pond, where Levin's remarkable physical strength and skill come out in all their glory, and Kitty's young and fresh beauty, combined with genuine sensitivity, make her seem the ideal mate.

D. Tolstoy gives this scene a kind of spiritual dimension with a lovely, light touch.

1. The heavily snow-laden Russian birches, in all their majesty, seem "dressed in beautiful edges of icons and solemn priestly robes" ("*Razubrany v torzhestvennye rizy*").

2. Tolstoy thus adds elements of Russian folklore, together with a religious feeling right out of the most beautiful part of Russian nature: the Russian winter.

E. Later, Levin is rudely awakened from this idyllic dream when Kitty turns him down.

III. Kitty's refusal deeply wounds Levin, who retires to his country estate.

A. The seemingly inevitable distancing of Moscow and Russian high society from Levin's life gives us a chance to concentrate on the realities the Russian countryside, which Tolstoy considered the genuine center of the Russian spirit.

B. Levin's old friend Oblonsky comes out to pay a visit, and they quickly find themselves united in the common pursuit of the Russian aristocracy, which we have already seen in *War and Peace*—the hunting of animals.

C. All of a sudden, Oblonsky brings up the avoided topic of Kitty. Levin learns that Kitty has been jilted by Vronsky and is seriously ill. Naturally, the news disturbs him.

D. But we know we are in a novel by Tolstoy when we learn that the news is even more disturbing to someone else, Laska, the retriever dog, who lifts her ears in canine disgust.

    1. She wonders to herself how these stupid people can take a time like this, when the birds are overhead, to talk about irrelevancies.

    2. Somehow, once again, Tolstoy makes the verbalization of animals as important, if not more so, as the chatter of human beings.

E. Somewhat later in the summer, when Levin's half-brother visits the estate and Levin reacts with some skepticism about the new political institutions in Russia, Levin decides that he needs a break from the frustrations of intellectual argument. To soothe his irritated temper, he picks up a scythe to participate in the mowing of the harvest.

F. In one of the most famous scenes by Tolstoy, we get a detailed description of physical labor on the Russian farm. Line by line and row by row, we see the workers attacking the mounds of grass. At first, the scythe feels clumsy in Levin's hands, and his body can barely withstand the unaccustomed strain. Little by little, he gets into the rhythm, and he finds that he can keep up with the peasants, who are no longer laughing at him.

G. Suddenly, Levin comes to a very Tolstoyan conclusion: As soon as he lost count of time and forgot to analyze what he was doing, his mowing went well and gave him pleasure. But as soon as he started to think about it, consciously trying to improve, the work went badly and he felt tired.

H. As in many other Tolstoyan moments, conscious thought was the enemy of good results. This rejection of conscious thought is, of course, stated by that very same Tolstoy who analyzes every action and feeling of his characters, even of the dogs and the horses! If one is looking for consistency, Tolstoy is not the place to look.

I. Thus, it is hardly surprising to discover that Levin, after enjoying the ordered attractiveness of the Russian countryside, abandons his idea of finding marital happiness with a peasant woman. As he sees Kitty riding by in a carriage, he realizes that she is the only possible woman for him.

IV. Having gone through the bitter disappointment of rejection, Levin now meets Kitty at the Oblonsky house in Moscow.

   A. Levin approaches Kitty at a card table, where she is using the chalk to draw circles on a green cloth.

   B. Levin takes the chalk and does the same thing that Tolstoy did when he proposed marriage: He writes the first letter of each word in the sentence that he wished to communicate to his prospective bride. She puzzles over it for a short time, then immediately understands that he is asking for a reversal of her previous refusal. She then communicates in the same way, and we understand that both of them are on the same wavelength.

   C. They marry and Levin discovers the deep discomfort of causing insult and hurt when he least expects it: Kitty is upset and angry when he comes home late. As he begins to remonstrate with her because of what seems to him her unreasonable reaction, he begins to realize that she has already become part of himself. His excited arguments against her are really arguments against himself.

   D. When a light-minded Vasya Veslovsky comes to Levin's estate and attempts to play the usual societal game of light flirtation with Kitty, Levin burns with inner fury.

      1. He quickly decides that Veslovsky must leave and confronts the man without any diplomatic niceties, although he knows that he will appear ridiculous in the eyes of the society around him.

      2. The whole episode has a slightly comic air to it, as observed by Oblonsky, but it is deadly serious to Levin.

   E. Later in the novel, Levin goes to visit Anna, when she is living in isolation from aristocratic society. To his surprise, he finds a kind of sympathy for her welling up inside of him.

IV. It is hardly surprising that the final Christian epiphany, which Levin claims to find, seems to be a temporary one. Like Levin, Tolstoy could never stop searching. This trait has been caught by Isaiah Berlin in his essay "The Hedgehog and the Fox."

   A. Berlin quotes an ancient Greek proverb: The fox knows many things, the hedgehog knows but one. The fox explores all aspects of the field; his defenses are all over the countryside. The hedgehog has one defense: his sharp quills.

   B. Berlin believed that all writers were either foxes or hedgehogs.

   1. The greatest fox was Shakespeare, because he explored all aspects of human nature.

   2. The greatest hedgehogs were Dante and Dostoevsky, because both saw one central salvation that illuminated their entire work.

   3. Tolstoy was a fox but would have liked to have been a hedgehog.

Suggested Reading:

Isaiah Berlin, *The Hedgehog and the Fox.*

Questions to Consider:

1. When the novel presents the ongoing and presumably permanent marriage of Levin and Kitty, Tolstoy is drawing a picture that might be called *Family Happiness*, the title of one of his later novels. How does he make it appear realistic in a way that avoids sentimentality?

2. In what way does the doomed affair of Anna Karenina serve as a contrast or, perhaps, reflecting mirror to the happy marriage of Levin and Kitty? Don't forget the novel's epigraph ("Vengeance is mine, saith the Lord...") and Levin's apparent sympathy for Anna near the end of the novel.

Lecture Twenty—Transcript
Family Life Makes a Comeback

In the last lecture, when we were talking about the ending of *Anna Karenina*, I tried to describe a little bit about the epilogue where Vronsky goes off to the Balkan wars with a toothache. Tolstoy expresses his deep skepticism about the whole policy in Russia of supposedly trying to help their brother Slavs in the Balkans but, in reality, actually trying to extend their power. This skepticism was expressed so strongly that at the end of the publication in which the whole novel *Anna Karenina* had been published, a man named Katkov, the editor, that is, decided he would not publish the epilogue, but would only summarize it for the benefit of his readers. He said, "Oh, after all, Mr. Tolstoy's novel is getting a bit too long so I'll simply summarize it and not print the whole thing." When Tolstoy heard about this, he composed a letter to Katkov where he said the following:

> Dear Mr. Katkov: With your usual honesty and sincerity as an editor, you said you wouldn't publish my epilogue in your journal because you said the novel was getting too long. It would be interesting to know why you published all six parts of the novel, which are very long, and then refused to publish the short epilogue, claiming it was too long. If it was so long, why did you publish the other parts? But for the benefit of those of your readers who are upset by its length, let me summarize:

> There was once a certain Anna Karenina. She lived in Petersburg. She got angry about many things. She fell in love with Count Vronsky and threw herself under a train.

> Sincerely yours, Leo Tolstoy.

Now, of course, this was a marvelous put-down to a somewhat conservative, if not reactionary, editor. What's interesting is that Tolstoy wrote the letter—we have the manuscript—but he never sent it. And, of course, he didn't send it because it would spoil the image of the all-loving Tolstoy, the Tolstoy that, at that time, many people thought was beginning to run for God, to run the universe. Now, of course, coming from a man who talks so much about conventionality and honest feelings and the openness of expression, this seems to be something of a paradox, if not a contradiction. And I do think that such paradoxes and contradictions did exist in Tolstoy's life in spite of all his arguments about being open and feeling into society.

But, in any case, in this novel, what I've talked about a little bit so far is the nature of love, that is, Tolstoy's notion of the nature of love, of passion and wild attraction. I've talked about that wild and wonderful attraction—also tragic, by the way—between Vronsky and Anna Karenina, which ended up, of course, destructively. There is, of course, as almost everybody knows, another love in this novel, and that is the love that ends up as conjugal love. That's the relationship between Kitty, about whom we talked earlier, and Levin, the other major character in this novel. You'll notice, by the way, the name Levin obviously has some connection with Tolstoy since his first name was Lev, so that Levin was simply an extension of that same name with "in" added to the end as very often happens in Russian names. Levin was a character who tries to look at everyone rationally, including himself, when he behaves less intelligently than he would like. At the same time, he is also a man of very deep feeling and real sensitivity, so the reader is drawn to him in a warm and friendly manner. He is obviously close to the author in many ways.

Now this is similar to something that happened in *War and Peace*, where Pierre Bezukhov, the major character that we saw who was so open to many different kinds of emotions, grows rather fat in the course of the novel. He lives the good life a bit too well. The name Tolstoy is very closely connected to the Russian word for fat. The Russian word is *tolstyi*; all you have to do is change the stress. Instead of *tolstyi*, it becomes *tolstoy*, so that Pierre could be Mr. Gross or Mr. Fat. Clearly there is a connection between Tolstoy and Pierre Bezukhov, as there is a connection between Tolstoy and Konstantin Levin.

Now Levin is somebody who lives in the country and you remember what the country means to Tolstoy and to most Russians in those days and, for that matter, perhaps even today. That's the real Russia, not the artificial life of a city but the genuine life in the country. Levin first comes into Oblonsky's office near the beginning of the novel because he wants to ask him about the possibility of making a proposal of marriage to Kitty. Oblonsky is sitting there, and as Levin walks in, he suddenly observes—and this is something particular to the structure of the Russian language—"*Ego skuchnaia, nikomu ne nuzhnaia rabota;*" translating it literally is his boring, daily, useless, not to anyone not necessary work. The very length and rhythm of the sentence gives you some idea about how Tolstoy and, of course, how Levin feels about the uselessness of the work of the bureaucrats. Of course, the first thing that catches Levin's eye are the fingernails of an associate named Grinevich. He has very long fingernails, ostentatiously beautiful, which would get in the way of any work that Levin would consider genuine work. Just imagine trying to work on an agricultural estate in the countryside, trying to work on the land with those long fingernails. That shows the distinction between the artificial side of life, as Tolstoy sees it, and the genuine real work that takes place in the countryside.

But even though Levin is attached to the countryside and can't think about working anywhere but on a farm and a land that is so important to Russia, at the same time he feels he can't live without the love of Kitty who, of course, comes from the city, who comes from Moscow. Oblonsky encourages him; he says, "Look, act fast. I think Vronsky is after her so go ahead and make your move." Then we have one of the most beautiful scenes, I think, that Tolstoy ever wrote; it's the scene where Kitty is on ice skates. Of course, she has her muff, is dressed in a beautiful dress; she is a young woman. The cold is bringing out the color in her cheeks. She is just the ideal of a young woman seen through the ideas of a young man. Remember before, when I said Tolstoy knows how to get inside a woman's head? In this particular case, she is certainly observed from the point of view of a man; she is the ideal creature for some man to fall in love with, innocent, beautiful, strong, athletic, well-dressed, and everything that would come to mind for the conventionally beautiful woman. So Levin meets her at the ice-skating rink and goes out on skates. He, himself, is a rather good skater.

As he gets out on the ice, he is looking at the heavily snow-laden Russian birches and all their majesty around them. Now you have to understand, American birch trees, from the point of view of Russians, are dwarves, very small and of a stunted growth. In Russia, the birch trees are huge with all the graceful beauty of the white bark and the light green foliage. The Russians call them *damskie pal'chiki*, the small beautiful fingers of women. Levin looks at these trees and they turn into *rizy*, which are the beautiful silver edges within icons. If you look at a Russian icon, you'll notice that in some cases the features of the religious figures of the icon are encased in a silver-looking metal. These silver-looking streaks, so to speak, which go through the center of the picture, only add to the depth and the wonder of the picture. Tolstoy manages to identify the feeling of this beautiful birch forest, under snow and ice, coming out of the most beautiful part of Russian nature, the Russian winter. Seldom has this been done in a more lovely and a more beautiful way. Of course, as readers, we can bask in the lovely Russian winter light; there is something magnificently attractive about this.

Tolstoy makes the most of it as the two are going gracefully skating along and then, as Levin is a very good athlete, he jumps over several barrels and shows that physically he is at one with nature and with his skates. He feels that somehow he is getting close to Kitty and he doesn't realize what's actually going on. One is left with a magnificent feeling from this particular scene. Of course, Levin goes on, living in his own little dream world, little realizing it's only a dream world, and he is awakened roughly from this idyllic dream when Kitty turns him down in anticipation of a proposal she expects from Vronsky. Levin realizes that his dream is simply not going to come true, at least in this part of the novel. In fact, at this point, it's no more than a dream. For Levin, of course, this is a very painful time in the course of the novel. Tolstoy makes it even more painful when he goes to Moscow and to an evening where the Countess Nordston is. Of course, Levin has always looked down on the Countess because she represents, for him, everything he doesn't like about the urban life and everything he thinks is the unreal life of the city. Of course, she knows he has been turned down and tries to take advantage of it now by making fun of him at his expense. She says, "Well, I see you've come back to our sinful Babylon in Moscow, have you?" Levin attempts to parry the jest; he says, "Well, I see you've taken my word seriously. You remember my remark about the sinful Moscow." And then he makes the faux pas of repeating it, saying the same thing twice. And of course, this is very clumsy in high society.

In short, Levin is not the man to make his way gracefully through high society. Of course, this gives him a great plus in Tolstoy's eyes. This becomes even more ironic if you remember Tolstoy's attitude about bureaucratic Petersburg, the home of Aleksei Karenin, Anna's real husband, and his cold conventionality. Moscow, with the Shcherbatsky family, the family of Dolly and Kitty, is very far from the sins of Babylon and much closer to the rustic warmth of Levin's countryside. Yet, in Levin's eyes, at this particular point it takes on an urban overcast. It is interesting how things change very quickly in Tolstoy's sight in the course of the novel.

Well, as we have already mentioned, Kitty refuses Levin, and he finds himself living in the country estate without a wife, without love. In spite of all his attachments to the country life, this becomes very painful. Then Oblonsky comes to the countryside and the two of them get involved in—well, perhaps you'd guess what's coming— they get involved in a hunt. You can't have a Tolstoyan novel without the attraction of a hunt. I notice at the present time, many people are against hunting because they see it as cruel to animals, but to understand this novel, you have to put yourself in the context of the 19th century, where the hunt meant being at one with nature; the hunt meant something very warm and very different from the way many people today look at it.

We get into a beautiful scene in nature. Oblonsky and Levin go out with their guns through the white young birches. "Venus, bright with silver streak, shining with her delicate glitter, appears low down in the west." As a matter of fact, this is a mistake by Tolstoy, when he says this is where Venus is, "high in the west, flickered by the red fire of Arcturus." Tolstoy's mistake is he puts Venus in the wrong part of the sky, as many critics have pointed out; so even a great observer like Tolstoy can sometimes make a mistake. But the vision we get in nature, the light of Venus and of Arcturus, is something very impressive. Of course, they are even happier, the human beings are even happier because each one of them brings down two snipes.

In the process, in the middle of these beautiful feelings, all of a sudden Oblonsky brings up the very painful subject for Levin of the situation of Kitty, who is now grieving because of what happened after her being jilted by Vronsky. Levin is embarrassed to be even talking about this and the two of them suddenly get distracted from the hunt. The one who, of course, makes a comment to him and says, "Hey, pay attention to the hunt," is, as you might expect, the dog. The dog suddenly talks to them and says, "Don't turn your attention to that. Stick with the hunt." Laska, the dog, is disgusted at their being distracted from the immediate business of the hunt. Again, you have the verbalization of an animal; again, you have nature in the woods and nature in man, obviously paralleled by nature in animals.

We get even closer to nature while Oblonsky is at the house. Levin's half brother is also there, a man named Koznyshev, who wants to talk about political institutions. Of course, the last thing in the world Levin wants to talk about at this point is political institutions; he tries to be polite to his brother but somehow he can't stick to it. Suddenly he decides, "I've got to get away from this and go out in the country." He picks up a scythe and decides to participate in the mowing of the harvest.

This mowing scene, again, is one of the most famous scenes by Tolstoy. We get a detailed description of physical labor on a Russian farm. Line by line, row by row, we see them attacking the mounds of grass. Now you understand what it means for a person unaccustomed to swinging a fairly heavy scythe, hour after hour, with the movement of the arms. If one is not accustomed to it, one gets stiff very quickly and it becomes very painful. Levin, in spite of the fact that he is in very good physical shape, soon feels this. The peasants understand how he feels, and little by little he begins to go into the rhythm. He goes swish, swish, swish, and suddenly Levin understands that by getting into the rhythm, by not thinking about what he is doing, he loses count of time and loses count analyzing his whole life and love. His whole being is suddenly lost in the magical rhythm of mowing through the grass. Suddenly it gets to a point where, he says, "I can't take one more step. If I take one more step I'm going to fall." And at that very moment he suddenly decides to stop. Clearly this is something that is picked up, not verbally, but through the feelings of the people around him. He knew he had to stop and it was at that very moment that they stopped. They dipped the blades of the scythe into water; he tasted that water and never did any water in his life ever taste as good as he thought then.

As in many other Tolstoyan moments, conscious thought was the enemy of good results. That task which is felt well is also done well or, to upset the old proverb, "The watched pot boils badly." This is, of course, stated by the very same Tolstoy who analyzes every action and feeling of his characters, even the dogs and the horses. If you're looking for consistency, I'm afraid Tolstoy is not the place to look; if you're looking for life, that's a different story.

So it's hardly surprising to discover that Levin, after feeling the ordered attractiveness of the Russian countryside, abandons his idea of finding marital happiness with a peasant woman. He sees Kitty riding by in a carriage; he realizes she is the only possible woman for him. Well, Levin girds his loins and decides he will now meet Kitty in the Oblonsky house, where Oblonsky has invited him with great enthusiasm. We suddenly see Levin in the situation very close to something that happened in Tolstoy's life. As a matter of fact, what Tolstoy does in this novel is repeat almost exactly word for word, syllable by syllable, what he said to Sophia Andreevna, his real wife when he proposed to her, naturally, how a Tolstoyan proposal would take place.

They were in Oblonsky's household in Moscow. Kitty, who now wants Levin very much to propose to her, has sat down at a card table which is covered with a green cloth. She is playing with chalk; she has covered the green cloth with patterns she made with the chalk. Levin suddenly picks up the chalk and, of course, this in translation, he writes the letters: W-Y-A-I-C-N-B-D-Y-M-T-O-N. He waits for Kitty to puzzle it out. She looks very hard as if to say, "What the devil is going on?" and suddenly it occurs to her, these letters stand for, "When you answered, it cannot be," which is the marriage, "Did you mean then or never?" She is so close to the way he feels and so sensitive to the way he feels that she deciphers these letters. So she takes the chalk and now it's her turn. She writes: T-I-C-N-A-O. Now it's his turn to figure it out and finally he reads it and says, "Then I could not answer otherwise." Then she writes another: T-Y-M-F-A-F-W-H, "That you might forgive and forget what happened." And it's clear that they will be married.

In preparing for the wedding, Levin decides that he must be absolutely open and honest with his new wife. He, therefore, gives her his diaries to read so she'll know what kind of a man she has chosen to share her conjugal life. To her horror, she reads of the many ways that he, as a young man, has strayed from the straight and narrow. This most especially includes many sexual episodes with women. This causes her to weep bitterly, but in the end she realizes that he has confronted his impulses and is ready to accept openly the challenges of married life. This episode is very close to what happened to Tolstoy, himself, when he married Sophia Andreevna.

Of course, Tolstoy goes into a very long description of the wedding. You understand that at a Russian Orthodox wedding each one is supposed to wear a crown, and they are united when these two crowns are tied together. Each person tries to put his or her crown lower than the other one, to show the other person was above that person in feelings. Levin is now attached to Kitty and begins to understand what a genuine conjugal relationship means in a person's life. This is something quite new for Levin. Levin is a man who is previously accustomed to having lived a very independent life, to doing whatever he wanted, going wherever he wanted, doing wherever he wanted. Now he constantly has to take into account the feelings of his spouse, with whom he has a conjugal relationship. One time he comes home late. He was out in the fields, was busy, didn't think of getting home on time. Kitty is very angry with him. She says, "How come you came home late? Don't you understand you made me worried? This is terrible. You can't do this kind of thing." Levin gets very angry; after all, it's quite reasonable for him to be out in the countryside. She has to understand that he had to do this. Suddenly they start fighting with each other and Levin discovers something very strange. He gets angry at Kitty because he thinks she is being quite unreasonably angry with him. Being angry with her, he suddenly realizes that, lashing out verbally to her, he is actually lashing out at himself. He realizes that he and Kitty, his body and Kitty's body, his soul and her soul, his nervous system and her nervous system have come together. They're as one. Anytime he lashes out against her or anytime he does anything to her, with her, he does it to, or with himself.

How does a person, who has previously been independent, manage to get into a life like this? This brings us back to the discussion we had when we were talking about the Underground Man and the difficulty of having freedom and love at the same time. Dostoevsky tries to work this out with the character of Christ in the notion of genuine Christianity. In Tolstoy's case, this will obviously be worked out in a very different way, so it's not so easy to be connected that way in spite of the fact that Levin wants to be free.

Then another thing happens: a man named Vasya Veslovsky comes to visit Levin's estate. You know that when you live in the countryside, it's nice to have visitors. Here a man has come along, dressed very stylishly in the Scotch plaid. He's a man who obviously knows what it's like to be in society, who knows what it's like to make people like you. He engages in—quite conventional for that time—a light flirtation with Kitty. He doesn't mean to do anything nasty with her, but, after all, Kitty is an attractive young woman and he tries to make her like him. This is his way of trying to fit into the household. Now, of course, in Levin's eyes, this is something absolutely outrageous; nobody else could get close to Kitty. It is he that is close to Kitty. That may be painful and a hard thing to deal with at times, but she is his conjugal wife. The two of them are close and anybody who tries to come in between is somebody who makes Levin deeply furious. They, that is to say, Veslovsky and Levin, go out in the field, Levin so angry he can't quite control himself. He takes some thick sticks and in front of Veslovsky's eyes he breaks these sticks to show what kind of muscles he has and what a difficult person he would be to tangle with. He also realizes he is making something of a fool of himself, particularly in the eyes of the society around him, but he knows he cannot stand for this. Finally, he brings to himself the courage to say, "Look, you're going to have to leave." Veslovsky says, "Why, I don't understand. Have I done something to offend you?" Levin answers, "Look, don't ask me to explain. Just leave."

This was a total breaking of all kinds of polite relationships in ordinary society. Veslovsky says, "But, please, explain to me what's going on." Levin says, "Look, don't ask for an explanation." And again he breaks another stick. He says, "Go." Well, Veslovsky has no alternative but to go back to the house, pack up his goods, higgledy-piggledy, as quick as he can. He put them in a trap, which is an old form for horse-drawn carriage. There he is, going away with his Scotch plaid hanging over the side—his baggage is all messed up on the trap—cutting a ridiculous figure. People look at Levin as if he's gone out of his mind. Oblonsky says, "What are you doing? What's the point of all this? You're behaving absolutely absurdly." Levin says, "Yes, I know I'm acting absurdly, but I'm acting the way I have to." Some hours later they are all laughing about it.

Well, it's all very well, of course, for Levin to be jealous and we can understand, I suppose, how he might be jealous. But then, a little bit later, Anna and Vronsky are staying on an estate that's not very far from where Levin is living. For some reason he decides to visit that estate. He has heard what Anna has done. In his own mind he condemns her very seriously since she is engaged in a relationship that no human being should. This is a real sin in Levin's eyes. He looks at her as a sinning woman, very much in light of that epigraph I told you about before, *"Mne otomshchenie, i az vozdam,"*

"'Vengeance is mine,' saith the Lord, 'and I will requite.'" It's the way a person from a very fanatical Christian point of view might judge a sinner. However, to Levin's amazement, when he actually meets Anna he finds a rather attractive woman—I don't mean attractive woman in the physical sense. He finds a woman who knows how to talk with him, who understands some of his ideas. Levin had very unconventional ideas about the way Russia should go, how farms should be run, and many different ideas of a great individualist. But to his amazement, Anna seemed to understand them at half a word whereas when he tried to talk to his half-brother, when he tried to talk to his fellow aristocrats, they thought, "My gosh, what a strange fellow." They couldn't make heads or tails of what he was trying to say.

Here was Anna, who was this person whom he had previously been ready to condemn, understanding him at half a word. He finds himself beginning to be taken in, and perhaps not only by words, perhaps by something else in Anna's personality. You can see why Vronsky was attracted to her; you can see why almost any man would be attracted to her. Only half consciously, seeing what's going on, he goes back home and he says to his wife—rather unwisely, I might say—"You know, the judgment that society is making on Anna is really not justified at all. This is a rather remarkable woman who is as much sinned against as she is sinning." Can you imagine his wife's reaction? She has the impression that Anna has succeeded, at least half way, in seducing her husband. And she is as furious as Levin had been to Vasya Veslovsky, who tried to engage in a light flirtation with his wife. So Kitty is furious with him, and all of a sudden he is getting a taste of his own medicine. That's not so pleasant; Levin feels that very deeply and very painfully.

Tolstoy shows us very clearly what genuine conjugal life is like. Yes, of course, there is deep love, attraction, and even satisfaction for two people working together for the sake of a family, for the sake of work on a farm, for the sake of whatever work has to be done with the family, and, of course, for the sake of their mutual love. But, at the same time, there are very deeply painful aspects of what he sometimes calls *semeinoe schast'e*, that is, family happiness, which, by the way, was a title of another novel that Tolstoy wrote later on. At the end of this novel *Anna Karenina*, Levin tries to work it out and, undoubtedly, so does Tolstoy. Somehow or other, Levin is going to have to find a Christian epiphany which, when he finds it, is going to solve his problems. At one point, he suddenly realizes that to be a believing Christian does not necessarily mean that you're not going to get angry, that you're going to avoid all human weaknesses, that you're going to become an angel rather than a human being. With this faith, Levin will be willing to face the world. This, by the way, is very close to a faith that Tolstoy thought he had worked out for himself. Of course, in Tolstoy's case, you can imagine how long this lasts, a day or two, until he finds a new faith that he turns to. Tolstoy's mind was of a sort that could never stop searching, seeking, and looking at aspects of all human life.

This has been caught in an essay by a very wise critic. That critic's name is Isaiah Berlin, who, unfortunately, died not too long ago—I think in the last year, year and a half. He was a remarkable man who was born in Latvia, which was part of Russia in those days, but brought up in England and worked at Oxford University. He wrote a remarkable essay that I strongly recommend that you read. It's very short and doesn't take very long. It's called *The Hedgehog and the Fox*, and the idea is something like this. He quotes an ancient Greek proverb that says, "The fox knows many things, the hedgehog knows but one." By that he means that the fox explores all aspects of the field—his defenses run all around the countryside—whereas the hedgehog has only that one central defense. Well, if your hands have ever been pierced by a hedgehog quill, you know what I'm talking about.

Isaiah Berlin says, "All writers have been divided into hedgehogs and foxes. The greatest fox was Shakespeare, whose characters run the gamut of all human beings from the apothecary to the noble to the peasant to the man to the woman to the old to the young, everyone. He's the fox; he explores all aspects of the field; he runs all across humanity, in every part of humanity, and every single character is individual, unique in its own way." And, of course, you know how Shakespeare animates his characters. On the other hand, the opposite of this would be the hedgehog, and the greatest hedgehog would be either Dante or Dostoevsky because both of them saw some central salvation which could be achieved and which illuminates their entire work. Dante, of course, finds it in Beatrice, that beautiful woman who he identifies with the Holy Mother of God and through whose beauty he feels he can get to a kind of Christianity and, of course, a kind of love that is the highest thing in the world and in the heavens above. Dostoevsky sees it in the idea of Christ, the most courageous, the most insightful, the most sensitive of anything that has ever hit this world. For Dostoevsky, Christ is that very, very special quality, which is the highest thing in the world and through which he will achieve his salvation. So that both Dostoevsky and Dante, in Isaiah Berlin's eyes, are beautiful examples of the hedgehog.

"Now Tolstoy," says Isaiah Berlin—and in my opinion, this is brilliant—"Tolstoy is born to be a fox, but he would like to make himself into a hedgehog. Here is the creator of *War and Peace*, who saw humanity from all directions and all corners of the field, whether it was the hunting field, the war field, or the family field; he was desperate to find some central idea which would illuminate the entire thing. Of course, at the end of *Anna Karenina*, he thinks he has found it, but it's not going to work because a genuine fox, as a writer, can never turn himself into a hedgehog."

Lecture Twenty-One
Tolstoy the Preacher

Scope:

From the 1880s onward, Tolstoy became more and more engrossed in the moral and religious problems he saw within and around him. He even went so far as to renounce and condemn his own masterpieces as vain incense burned at a false altar. Even then, however, he defined art marvelously as the *"chut' chut"* (that which is barely, barely expressed). In 1886 came *The Death of Ivan Il'ich*, and in 1891 appeared *The Kreutzer Sonata*, two masterpieces of the novella form that rivaled both Gogol' and Dostoevsky. In this period, we see Tolstoy as he was masterfully described by Gorky: "Tolstoy and God are like two bears in the same den." His home life became increasingly acrimonious, as his wife and most of his seven children started to do battle with the previously great literary artist, who now seemed to be running for the office of God Almighty. The climax came in 1910, when he secretly ran away from wife and home, contracted pneumonia on the train, and died in the stationmaster's office at the station in Astapovo—in biblical language: *"Zekher Tsaddik L'v'rokhoh"* ("The memory of the righteous is for blessing").

Outline

I. Among Tolstoy's interests up until the 1880s was an interest in country life. He believed in physical labor but also in the benefits of agricultural machines to ease the lives of serfs.

   A. This theme is present in *Anna Karenina*.

   B. Tolstoy was also interested in the education of the peasantry and put his ideas into many articles.

II. In the 1880s, Tolstoy experienced a distinct change in his interests and in his writing. He even went so far as to denounce his previous writing as immoral and vainglorious.

   A. The true nature of art he redefined as a Russian expression very difficult to translate: *chut' chut'*, meaning something like "barely, barely," or "the wee bit." It was a kind of call for minimalism, the slightest, most sensitive effort to communicate an idea or a feeling.

B. In this later period, Tolstoy's two most impressive works were in the novella form, a kind of long short story, or short novel: the Russian word is *povest'*. It is a favorite form of the Russian masters, represented by many 19th-century Russian masterpieces, as we have already seen in Gogol's *Overcoat* and Dostoevsky's *Notes from the Underground*.

III. In 1886, Tolstoy published *The Death of Ivan Il'ich*, a story that deals with one of the author's two main obsessions. In this case, it is the inevitability of death, no matter how hard we struggle against it.

A. The story juxtaposes, almost diagrammatically, the life and death of a seemingly comfortable St. Petersburg legal bureaucrat, whose death announcement is read in the beginning of the story by his colleagues and friends.

B. Their thoughts are all centered on what positions they may gain as a result of his absence, just as the widow's thoughts are all concentrated on how much money she can get from the government, a scheme that she has very cleverly and earnestly tried to work out.

C. No one, it seems, has been willing to concentrate on the topic so important to the author of the tale: What is the nature of death itself, and how is it connected to the life of the formerly living human being?

D. Tolstoy takes us back to the life and career of the title character: how he made himself respected through observance of all the conventions of his social class.

    1. Everything was done in accordance with the expectations of a career and of a family whose real feelings and desires were always kept at arm's length.

    2. We are reminded of Karenin's St. Petersburg, though bereft of the genuine life force and passion of an Anna Karenina.

E. Just as Ivan Il'ich seems to have solved his financial problems and to have established his ideal comfortable home with its beautiful furniture, he slips while setting up a curtain and falls with considerable force on his side.

F. The initially minor pain gradually takes on an intensity that can no longer be ignored, and Ivan must face the fact that he is dying. What Tolstoy describes, in agonizing and precise detail, is death by cancer.

G. Nothing is able to bring relief, most especially not the agents whom Tolstoy has held in contempt for his whole career: doctors and lawyers. None of them can face the fact of death; they hide behind jargon like "floating intestines" and "binary state pensions."

H. We can make comparisons with similar scenes in Tolstoy's other novels.

I. Ivan begins to understand a little bit about the nature of his life when he contemplates the classical example of the syllogism: "All men are mortal. Caius is a man; therefore, it must follow that Caius is mortal."

    1. Ivan considers that all very well for Caius. Let him die if he so wishes. What does Caius know about Vanya's mama's dress with the rustle of its silken folds, about Vanya's love for tarts, his loves, his skills?

    2. Here, we get a breath of the old mastery of Tolstoy in bringing our deepest feelings and fears, as well as pleasures, to light.

J. Through the worst pains of a drawn-out death, Tolstoy leads us mercilessly, yet with enough glimpses of compassion, to the final hours, when Ivan cries out desperately that he doesn't want it, death, to take over. In Russian, "I don't want" is *Ia ne khochu*, and Ivan becomes stuck on the final vowel, *uuuuu*, which he moans through the house so that no one can miss its sound.

K. At the very last minute, there was no fear, because in place of death, Ivan saw light and felt a certain kind of joy, and he could no longer find his former customary fear of death. For him, becoming dead meant that death no longer existed. In all of Tolstoy's many scenes of death, this was the closest he came to the kind of transcendence that he sought.

IV. The second great obsession with which Tolstoy continually struggled was the passion connected with physical sex.

   A. In the case of Anna Karenina, as in the first unhappy marriage of Pierre Bezukhov, Tolstoy recognizes the depth and the power of lust.

   B. There is a marvelous scene in *War and Peace*, in which Pierre Bezukhov proposes to La Belle Helène, the daughter of Prince Vasilii. Pierre knows that he is doing something wrong. His lust won't make a happy marriage, but he can't help himself. He can't even remember to say, "I love you." The marriage is indeed unhappy.

   C. A novella published in 1891, *The Kreutzer Sonata*, shows Tolstoy expressing his most ferocious views and feelings on the subject. This novella is, in some ways, very unpleasant reading, showing an older Tolstoy expressing deep disenchantment with marriage and even with physical love. Yet, at the same time, it is one of his most powerfully expressed works.

   D. Interestingly, the narration of the story takes place in a railroad car.

   1. Clearly, Tolstoy sees the railroad as a destructive force within Russia, a blindly onrushing machine that crushes human life and has none of the charm of the carriage, pulled by a horse, a living organism with a sense of smell and direction.

   2. We saw this negative association not only in the self-destruction of Anna Karenina but also in the unsuccessful attempts of Oblonsky to get into the commercial direction of the newly established Russian railway companies.

   E. The story opens under an epigraph taken from the book of Matthew. It is the famous warning by Jesus about anyone who looks upon a woman with longing: Such a person has already committed adultery in his heart.

   F. The narrator, riding in the train, looks about him and cannot help but notice an especially nervous man with extraordinarily brilliant eyes. He resists almost all attempts to open conversation, but when the general discussion turns to a theme much discussed in Russia at that time, the position of women in society and the nature of love and marriage, the old man suddenly becomes extremely articulate.

G. It turns out that he is a man connected with a well-known scandal in Russia at that time: He murdered his wife. When other travelers in the railway car manage to leave his presence, he goes into a long, passionate recounting of the events and feelings leading to the murder.

H. He argues that the maintenance of conjugal love is impossible, that physical love between a man and a woman, even in marriage, can only lead to the worst kind of sin and degradation. When his interlocutor objects that such an extreme position against physical love could lead to the end of the human race, the passionate man agrees and says that would be a good thing, long predicted by all religions and the discoveries of science.

I. He also argues paradoxically that women have domination over the world, simply because of the fact that men have all the rights. By acting on the passions of men, women subdue them and gain a terrible power over them. In this way, they exact vengeance for the submissive role that society has attempted to assign them.

J. He makes a curious analogy between the position of Jews and the position of women in Russia. Just as Jews, who are forced to be petty merchants, use their financial power to avenge their humiliation, so women use their position as objects of sensual desire to bring about the slavery of men.

K. In many other instances, Tolstoy showed considerable sympathy for the problems of Jews in tsarist Russia. Here, his character makes a statement about so-called Jewish financial power that one would ordinarily expect in anti-Semitic propaganda. One can explain this aspersion, it seems to me, by the extreme passions aroused in the character of the story.

L. The man's wife had been performing music in their house with a handsome young man who was also a fine musician. The husband describes the terrible passion expressed in Beethoven's *Kreutzer Sonata*. He describes so effectively how Beethoven's art transports the listener to another realm of consciousness that the reader can see how his wife was swept away by her passion for the young man.

M. It is only a matter of time before the husband discovers the real attraction between them, and Tolstoy describes in agonizing detail how the husband's knife enters his wife's flesh under the ribs. This description is all the more terrible when we realize that Tolstoy was dictating the story to his own wife.

N. In a sequel to the story, Tolstoy replies to the understandable dismay expressed by many of his readers. He reiterates, quite explicitly, that physical love is an unworthy object for men and women, even within the marriage bond.

O. Within this story, we see quite explicitly Tolstoy's position taken to the extreme: The end of the human race would not be a bad thing—it might well be an end to be desired. This message is a hard one to take from the author who created the intense and loving world of *War and Peace* and *Anna Karenina.*

V. Tolstoy lived out his remaining years in the last decade of the 19th century and the first decade of the 20th. His household had become world famous and a place for widespread pilgrimage.

A. An event took place that was probably painful to Tolstoy and certainly to his family. He had published a novel called *Resurrection.* In it, he described a mass in an unspiritual way, which the Church found offensive. He was excommunicated.

B. In 1910, Tolstoy decided he could no longer bear his domestic situation. He quietly left the house one night, without informing his family, and set out on the road, presumably toward a monastery.

C. Tolstoy fell ill on the train that he took and was taken into the stationmaster's office at the city of Astapovo. He was mortally ill. After his death, the Church refused him burial in hallowed ground, as he was officially a heretic and had not confessed his sin.

D. His coffin rests in an ivy-covered knoll. He had specifically requested to be buried under a stick that he and his brother had found when they were children; they called it a stick of reconciliation and love.

Suggested Reading:

R. F. Christian, *Tolstoy: A Critical Introduction*.

Donna Tussing Orwin, ed., *The Cambridge Companion to Tolstoy*.

Questions to Consider:

1. In *The Death of Ivan Il'ich*, Tolstoy talks about fear in the anticipation of death as contrasted with the appearance of light, without fear, in the actuality of death. Can this be compatible with the Christian idea of resurrection, or is Tolstoy talking about something totally connected with our living senses? Keep in mind that the author could not be buried in Church-hallowed ground.

2. In his examination of sexual lust in *The Kreutzer Sonata*, Tolstoy talks about women's terrible power, which they attain as a kind of sexual vengeance over men, who have taken away many of their rights. Would such an argument find agreement in the contemporary women's movement?

Lecture Twenty-One—Transcript
Tolstoy the Preacher

In this lecture I would like to talk about the later Tolstoy, after the production of the two most famous and great novels, the Tolstoy of the 1880s to the time that he died in 1910. To understand this, it seems to me you also have to understand the context within which he was working. In the first place, of course, there was the domestic context. Remember that his wife, Sophia Andreevna, had once upon a time, back in the 1860s, recopied the manuscript—by hand—recopied the manuscript of *War and Peace* seven separate times. It's hard to imagine that, of course, before the days of the typewriter, before the days of the computer. She had recopied that novel seven times so he could correct it to the extent that he wanted. At the same time, she also bore him 13 children, seven of whom lived to adulthood. It's a rather painful fact to have to say that at the end of his life, at the age of 82, he died on the road, running away from his wife. That is, I must say, a little bit hard to take.

Then, of course, there is the fight over the legacy. In the 1880s and '90s, there grew up groups called the so-called "Tolstoyans," in Russian, *Tolstovtsy*, the followers of Tolstoy. They thought that they had somehow a kind of lock and key on the doctrine of Tolstoy that he was developing: the doctrine of non-violent resistance to evil, the doctrine of a kind of Christianity that was somewhat different from the Eastern Orthodox Christianity that most Russians knew. And there came to be great fights between the Tolstoyans, the so-called followers of Tolstoy, and people within his household, particularly with his wife. There was even a fight over who had the rights to the manuscript. Finally, Tolstoy, in disgust, said to his wife, "Look all right, you take the manuscripts. I put them entirely in your hands." And she said, "Oh yes, that's very nice. You think that money is the root of all evil and you want to give it to me. You want to give me the root of all evil." Even giving her the rights to the manuscripts, of course, was not satisfactory to what she wanted from him. Obviously, what she wanted from him was a continuation of the love that had existed earlier and, of course, he was now a very different man.

Sometime, when you go to Moscow, visit the Tolstoy house, which has been preserved as a museum. Of course, he had his estate at Iasnaia Poliana, which is to the southeast of Moscow, near the city of

Tula. There is also a house in the city of Moscow proper, not far from the Ministry of Foreign Affairs. If you go into that house, what you see first of all is a great bear with his paws—a stuffed bear obviously—with his paws outstretched, with visiting cards of people who came to meet Tolstoy at that particular time. If you look at the rooms, you'll see that most of the rooms are furnished in a way that we would consider Victorian, a way that we're very accustomed to when we know Victorian houses. If you go to the back of the house, you see one room that's very, very spare with just a wooden desk and a wooden table, with instruments for making shoes. Those rooms that are decorated like the Victorian rooms, those are the rooms decorated by his wife. That room that has the instruments for making shoes and just a bare table and a bare desk, that's, of course, Tolstoy's room. And the very setup of those rooms, the very decoration of those rooms, gives you an idea of the distinction between his personality and the personality of the family and his wife. Of course, she had no choice; she had to raise those children. She had to take care of them. It became a very difficult situation.

There was also, of course, the question of agriculture. As you know from our discussion of *Anna Karenina* and, to a certain extent, of *War and Peace*, Tolstoy was very much interested in what happened in the countryside, which he considered the heart, the soul of Russia. On the one hand, he really did believe in physical labor, in human labor. It was the human element, it seemed to him, that made the importance of agriculture and, yet, this was a time when machines were beginning to come into agriculture, and Tolstoy was interested in perhaps using those machines not to replace the laborers as some of his neighbors wanted to do but—you have to remember now, this is after the abolition of serfdom which happened in the 1860s—Tolstoy wanted to use these machines not to abolish the labor, not to throw the people off their land, but rather to make agriculture more productive in the interest of these very people. But, of course, the peasants didn't understand this very well; they would often sabotage the machines. They didn't understand them, they didn't want them coming in, and it became quite a struggle, the whole business of the organization of agriculture, which he discusses in some detail in *Anna Karenina*.

Then, of course, there was the question of education. The tsarist regime deliberately kept the vast majority of its population in illiteracy because the tsar thought this was to his advantage. That way, he could control the population more easily. Tolstoy saw this as a distinctly immoral position; he was interested in the education of the peasantry. But, of course, he realized that if they got a certain kind of education it would do them no good—they couldn't use it. There was no place for them to go; there was no place to use the education. And he worked very hard to work out an education that would be appropriate for these very peasants. And if you examine some of the books that he did, you'll find some very interesting ideas about how people who previously had been illiterate, people who have to work the land, who don't have a chance to get into an urban society, nevertheless can become literate and educated. Tolstoy was deeply involved in that and had many articles about it, many polemics with others interested in education. This was a very important part of his life.

And then, of course, there was the literary side. You have to remember one of the most interesting things about the background of literature in Russia in the 19th century is that there were many, many fine writers who were born not only within a few years of each other, that I, mostly in the 1820s, the very early 1830s, but even lived—given the vast extent of Russia—within a rather close distance from each other. There were, of course, the names that you certainly recognize in Tolstoy, Dostoevsky, Turgenev. There was also Goncharov about whom we're not talking in this course but a very important writer, and many others. It's interesting that they were all born roughly within five or 10 years of each other, and most of them died in the 1880s. Tolstoy was the great exception; Tolstoy lived on until 1910, in other words, 25 to 30 years after the death of most of the others. Of course, his relationship with those writers is very interesting. We're going to discuss that when we come to Turgenev. But here he was, in the context of this great literature, himself having produced two novels that not only gathered the attention of the reading public of Russia but of the entire world, and yet this very same Tolstoy, in the 1880s and the 1890s, suddenly denounced his novels and denounced literature in general. He said, "It was an immoral thing. It pulled people's attention away from the really great moral problems of life." And, as a matter of fact, at one point he wrote an essay called, *Chto Takoe Iskusstvo?*, *What is [the Nature of] Art?* And Tolstoy finally came to the expression: the nature of art is the expression of the *chut' chut'*, in Russian, something not very easy to translate. It means "barely, barely," or "the wee bit." It was kind of a call for minimalism, the slightest, most sensitive effort to communicate an idea or a feeling. This *"chut' chut'*," or "barely, barely," or something very like, that one could just—"What turns," he said, "what turns ordinary prose into artistic prose, it's the tiniest, tiniest of details." And that's the *chut' chut'* which Tolstoy is talking about.

Under the influence of these ideas he turned—I'm almost tempted to say this is the period of Tolstoy the preacher—he turned to the idea that the most important thing in writing was preaching morals to people, preaching to them how they should live. The first really masterwork of this period is a work called, *The Death of Ivan Il'ich*, which was published in the early 1880s. In 1886, Tolstoy published *The Death of Ivan Il'ich*; this is in the form of a *povest'*, as you may remember, what they call a novella. The two novellas I'm going to talk about, it seems to me, are actually at the very high level that we saw before in Gogol and in Dostoevsky and, of course, also in some of the *povest'* by Pushkin.

The Death of Ivan Il'ich deals with one of the two great obsessions in Tolstoy's life. The first obsession was with the problem of death. It seemed almost scandalous that death was inevitable for every human being, no matter how hard we struggle against it. And the story juxtaposes almost diagrammatically the life and death of a seemingly comfortable Petersburg legal bureaucrat, whose death announcement is read in the beginning of the story by his colleagues and friends. Of course, their thoughts are all concentrated on what they may gain as a result of his absence, just as the widow's thoughts are all concentrated on how much money she can get from the government, a scheme which she has very cleverly and earnestly tried to work out. They are all concerned with what they can get out of the death.

No one, it seems, has been willing to concentrate on the topic so important to the author of the tale. What's the nature of death itself? How is it connected to the life of the former living human being? And so in order to do this, Tolstoy takes us back to the life and career of the title character, Ivan Il'ich, how he made himself respected by going through all the conventions of a society. Remember before we talked about comme il faut; his life is comme il faut to the nth degree, everything completely according to the expectations of a career and a family, whose real feelings and desires are always kept at arm's length by a Russian legal bureaucrat. We see Karenin's Petersburg. You remember Karenin, the successful bureaucrat, bereft of the genuine life force and passion of Anna Karenina, but through the eyes of Alexei Karenin. Just as Ivan Il'ich seems to have solved his financial problems, to establish his ideal comfortable home with beautiful furniture, you understand how he struggled for this; he spent his life working very, very hard to make a career to get the necessary money, to make the necessary connections, all those things that a bureaucrat has to do. In the process of setting up this redecorated house, he slips while setting up a curtain and falls with considerable force on his side. The initial minor pain gradually takes on an intensity which can be ignored less and less. You feel more and more deeply how that pain is going through his body, and Ivan faces the fact that he is dying. What Tolstoy describes in agonizing and precise detail is death by cancer. And, by the way, many doctors have examined this and noted just how accurate his view is. Nothing is able to bring relief, most especially the agents whom Tolstoy has held in contempt for his whole career, doctors and lawyers. None of them can face the fact of death. They hide behind jargon like "floating intestines" and "binary state pensions."

If you think back to the works that we've already examined, you can get some examples that compare with this. You think of the death of old Bezukhov in the first part of *War and Peace*, a death which brings terrible suffering to Pierre Bezukhov, who is the illegitimate son of this old man. There has been a great love relationship between them, and he sees the old man helpless on the bed, trying to turn him over. He does his best to try to help to relieve the pain of the old man, but he can't do it. And finally, of course, he has to face the death; he has to face the actual physical death. And, of course, the actual physical death is a terrible thing, but equally terrible is the fact that there was a will that names Pierre as the inheritor, which goes against the custom at that time because illegitimate sons were not normally able to inherit. And, of course, other people, particularly Prince Vasilii and the nieces, try very hard to keep that will out of the hands of the people who were defending Pierre. So the deep feelings that Pierre has about the death contrasts to the legalities of the will and the legalities around death, the legalities taking us away from the real question.

When it comes to doctors, we think of Natasha, who is plunged into a terrible sickness after the awful trick that Anatolii almost succeeds in playing on her, that we talked about before. Nobody knows how to cure her; nobody knows how to bring her out of the depression and the horrible feelings and the illness that she falls into. Doctors come and, of course, doctors' attempts are of no avail; the only thing that will cure her, says Tolstoy, is nature itself. And then we remember Karenin going to a lawyer's office and, of course, Karenin, in spite of all of his surface coldness, is deeply disturbed by his loss of Anna, and all the lawyer can concentrate on is trying to catch moths which are in his office. And the lawyer wants to laugh at Karenin—he sees him as rather ridiculous—and to cover up the laughter he reaches for a moth and claps his hands to try to do this.

The one exception in the story that we're talking about, that is, in *The Death of Ivan Il'ich*, is Gerasim, a peasant who willingly brings relief with his cheerfulness and willingness to hold up Ivan's legs—and Ivan's youngest son who still has the innocence of youth about him. Ivan begins to understand a little bit about the nature of his life when he contemplates the classical example of the syllogism. You remember the syllogism: "All men are mortal. Caius is a man; therefore, it must follow that Caius is mortal." You have the general proposition, the particular proposition, which is a part of it; therefore, the particular has to share with the general. Caius is mortal. "Well" says Ivan Il'ich, "that's all very well for Caius. If he wants to die, let him die. But what about Vanya?" You understand, "Vanya" is the diminutive of Ivan. "What about Vanya? What did Caius know about the rustle of the dress of his mother? What did Caius know about Vanya's love for tarts, his loves, his skills?" Once again, we get the Tolstoy that deals with the physical details: the silk dress of the mother, the tarts that he ate as a young man. Here we get a breath of the old mastery of Tolstoy and bring our deepest feelings and fears, as well as our pleasures, to life.

Throughout the worst pains of a drawn-out death, Tolstoy leads us mercilessly, yet with enough glimpses of compassion, to the final hours when Ivan cries out desperately that he doesn't want it; he doesn't want to die, in Russian, "I don't want," *la ne khochu*. But somehow he gets stuck on the syllable, "uuuuu." You remember Anatolii with his amputated leg, *la ne khochu*, and that "uuuuu," moans through, resonates through the house so that no one can miss its sound. And, of course, the poor widow is driven to distraction, that "uuuuu," that very physical sense of what the pain of death might mean. And yet, at the very last minute there was no fear, because in place of death he saw light and a certain kind of joy. And he could no longer find his former customary fear of death. For him, becoming dead meant that death no longer existed. By overcoming death, he conquered death—by the way, a very Christian idea, a hymn that's sung in Russia at Easter time. And in all of Tolstoy's many scenes of death, this is the closest, it seems to me, that he came to the kind of transcendence that he so desperately thought—and mistakenly thought—he had at the end of *Anna Karenina*. It's a very powerful story.

The second great obsession with which Tolstoy continually struggled was the passion connected with physical sex. Now at this point you might say, "Well, he was obsessed with sex and death. What else is there in life?" And you may have a point. In the case of *Anna Karenina*, as in the first unhappy marriage of Pierre Bezukhov, Tolstoy recognizes the depth and the power of lust. There is a marvelous scene in *War and Peace* where Pierre Bezukhov is proposing to—remember la belle Helene—the extraordinarily beautiful and, by the way, very sexy daughter of Prince Vasilii—by the way, very well played in the American film by Anita Ekberg. I think she was perhaps the best actress in that film. Pierre knows that he is doing something wrong; he knows that this is not the woman for him, that this lust that he's obsessed by is not going to be the source of a happy marriage, and yet he can't help himself. And as he gets close to her, she suddenly rips off his glasses. She says, "Take off these glasses," and she kisses him, and he says, "You know, I know there is something that is said at a time like this and I can't think of what it is." He thinks and suddenly he says, "*Je vous aime.*" It comes out and they're engaged. Of course, it turns into a very unhappy marriage, a marriage which is the torture of Pierre Bezukhov's life. The pain is only ended with the death of la belle Helene herself.

Even Levin, himself, in the diaries which he showed his intended bride, suffers from the call of the flesh. He tells Kitty all the terrible things he did as a young man. In a novella published in 1891, *The Kreutzer Sonata*, obviously referring to a work by Beethoven, Tolstoy expresses his most ferocious views and feelings on the subject. This novella is in some ways very, very unpleasant reading, showing an older Tolstoy expressing deep disenchantment with marriage and even with physical love. Yet, at the same time, it's one of his most powerfully expressed works. It's interesting that the narration of the story takes place in a railroad car. Clearly Tolstoy sees the railroad—you remember *Anna Karenina*—Tolstoy sees the railroad as a terribly destructive force within Russia. He contrasts it to transportation by horse. A horse is a living organism. A horse can smell. A horse has a sense of direction. The locomotive, of course, is an iron monster which can only go on the tracks and which works as a machine. And this monster is something terribly heavy and terribly threatening. It stands in many, many ways as a statement about death.

And, of course, we remember that Oblonsky tried very hard to get into the commercial direction of the newly established Russian railway companies in his life. The railroad is no place for a living in a sympathetic character like Oblonsky, according to Tolstoy. The story opens on an epigraph taken from the book of *Matthew*. It's the famous warning by Jesus about anyone who looks upon a woman with longing, such a person has already committed adultery in his heart. The narrator of the story, riding in the train, again in a railroad train, looks about him and can't help but notice an especially nervous man with extraordinarily brilliant eyes. He resists all attempts to open conversation, but when the general discussion turns to a theme of great concern in Russia at that time—of course, it'll seem very familiar to us—the position of women in society and the nature of love and marriage, the old man suddenly becomes extremely articulate.

It turns out he is a man connected with a well-known scandal in Russia at that time; he has murdered his wife. And when the other members of the car leave his presence, he goes into a long, passionate recounting of the events and feelings leading up to the murder. He argues the maintenance of conjugal love is impossible, that physical love between a man and a woman, even in marriage, can only lead to the worst kind of sin and degradation. When his interlocutor objects that, well, such an extreme position against physical love could lead to the end of the human race, the passionate man agrees and says that would be a good thing, long predicted by all religions and the discoveries of science.

He also argues paradoxically that women have domination over the world, simply due to the fact that men have all the rights. "By acting on the passions of men," he says, "the woman subdues them and gains a terrible power over them." In this way, she exacts vengeance for the submissive role which society has attempted to assign her. I'm not sure how contemporary thought would deal with this argument. He makes a curious analogy between the position of Jews and the position of women in Russia. He says Jews who have to face terrible repression in Russia are forced to be petty merchants. They use their financial power to avenge their humiliation in the same way women use their position as objects of sexual desire to bring about the slavery of men.

While Tolstoy, in many other instances, showed considerable sympathy for the problems of Jews in Russia, including, by the way, a very interesting letter to Sholom Aleichem, the famous Jewish writer himself, here his character is making a statement about so-called Jewish financial power which you would ordinarily expect to meet in anti-Semitic propaganda. One can explain this, it seems to me, not only in Tolstoy's case but also in Dostoevsky's case, by the extreme passions aroused in the character of the story that somehow deal with the subconscious feelings that many Russians have about people of other nationalities and other cultures.

It turns out that the man's wife had been performing music in their house with a handsome young man, who was also a fine musician. The husband goes on to describe the terrible passion expressed in Beethoven's *Kreutzer Sonata*. He shows so effectively how Beethoven's art transports the listener to another realm of consciousness that the reader can see how the wife is swept away by her passion for the man. It is interesting, by the way, that some of Beethoven's most powerful music was sponsored and inspired by Razumovsky. Some of you may know the middle quartets of Beethoven, the Razumovsky quartets, which were done because the Russian Ambassador to Vienna recognized in Beethoven a very powerful talent and commissioned him to write quartets with Russian themes. Beethoven used a Russian theme for the first and the second quartet, but the third one, he made up his own Russian theme—so much for Russian themes according to Beethoven.

Well, it's only a matter of time before the husband discovers the real attraction between them. And Tolstoy describes in agonizing detail how the husband's knife enters his wife's flesh under the ribs. This is all the more terrible when we realize that Tolstoy was dictating the story to his own wife, to Sophia Andreevna, who had done what I told you before, had to go through the experience of hearing this powerful tale of a husband sticking a knife into the body of his wife. As you might imagine, the story aroused tremendous dismay among Tolstoy's readers and I must say I understand how they felt. In replying to this, Tolstoy replies explicitly that physical love is an unworthy object for men and women, even within the marriage bond. Within this story we see quite explicitly Tolstoy's position taken to the extreme. The end of the human race would not be a bad thing. It might even be an end to be desired. You know, this is a hard message to take from the author who created the intense and loving world of *War and Peace* and *Anna Karenina*. It's at one and the same time deeply dismaying and deeply moving and that's as much a part of the genuine Tolstoy as is the kind of love that we've talked about in these other novels. I think I've made this point before, but here we see it come wildly and flamingly to the front. There is something in Tolstoy that drives us away at the very same time that there's a talent and a notion of love and a notion of family life that draws us in in a way that very few other writers can do. This tension is part, it seems to me, of the great power of his writing.

Tolstoy lived out his remaining years in the last decade of the 19th century and the first decade of the 20th. His household had become world famous and a place for widespread pilgrimage. Many musicians visited Tolstoy. Tolstoy obviously had a very peculiar kind of obsession with music. There is the famous incident of Wanda Landowska, the great Polish harpsichordist, who came to visit him and his very moved reactions to what she did. There is also a very interesting description by Sergei Koussevitzky, who later on became the very famous, internationally famous, conductor of the Boston Symphony Orchestra, who tells how, in his younger life in Russia, he and a group of musicians went to play for Tolstoy, and when they played, he describes the tears that came to Tolstoy's eyes, the deep emotion that he felt through music. And then later on, we read in Tolstoy's diary a description of that very same moment, and Tolstoy describes it in a much drier and a much more condemning way. "Well, these people thought they came to me with music. The music was not at all good; there was just one small part of it was any good. The rest of it, I had to suffer through." The difference, of course, between what he said to them and what he really felt again is somewhat hard to take in an author who emphasizes so strongly the expression of natural feeling.

Tolstoy, of course—by this time, the estate at Iasnaia Poliana stood in the imagination of the world for something very, very broad and very, very powerful. It seems that the whole world came to the door of Tolstoy. It seems that everybody was interested in what he had to say. He had correspondence with people all over the world and, by the way, he was fluent not only in Russian but also in French, German, and English. And this was very, very impressive.

But, at the same time, an event happened that was very painful probably to Tolstoy and certainly to his family. Tolstoy had published a novel called, *Resurrection, Voskresenie*, where, among other things, he described a mass, not as the church saw it, the necessary proper respect towards the mass and the deep feelings experienced by the words of Christ and the words of the gospel that are done by the mass; rather, he concentrated on the fine leather boots of the priest and the noise that these boots made when they squeaked as the priest moved, making certain motions which might be prayer. But, of course, as far as Tolstoy was concerned, they were simply physical movements. Tolstoy does this quite often in his novels; where he reduces things that we normally see as part of something that makes sense, he takes the thing that makes sense out of it and all you see are physical motions, as if it were seen by somebody from another culture who was completely unaware of what those motions meant.

The church found this very offensive, and eventually Tolstoy was excommunicated from the Russian church. As a matter of fact, there were several cartoons at the time that showed a tiny, tiny church being surmounted by a huge Tolstoy, who was much bigger than the church. And, of course, Tolstoy had a somewhat larger notion, a somewhat different notion of Christianity, a notion, as he saw it, of the way Christ would deal with the world. It's almost a reprise of Dostoevsky's "The Grand Inquisitor"; the presence of Christ in the world is sometimes very, very difficult for those who claim they want to follow Christ. Of course, the Orthodox Church saw Tolstoy as some kind of a heretic. Tolstoy believed that this was the only genuine kind of Christianity. And then, of course, came the famous death of Tolstoy when he ran away from the house. He was on a railroad on the way to the famous monastery when he took ill—he took sick—and the dying Tolstoy was put on the bed of the stationmaster at a city called Astapovo. And, of course, when people heard that he was dying, the whole world came, including his wife, who was trying to find him. They wouldn't let his wife come to him. They were afraid the shock would kill him.

He died, and he could not be buried in hallowed land. Instead, he was buried on a small knoll in the midst of a birch forest which he had once planted, the white birch bark contrasting with the dark green of the ivy on that knoll, and he's buried under a famous stick that he and his brother had found. They called it the "stick of reconciliation and love." And so instead of being given a church burial, he was buried under the stick of reconciliation and love.

Lecture Twenty-Two
Ivan Sergeevich Turgenev, 1818–1883

Scope:

Turgenev had both the pleasure and pain of being the contemporary of Tolstoy and Dostoevsky. Although in his day Turgenev was generally considered the best of Russian prose writers, especially by his Western friends Gustave Flaubert, and Henry James, the Russian now tends to be depicted by a faintly concealed condescension, the poor relative of his more talented compatriots. This depiction is grossly unfair, as anyone who has read Turgenev's prose with half a heart can testify. Yet life itself seemed determined to put Turgenev down. He was once challenged by Tolstoy to a duel, and he was branded as a coward when he wisely avoided such a potential tragedy. Later, there was the famous reconciliation at Iasnaia Poliana, lasting until one of them lost a game of checkers! Dostoevsky never forgave Turgenev's kindness in lending money when Dostoevsky desperately needed it. Later, the religious writer savaged Turgenev as Karmazinov in the novel translated as *The Possessed*. Such are the literary rewards of liberal kindness!

Outline

I. In almost all the Russian writers we have thus far examined, one of their outstanding characteristics was a strength of conviction, the notion that they had an idea or a theme of vital importance, which they would communicate directly, no matter what the consequences might be. In the case of Turgenev, we find a genuine contrast to this kind of extreme passion.

    A. Turgenev, with the temperament of the true liberal, the man who found himself between the extremes of public opinion, often ended up in the middle of his society's polemics, attacked and even cursed by both sides or, even worse, praised for exactly the wrong reasons, or so it seemed to him.

B. He was born into a fairly wealthy landowner's family, in the old Russian province of Orel. His mother had the reputation of being a very harsh mistress over her serfs, not hesitating to order severe corporal punishment for the slightest infractions. Her son early experienced a deep revulsion against such actions and felt estranged from his social background. All his life he would argue against human slavery.

C. At the same time, he well understood that his livelihood and material welfare depended to a large extent on the money brought in by the family estate.

   1. His mother was well aware of both his attitude and his dependence. She attempted to use the income from the estate as a means of control over the actions and opinions of her son.

   2. The result was, of course, as long as she lived, a very strained and unpleasant family situation. It is no accident that the strong characters in Turgenev's novels are women.

D. In the 1840s, he began to write a series of stories, ostensibly about his hunting expeditions in the Russian countryside. When they were collected and published together under the title *Notes of a Hunter*, it became clear that the stories portrayed the miserable situation of the Russian serfs, who were still languishing in slavery.

E. The book brought him considerable fame, and many people believe it played a significant role in preparing Russian public opinion for the Grand Emancipation of 1861, the legal and official end of serfdom in Russia.

F. Of course, Turgenev was then seen as an ally of those who wanted to reform tsarist Russia and move it in the direction of Western European parliamentary democracy.

   1. There were also those who were more radical and wanted to see some form of socialism in Russia. Many of them looked upon Turgenev as a supporter.

   2. By this time, Turgenev had inherited his family estate and could afford to give monetary assistance.

G. As his reputation continued to grow in the 1860s, Turgenev was seen by his friends and colleagues in the West, particularly Gustave Flaubert and Henry James, as the best of the Russian writers.

    1. For at least a generation, Turgenev was the outstanding representative of Russian literature as Western readers understood it.

    2. To his considerable credit, Turgenev tried hard in the West to popularize the works of his great Russian contemporaries, particularly Pushkin and Tolstoy.

II. His personal relationships with Russian writers were more complex and sometimes even stormy.

A. Dostoevsky initially admired Turgenev's work, but then Turgenev made the mistake of lending Dostoevsky money, which he desperately needed. This generosity triggered a hostile reaction against Turgenev, as Dostoevsky took it to mean that Turgenev looked down on him.

B. The result was a vicious satire of Turgenev in Dostoevsky's passionately anti-revolutionary novel *The Possessed.* In the midst of a text about diabolical and murderous political radicals, Turgenev appears lightly disguised under the name Karmazinov. He is pictured as a weak, fading writer, desperately pandering to the Russian radicals.

C. The situation was further aggravated by many ironic statements Turgenev made about the state of tsarist Russia and its backwardness. Dostoevsky found them deeply insulting.

D. Turgenev's relations with Tolstoy were not much easier. In a discussion between them, Tolstoy caused anger to flare by a deprecating remark about some charitable actions described by Turgenev. Hot words led to a challenge to a duel. Tolstoy agreed, on condition that the weapons be rifles, not pistols. Turgenev wisely managed to avoid the duel, and Tolstoy spread the word that his contemporary was a coward.

E. Some years later, when Tolstoy was already in his preaching mode, he wrote to Turgenev in France, requesting and urging a reconciliation. Turgenev agreed to a friendly visit at Tolstoy's estate. Rumor has it that the tearful reconciliation lasted until Turgenev was victorious in a game of checkers!

F. In defense of Turgenev, it can be said that later, in 1883, when he was on his deathbed, he wrote a deeply moving letter to Tolstoy, begging him to return his great talent to literature for the sake of Russia's welfare.

III. Unlike either Tolstoy or Dostoevsky, Turgenev's most impressive writing appears in his shorter works, where there is less need for the development of character and where a strong feeling of a particular time and place can be emphasized.

A. One of his most impressive novellas came in 1860, with the publication of *First Love*.

    1. It is an incredibly tender and beautiful evocation of adolescent passion, and it presents many of the themes and problems central to Turgenev's work and talent.

    2. It is ostensibly written in nostalgic retrospect by the protagonist of the story in response to his friends' request to hear the story of his first love, which was "not exactly ordinary."

B. He starts off with the vaguely formed but deeply felt sensual stirrings of a bashful 16-year-old boy:

> …obraz zhenshchiny, prizrak zhenskoi liubvi…ne voznikal opredelennymi ochertaniiami v moem ume, no … tailos' polusoznannoe, stydlivoe predchuvstvie chego-to novogo neskazanno sladkogo, zhenskogo…

> The image of a woman, the phantom of a woman's love…almost never came well shaped or formed into my spirit…but somewhere there was rising up a half recognized, guilty foreboding of something new, inexpressibly sweet, and feminine…

Seldom has the first stirring of sensual love been so well caught in literature.

C. At a time when these feelings are rising up in the heart of the youngster, who is still partly a boy and partly a man, he and his family move into a summer house near a famous Moscow park. Their new neighbors turn out to be the family of an impoverished princess, who has an imperious and very attractive 21-year-old daughter, Zinaida.

D. After the boy changes his name from the Russian Vladimir to the Polish Woldemar (which she thinks more romantic), Zinaida proceeds to make Vladimir a part of her subservient male company, rewarding him sometimes with tender kisses and sometimes with minor sadistic inflictions of sharp slaps and blows.

E. The young man's entire consciousness could not have been in greater bondage to her image than it was at that time of his life. The nature of love becomes closely associated with a situation of total slavery—in this case, of the young man to the attractive young lady.

F. But the young man must also keep up relations with his parents in the summer. Particularly troublesome to him is his relationship—rather, the absence of a real relationship—with his father.

    1. The older man knew how to be charming when he so wished, but he never tolerated consistently close communication with his son.

    2. The young man does notice, however, that the father knows how to talk with Zinaida.

G. It becomes clear that Zinaida is increasingly bothered by some mysterious feeling; she even seems, for some reason, to be apologetic to the young man.

H. It soon turns out that a mysterious stranger, appearing before the young man's eyes as he is watching Zinaida's house at night, is none other than his father. The protagonist suddenly realizes that he and his father are enamored of the same young woman.

I. Such relations cannot be kept secret for long, and soon the mother learns, from a letter written by a jealous follower of Zinaida, about the unfaithfulness of the father.

J. During the ensuing chaos, the father takes the son on a horseback-riding expedition. In the midst of this episode, the son sees his father striking the arm of the beautiful Zinaida with his horsewhip. Her reaction is to kiss the welt caused by the blow.

K. Many years pass, and the protagonist, no longer a young man, thinks back on the episode, with the consciousness that he had been introduced to the nature of true love.

IV. In Turgenev's writing, the genuine power of will is almost always exercised by a woman. His male characters, or at least those who are Russian, are capable of wonderful, sometimes even powerful, speech. But when it comes time for action, something always goes amiss.

A. Turgenev wrote an essay called "Hamlet and Don Quixote," in which he saw people as combinations of both these personalities.

B. This duality is visible in *First Love* and would become a much stronger theme in *Fathers and Sons*, which deals with conflicts between generations.

Suggested Reading:

Leonard Schapiro, *Turgenev: His Life and Times*.

Ivan Turgenev, *First Love*.

Questions to Consider:

1. Why does a classical liberal like Turgenev, who only wanted to help Dostoevsky by lending him money when he badly needed it, end up bearing the lash of the powerful writer's anger and contempt?

2. How does Turgenev make the bashful 16-year-old boy in *First Love* bear the tender and universally recognized symptoms of early and fresh passion?

Lecture Twenty-Two—Transcript
Ivan Sergeevich Turgenev, 1818–1883

In almost all the Russian writers we've examined thus far, one of their outstanding characteristics was the strength of conviction, the notion that they had an idea or a theme of vital importance which they would communicate directly, no matter what the consequences might be. It's interesting that Tolstoy as a young man said to the people around him, who were literary people and who liked to involve in discussions, he said, "You think you have convictions. I'll tell you what a conviction is." This is the Tolstoy who came back from the Crimean War and was carrying a sword. He said, "Conviction is when I stand here with my sword and say I will defend this with my life. No matter how many people you send against me, I will defend it until I'm killed. That's what real conviction is. You people don't know what genuine conviction is." Of course, Tolstoy was very young when he did this. I'm sure if it was a little bit later, he probably wouldn't have said it quite so strongly, but this is the way he felt, that he felt his convictions with such a passion and with such deep emotion that they simply couldn't be wrong. They couldn't be contradicted except, naturally, by himself later on, when he changed his mind.

Dostoevsky also was a very powerful dialectician. When he took issue with somebody, when he argued in the press in the diary of a writer and that kind of thing, there was a tremendous passion behind it and he thought he knew just exactly what he said. It's no accident that Tolstoy and Dostoevsky, they had some kind words to say about each other. As I think I told you earlier, Dostoevsky, very early on, recognized Tolstoy's talent, and Tolstoy said Dostoevsky showed how people who felt deeply—in Tolstoy's opinion—Dostoevsky expressed how people, really people who felt deeply and who didn't come from a rich background, just exactly how they felt. But it's probably not an accident that, at least knowingly, there was never a meeting between them. God knows what would have happened; they might have killed each other had they met each other. There was one incident that's been reported that we're not sure how real it was. Supposedly, when Dostoevsky gave a lecture one time, Tolstoy entered the room incognito; he didn't want Dostoevsky to know who he was but he wanted to hear the lecture. After the lecture, Dostoevsky was told that Tolstoy was in the room. He said, "Good heavens, why didn't he come to me? I would have liked to have met him." But Tolstoy took good, great pains to see to it that they never met, and probably for good reason.

In the case of Turgenev, whom we're going to deal with now, we find a genuine contrast to this kind of extreme passion. Turgenev has the temperament of the true liberal, a man who found himself between the extremes of public opinion, often ending up in the middle of society's polemics, attacked, and even cursed, by both sides, each one of whom thought that he should really be on their side but was really on the other side or, even worse, he sometimes found himself praised for exactly the wrong reasons, or so it seemed to him. People found grist for their mills in what he wrote when he didn't intend for them to have that particular grist. Turgenev was perhaps, psychologically, a somewhat weaker man than either Tolstoy or Dostoevsky and, of course, the relations could sometimes get very strained, and even in some cases mortally dangerous. He was not a man who easily got involved in fights, and, of course, sometimes he tried to avoid fights, which made other people think that he was even somewhat cowardly.

It was, of course, in some ways, a blessing to have been born in that marvelously creative time of Russian literature. Think of the 1860s. In one decade we had *Fathers and Sons* by Turgenev, which we'll be discussing in the next lecture, we had *War and Peace* by Tolstoy, and we had *Crime and Punishment* by Dostoevsky, three extraordinary masterpieces in the course of 10 years. Imagine what it must have felt like to live at that time. You might almost think, "Oh, well, there's nothing to it. We will have one masterpiece after another." It might even have been hard to realize just how extraordinary those times were. And, of course, for Turgenev, this was both a blessing and a curse, a blessing in that he had a chance to take part in it; and his reputation too, particularly at that time, was very hard, a curse, because it wasn't easy for him to navigate his own way through the high passions and harsh issues of the time.

He was born into a fairly wealthy landowner's family in the old Russian province of Orël. And by the way, the literary museums are very well kept in that area. If you ever go to visit Russia, it's a wonderful place to visit. His mother had the reputation of being a very harsh mistress over her serfs, not hesitating to order severe corporal punishment for the slightest infractions of what she considered to be necessary rules. Her son, early, experienced a deep revulsion against such actions and felt estranged from his social background. All his life he would passionately argue against human slavery; this was a very big issue for Turgenev. And, of course, the power of his mother was also something very, very hard to deal with. She wasn't too happy about the career of her son and there were various times when she even threatened to cut him off from the inheritance because she didn't like what he was doing. And, of course he, himself, well understood that his livelihood and material welfare depended to a large extent on the money which the family estate brought in. His mother, naturally, was well aware both of his attitude and his dependence and she attempted to use the income from the estate as a means of control over the actions and opinions of her son.

The result, of course, as long as she lived, was a very strained and a very unpleasant family situation, and the existence of a very strong and perhaps, in many ways, cruel and harsh mother obviously had much to do with Turgenev's attitude towards women, Turgenev's attitude towards life in general. It's certainly no accident that the only really strong characters in his novels were women, that all of the men in one way or another have fatal weaknesses, with perhaps one exception, but that particular man is not a Russian but rather a Bulgarian.

His position was hardly ameliorated by the fact that, as a young writer in the 1830s and 1840s, he fell desperately—and, it turned out, permanently—in love with a French opera diva, Pauline Viardot. This caused him to spend many years in France in her household, together with her husband, in what the French traditionally call a ménage à trois, that is, a household with two husbands and one wife. Pauline Viardot must have been a very fine singer and certainly, at least in her youth, was a very beautiful woman, and the relationship between Turgenev and Pauline Viardot tells you a lot about his description of love in his novels, his description of men and women in his novels, and so on.

In the 1840s he began to write a series of stories, ostensibly about his hunting expeditions in the Russian countryside and they were collected and published together under the title of *Zapiski Okhotnika,* or *Notes of a Hunter*—notice the use of that word, *zapiski*. You remember we talked about that in Dostoevsky's *Notes from the*

Underground. It's not something that presumably is a planned work of literature, not something that's a form over which the author has labored, but rather the jottings, the immediate jottings, of someone's immediate impressions. It seems to take on a life that pretends to have a greater reality than the normal kind of literature that you write. There's nothing any more real about *zapiski* or jottings than there is about a planned novel, but he tries to give you that impression. This is a literary device. It became clear the stories portrayed the miserable situation of the Russian serfs, who were still languishing in slavery. Remember, this is the 1840s; the liberation came in the 1860s.

The book brought him considerable fame and many people believed it played a considerable role in preparing Russian public opinion for the grand emancipation of 1861, the legal and official end of serfdom in Russia. In describing the serfs, Turgenev obviously had a very close understanding of them. It's a curious thing that the serfs—who, in many ways wanted, many of the serfs at least, wanted liberation and desperately wanted land, not under the conditions of serfdom but land which they could control themselves—you would think that they would be opposed to the aristocracy, and yet, having worked the land together in a kind of teamwork with the aristocracy for many hundreds of years, in a certain sense they were closer to the aristocracy than they were to anyone else. At one and the same time, there was a hostility between the two classes and a very deep kind of attraction.

Turgenev once explained this in a rather curious story. It has a kind of horrible twist to it and yet I think it illustrates this very clearly: He imagines that one day, while he was having tea on his estate and enjoying the nature and the fine food and all, all of a sudden a group of peasants would come up to him and say, "Oh, master, please enjoy your tea, enjoy your food, enjoy nature, enjoy everything, because when you're finished we're going to hang you." And, of course, that hostility which lay underneath the closeness, or perhaps the closeness that lay underneath the hostility, was something that Turgenev explored very carefully and very extensively. The picture of nature that you get in *Notes of a Hunter* is really quite extraordinary. Turgenev had a feeling for the Russian countryside, a feeling for the magnificent woods, a feeling for the great plains, a feeling for the whole rows of wheat, that was really quite extraordinary and it made the reader get a sense of what the rustic, what the rural part of Russia was like, in some way comparable to that famous scene of mowing that I've talked to you about before in the scene of *Anna Karenina*.

Both Turgenev and Tolstoy shared this characteristic that, in Russian, was called, *gnezdo derevnia* [sic *dvorianskoe gnezdo*], that is, a "nest in the countryside." What they had was a parcel of land—a piece of land—which gave them a sense of being rooted in the country. Whatever happened in the city, whatever happened in politics, whatever happened in their lives, they could always go back to that land, they could always go back to that estate. It was always there and for them; it was very powerful.

Of course, when we talk about serfdom, we also have to remember that there were very, very rich families—for example, the Sheremet'ev family. Maybe some of you have visited Moscow as tourists at one time or another, perhaps doing work in Moscow. You went through an airport. You may have noticed it was called Sheremet'evo; it is named after that famous Sheremet'ev family, which, as one family, controlled over three million serfs. Try to imagine one family in control not only economically, not only from the point of view of agriculture, not only from the point of view of the organization of lives, but even sexual power over three million people. It's hard to conceive and, of course, if you begin to conceive it, you get some notion of what the problem of serfdom became in Russia in the 19th century and what it meant to publish that book, *Notes of a Hunter*, and, of course, going in the direction of the liberation of the serfs. You can also appreciate what it felt like for the aristocracy to live after the liberation, when all the organization which they had known was totally destroyed and they had to go in a different direction which they couldn't possibly see.

If you understand this, you begin to realize how many very, very sharp and fundamental changes there have been in Russia in the last 100 or 150 years and, of course, we're living through something very parallel to that, at least in psychological terms, right now. Of course, Turgenev was then seen as an ally of those who wanted to reform Tsarist Russia and move in the direction of Western European parliamentary democracy. In those days, there were two groups that were formally defined. There were the so-called Slavophiles; that is, people who were lovers, as they saw it, of the past in Russia. Mind you, they often distorted the past to fit their ideology. And then there were the so-called Westernisers, of whom Turgenev was a very important member, who wanted to see Russia go in the very parallel direction that had happened in Western Europe. They wanted to see a more democratic form of government; they wanted to see more development of an urban economy; they wanted to see an education which was done in the European style rather than the old Russian style and, of course, Turgenev was a very important supporter of these Westernisers.

Now, mind you, there were also those who were much more radical and wanted to see what, in those days, they called socialism in Russia. Of course, it changed radically after Turgenev's lifetime when Marxism came to Russia. Many of them looked upon Turgenev as a supporter, and by this time Turgenev had inherited his family estate and could afford to give monetary assistance. As his reputation continued to grow in the 1860s, Turgenev was seen by his friends and colleagues in the West, particularly Gustave Flaubert and Henry James, as the best of the Russian writers. For at least a generation, as far as the Westerners were concerned, Turgenev was the greatest and the most outstanding representative of Russian literature, as Westerners understood.

Now in spite of his often hostile relationships towards his fellow Russian writers, it seems to me, very much to Turgenev's credit, that he tried very hard in the West to popularize the works of his great Russian contemporaries, particularly Pushkin and Tolstoy. Of course, obviously he had no personal relationships with Pushkin, who had died long before, but Turgenev tried very hard to get Westerners to understand Pushkin. Of course, Westerners could read Russian prose; it was much, much harder to read poetry. And, of course, I've already told you how difficult it is to translate Pushkin's poetry into a foreign language. Turgenev tried very hard, even translating himself some of the works of Pushkin for Flaubert, and Flaubert's famous reply was, *"Alors, il est plat, votre poet?"* "He's rather flat, your poet, don't you think?" As hard as he tried, Turgenev couldn't get across that brilliant simplicity and rhythm of Pushkin's language.

Of course, when it came to Dostoevsky and Tolstoy, Turgenev had had very hostile relations with them, but nevertheless he tried to get their works across to the Westerners and, of course, that led to the remark I think you've already heard from Henry James, that

"Tolstoy's novel is like the hitching together of an elephant and a carriage," a carriage, of course, which should be hitched to a horse. Dostoevsky initially admired Turgenev's work, but then Turgenev made a fatal mistake: he lent Dostoevsky money, which Dostoevsky desperately needed. It's interesting that sometimes, if you want to make an enemy, do somebody a favor. This was very much the case with Dostoevsky. Turgenev's generosity to Dostoevsky, when Dostoevsky was desperately in need, triggered a hostile reaction against Turgenev since Dostoevsky took it to mean that Turgenev looked down on him. As a matter of fact, in one of Dostoevsky's famous novels, *The Possessed,* or *The Devils,* which unfortunately I haven't had time to talk about in this series of lectures—it was a very powerful novel —there is a character named Karmazinov—notice how, in some ways, it's almost close to the name he later used for his latest novel, *Karamazov*—Karmazinov, who is a disgusting writer who seeks a cheap kind of publicity, who gives the kind of concerts that Turgenev was very famous for giving publicly, who doesn't know how to engage in the kind of kissing that Russians are involved in. It's a very nasty and passionately anti-revolutionary novel, where Turgenev appears lightly disguised as this Karmazinov, a weak, fading writer, desperately pandering to the Russian radicals, and not a very kind thing to do to a man who had really been very kind to Dostoevsky.

And, as a matter of fact, matters were not helped when Turgenev later said that if the Crystal Palace in London, which showed all the conventions useful to mankind, were destroyed, Russia would lose absolutely nothing because Russia had never contributed to them. Dostoevsky found that an insult to the Russian national honor and he became very, very angry.

Turgenev's relations with Tolstoy were not much easier. There was a time when Turgenev was bragging about the charitable actions of his niece and Tolstoy thought that this was something false, something that didn't really come with charity. Turgenev got very angry. Words led to a challenge, and Tolstoy challenged Turgenev to a duel on condition the weapons be not the kind of pistols they normally use but rather rifles. He wanted to kill him. Turgenev wisely managed to avoid the duel, and Tolstoy spread the word that Turgenev was a coward. Later on, when Tolstoy was already beginning to get into his preaching mood, in the 1880s, he wrote to Turgenev in France, requesting a reconciliation. He said, "Look, Ivan Sergeevich, you are a better Christian than I am. I know you have forgiven me already. Come visit me in Russia and give me a chance to forgive you." Well Turgenev came and there was a cheerful reconciliation, which lasted until Turgenev beat Tolstoy at a game of checkers. As we can see, sometimes the temperaments of great writers can be at the level of very immature human beings—I would say, rather, three-year-olds. In additional defense of Turgenev, I would like you also to know that in 1883, when he was actually on his deathbed, he wrote a deeply moving letter to Tolstoy, begging him to return his great talent to literature for the sake of Russia's welfare.

Unlike Tolstoy and Dostoevsky, Turgenev's most impressive work appears in his shorter works, where there is less need for the development of character and where strong feeling of time and place can be emphasized. One of his most impressive *povest'* or novellas came in 1860, with the publication of *Pervaia Liubov'*, or *First Love*. It's an almost incredibly tender and beautiful evocation of adolescent passion. And it presents many of the themes and problems central to Turgenev's work and talent. It's ostensibly written in nostalgic retrospect by the protagonist of the story in response to his friends' request to hear a story of his first love, which, as he put it, was not exactly ordinary. As a matter of fact, he won't even tell it to him. He insisted he'll write it down and send it to him. He starts out with vaguely formed but deeply felt sensual stirrings of a bashful 16-year-old boy:

> *...obraz zhenshchiny, prizrak zhenskoi liubvi...ne voznikal opredelennymi ochertaniiami v moem ume, no...tailos' polusoznannoe, stydlivoe predchuvstvie chego-to novogo neskazanno sladkogo, zhenskogo...*

> The image of a woman, the phantom of a woman's love almost never came well shaped or formed in my spirit. But somewhere there was rising up, a half-recognized, guilty foreboding of something new, inexpressibly sweet and feminine.

As I said before, seldom is the first stirring of sensual love been so caught in literature. At a time when these feelings are rising up in the heart of the youngster who is still partly a boy and partly a man, he and his family move into a summerhouse near a famous Moscow park. Their new neighbors turn out to be the family of an impoverished princess who has an imperious and very attractive 21-year-old daughter. The young man is called Vladimir, but she insists on calling him Woldemar, the Polish form, in her opinion a more romantic form of the name.

This young woman named Zinaida, Zinaida Aleksandrovna, has surrounded herself with young men, all of whom adore her, and she lords it over them in a way that very much appeals to the nature of this young man. He, too, wants to be a part of her subservient male company and he feels very good when she sometimes rewards him with tender kisses and sometimes slaps his face and even—she doesn't do this to him, but to others—sticks a pin in one of their hands. In describing the feelings and the nature that exists at this time, I'd like to give you a quote that gives you a sense of Turgenev's style.

> A thunderstorm, I thought, and I was right; it was a thunderstorm. But it was a very long way off and no thunder was to be heard, only dull, long, sheer lightning lit up the sky incessantly. It did not flash so much as flutter and quiver like the wings of a flying bird. The lightening did not cease for a moment; it was what the common people call, "Sparrow's night" [*vorob'inaia noch'*]. I gazed at the silent sandy plain of the dark mass of the *Neskuchnyi* garden [the gardens won't allow boredom] at the yellowish facades of distant buildings, which seemed to be quivering with every feeble flash. I gazed and could not tear myself away. That mute lightning, those temperate flashes, seemed to be in accord with the mute and secret emotions that were flaming up inside of me.

The use of the sparrow night, the use of the lightning, the use of nature, which somehow is outside, and at the very same time inside the young man's imagination, is something really quite wonderful. Furthermore, Turgenev uses Pushkin in a most extraordinary way. When the young man is thinking about Zinaida and wondering why it is that one moment she seems to be very close to him, another moment very far away, he suddenly thinks of a Pushkin poem and he starts to sing it to her. The poem, of course, has been put to music by Glinka, the famous Russian composer, but I would like you to hear it in the tune of a little-known composer, a little-known American composer of the 20th century.

Ne poi, krasavitsa, pri mne
Ty pesen Gruzii pechal'noi:
Napominaiut mne one
Druguiu zhizn' i bereg dal'nyi.

Uvy! napominaiut mne
Tvoi zhestokie napevy
I step', i noch' – i pri lune
Cherty dalekoi, bednoi devy.

Ia prizrak milyi rokovoi,
Tebia uvidev, zabyvaiu;
No ty poesh' – i predo mnoi
Ego ia vnov' voobrazhaiu.

Ne poi, krasavitsa, pri mne
Ty pesen Gruzii pechal'noi:
Napominaiut mne one
Druguiu zhizn' i bereg dal'nyi.

He talks about Georgia in the Caucasus, a song which is being sung about Georgia, which reminds him of a woman who lived there at a different time and a different place. And he sees before him, in these rather stern and sometimes even harsh chanting, the steppes, that is, the plain, the night, and in the light of the moon, the features of a far-off young woman. And he remembers a very dear specter, "And having seen you, I forget it, but as soon as you sing in front of me, the specter arises once again." The specter, of course, is the beautiful woman that Pushkin traveled with at that time. It's a beautiful evocation of the feelings that Turgenev is trying to get across.

His entire consciousness, that is, the consciousness of the young man, could not have been in greater bondage to her image than it was at that time of his life. The nature of love becomes closely associated with a situation of total slavery—in this case, of a young man to the attractive young lady —but the young man also has to keep up relations with his parents in the summer. Particularly troublesome to him is his relationship to his father or, I should rather say, the absence of a real relationship. The older man knew how to be charming when he wanted, but he never tolerated consistently close communication with his son. But the young man does notice, contrary to what he thinks, that the father knows how to talk with Zinaida, with the beautiful young woman. It even becomes clear that

Zinaida is increasingly bothered by some mysterious feelings. She even seems, for some reason, to be apologetic to the young man because she can't give him the kind of love that he wants.

He broods over this for a long time. He feels the ambivalence of the situation; he feels it very hard somehow to make contact with her, and one of the other men who is around Zinaida says to him, "You know"—by this time he has been appointed a page to Zinaida; he's her page and, of course, that means he has to do exactly what she says—the young man says, "You know, a page has to be very alert, very aware. He has to keep his eyes open both day and night." The young man ponders, says, "Why day and night?" But when Zinaida makes an arrangement to see him at nighttime sometimes, he goes out and he watches very carefully and, to his amazement, and perhaps horror, he sees that another person is coming to Zinaida at night and, of course, that person is none other than his own father.

He suddenly realizes that he and his father had been enamored by the very same young woman. Well, such relations can't be kept secret for very long and soon the mother learns from a letter written by a jealous follower of Zinaida about the unfaithfulness of the father. In the midst of the ensuing chaos, the father takes his son on a horseback-riding expedition. In the midst of this episode, the son sees what, to him, is a truly shocking and horrible sight. The father leaves the horse with his son and goes off to talk with Zinaida, thinking, of course, that the son won't follow him and watch him, but the son does follow and watch him, and they get involved in what looks like an increasingly exciting conversation, and suddenly the father takes the horsewhip that he has in his hand and strikes Zinaida across the flesh of her arm, and her reaction is to kiss the welt caused by the blow.

This is something that is very, very hard for the young man to take. How could his own father possibly act this way towards a woman whom the father obviously appreciates and whom the father has even defended in certain conversations with the mother, whom the father—a man who can have relations almost with nobody around him—finds a way of having a relation with this woman. You would think that their sensitivity would lead them together, and all of a sudden he beats her with a horsewhip. To say it's traumatic for the son is, of course, putting it very, very mildly.

In the course of the story, the man telling the story from the very beginning says:

> Many years passed by and the protagonist, no longer a young man, thought back on the episode after the deaths of the other people in the story—the father dies; the young woman dies—and he realizes that he has been introduced to the nature of true love, a love which can have terribly cruel aspects as well as tremendously tender and tremendously slavish aspects, all into one large bundle.

In Turgenev's writing, the genuine power of will, as I said before, is almost exclusively exercised by the women. His male characters, at least those who were Russian, are capable of wonderful, sometimes even powerful speech, but when it comes time for action, something always goes amiss. Turgenev wrote a very famous essay called, "Hamlet and Don Quixote." Hamlet is the one who is always thinking, always pondering, always wondering how things will work out. Don Quixote is the one who takes action, even when action is not called for. He doesn't think; he acts. And according to Turgenev, people are made up of combinations between Don Quixote and Hamlet. And, of course, in the story, you see the beginnings of this.

We're going to see it much more powerfully in perhaps Turgenev's most powerful novel, which we'll examine next time, in the next lecture, called, *Fathers and Sons* or, in Russian, *Ottsy i Deti*, *Fathers and Children*, where we see how these dynamics play themselves out in the conflicts and the relationships that exist between two different generations.

Lecture Twenty-Three
The Stresses between Two Generations

Scope:

In addition to a series of extremely finely crafted short stories and novellas, Turgenev wrote several relatively short novels. One of them, *Fathers and Sons* of 1861, was destined to become one of Europe's defining moments in 19th-century prose. Both Tolstoy and Dostoevsky, as well as many Western writers, took the form and ideas of this novel as a basis for their own work. With his invention of the political word *nihilist*—one who wants to destroy all present institutions—Turgenev managed to touch the essence of the biblical question from Genesis 22:1–18, the story that relates Abraham's willingness to sacrifice his only son. Any binding (the Hebrew title *Akedah* means "binding") between generations requires not only accord but also friction that can even threaten to become mortal. It is the latter that we see in *Fathers and Sons*. Bazarov and the Kirsanov family become the modern characters in this universal drama.

Outline

I. In Russia, the decade of the 1860s was an extraordinarily creative time for literary prose. The most outstanding prose artists of that time were clearly Dostoevsky, Tolstoy, and Turgenev. In no small way, they were all caught up in the themes of the polemics between generations and among the political and ideological groups, which each had their own programs for the future of their rapidly changing country.

    A. The relatively open and liberal regime of Tsar Alexander II made it possible to debate many of these issues openly, and the Russian writers jumped into the fray with blazing polemical pens. Turgenev dealt with the great theme of the relationship between generations in his most famous novel, *Fathers and Sons*, which had extraordinary influence, most especially on Dostoevsky.

B. It is a theme that goes back to the biblical story of Abraham and Isaac. The Hebrew title of the story is *The Binding*, which implies both the idea of connection and the idea of rebellion. Written in 1861, *Fathers and Sons* straddles many of the most hotly debated issues of the day, thereby calling down on Turgenev's head intense fire from all sides of the political spectrum.

C. The novel takes place in the countryside, on the estate of the Kirsanov family. We first observe the place through the eyes of Nikolai Kirsanov, who is excitedly awaiting the arrival of his son, Arkady, just coming back from student life at a large Russian university.

    1. In the father's strong emotions, we experience not only the delight of a family reunion but also a certain trepidation.

    2. After the death of his wife, Nikolai has entered into close relations with a young woman from the lower class, and the two of them already have a young child, a new and unexpected brother for Arkady.

D. The situation is made even more complicated by the fact that Arkady has brought a guest to the house, a young man named Bazarov. One of Turgenev's most famous characters, the young guest represents the new, radical thinking of a younger Russian generation, just coming out of the universities.

E. It does not take Bazarov long to let the older generation know, in a deliberately offensive tone, that he holds all of their most cherished convictions in deep contempt. He proudly adopts the title of *nihilist*, a word rather new to the ears of Nikolai and his brother, Pavel.

F. Near the beginning of the novel, the fathers and sons get into a passionate and heated argument about the perceived worth or, rather, the complete absence of worth in the most cherished convictions of the older generation.

G. Nikolai, and even more strongly his brother, Pavel, are proud of their liberal notions and proposals for reform in Russian society. It is, after all, very close to the time of emancipation for all of Russia's millions of serfs. Pavel defends the notion of aristocratic *noblesse oblige*, a well- defined, stable society in which cultured and beneficent aristocrats tend to the needs of their less fortunate countrymen.

H. Bazarov responds with unconcealed contempt for what he sees as aristocratic condescension and incomprehension toward the lower classes. He brushes aside their notions of social philanthropy, proudly boasting that he understands the peasantry a thousand times better than any of them could possibly know.

I. Furthermore, he absolutely denies the presence of anything positive in Russian culture or society. All of it has to be destroyed, he believes, turned into *nihil*, or nothing. Only then can a better society be conceived. In order to do this, even Russian poetry must be destroyed. Only materialist science can offer ideas and concepts of value to Russian society.

J. In a way, this point of view reminds us of Turgenev's own statement, which infuriated Dostoevsky. At that time, there was a building in England called the Crystal Palace, which supposedly contained all of the useful inventions known to humankind. Turgenev said, rather sarcastically, that if that palace were to burn down, Russia would not have lost any of its own contributions. Such was the approach of Russian radicals toward their own national history.

K. Turgenev's novel expresses the extreme conclusions drawn by the nihilists. And Bazarov seems to be one of the strongest male characters drawn by Turgenev.

II. In contrast to the atmosphere of Bazarov's polemics against the older generation, Turgenev gives us a picture of Russian feminine society in the countryside of the 1860s. He compares a caricature of what the Russians would then have called a liberated woman with a female character who turns out to be the strongest figure in the novel.

A. When the two young men leave the Kirsanov Estate, they go to visit a woman named Evdoksiia Kukshina, described as a truly emancipated, progressive woman. She soon turns out to be the kind of person who scatters pronouncements and questions in the air, without the slightest intent of intelligent communication.

B. She dismisses the notions of almost all serious contemporary thinkers. All of this rejection is put forward in the name of materialism and progress.

C. Bazarov has sense enough to take her very lightly, in spite of her seemingly materialist views. But he does not hesitate, rather cynically, to take advantage of her hospitality, especially her good champagne.

D. The action at Kukshina's house is rather abruptly interrupted by the mention of another woman's name, Anna Odintsova. When Bazarov hears their description of this beautiful lady, he understands instinctively, almost immediately, that a very different person is in view. In spite of his extreme expressions of nihilism, he obviously has a genuine sensitivity for understanding people.

E. After the two young friends actually meet Odintsova, Bazarov responds to Arkady's question about the first impression made by the beautiful lady: what a delectable body—perfect for the dissecting table! Arkady expresses disgust, but the reader understands that something rather different is happening inside Bazarov, something that the nihilist finds uncomfortable.

F. When the two of them go to visit her estate, it soon becomes obvious that Odintsova's beauty and intelligence have entered deeply into Bazarov's imagination. The nihilist is nowhere nearly so consistent as his arrogantly ejaculated arguments would make the older generation believe. Furthermore, he is intelligent enough to realize the genuine strength and intelligence of the beautiful woman, who is obviously worthy of a far better position than a body on a dissecting table.

G. Bazarov eventually opens up to show his passion for Odintsova, but she, in spite of her attraction to his powerful personality, rejects his offer of closeness. She is not ready for the complexities of a genuinely intimate relationship.

III. At this point, Turgenev takes us to a still different version of the older generation: He shows us Bazarov's parents, an old-fashioned medical doctor with his wife, a warm-hearted, plump country lady who knows how to prepare and set a marvelous traditional Russian table. Turgenev describes the two of them with obvious attraction and delight.

A. The conversation between the two generations is quite different here from what it was at the Kirsanov estate.

    1. Here, the older man is trying to convince his son, who also will practice as a medical doctor, about the efficacy of medicine in previous days.

    2. Bazarov reacts with skepticism, but without any of the arrogance he displayed earlier. We understand that he respects what his father does, in spite of the nihilist's words toward medicine in general.

B. Furthermore, it is equally clear that the elder Bazarov has great respect for an earlier generation of Arkady's family, a general under whom the doctor had served. He brushes aside his son's attempt to dismiss that generation with nihilist talk.

C. Turgenev makes it clear in this scene that the work of the older generation cannot be simply dismissed, even in the context of a younger generation that wants to change everything in the world. The doctor has respect for the force and energy of the young people, but he also has a decent amount of self-respect.

D. The real literary fireworks are reserved for Bazarov's mother, a "genuine Russian woman of the old school," who might well have lived 200 years earlier. Her evening meal was incomparable, with all the flourishes of the old school of cooking.

E. She was full of the old Russian folklore, with all kinds of superstitions expressed in marvelously spontaneous and poetic ways. She knew the devil lurked in still water, so she washed her face only in running water; she wouldn't eat watermelon, because when cut in half, it reminded her of the head of John the Baptist.

F. As Turgenev interjects, such women are increasingly harder to find. God knows if that is a good or a bad thing. The reader certainly infers the positive side of this proposition.

G. It is indicative of her strong influence on the subconscious of her nihilist son that her presence causes him to lose a night's sleep thinking about Odintsova's recent rejection of his advance. The traditions that she embodies go very deeply into his character and the real character of the younger generation.

H. When the young people abruptly decide to leave the parents' house, it is Bazarov's mother who expresses what the older generation feels in losing its young people; it is also she who comforts her husband when he realizes how alone he feels in the parting with his son. Clearly, Turgenev has a deep association with the feelings of this old-fashioned Russian couple.

IV. Turgenev then plunges the reader into the internal contradictions of Bazarov's character. Although upholding the stubborn consistency of his own opinions, the young nihilist manages to antagonize and even threaten physically his close friend Arkady. When they return to the Kirsanov Estate, he even manages to get involved with Fenya, the young mistress of Nikolai Kirsanov.

A. When Pavel, Nikolai's brother, who has had bitter arguments with Bazarov, notices how warmly Fenya reacts to Bazarov, he decides to take matters into his own hands. He will provoke the young man to an old-fashioned duel.

B. Bazarov realizes that the very idea of a duel is absurd to a man of his principles, but he is also determined not to let himself be insulted by these condescending aristocrats.

C. The result is a duel in which Bazarov wounds Pavel, then insists on dealing with the wound as a young medical doctor would. Pavel ends up wearing the bandage set by the person whose principles the older man hates, and Bazarov ends up by participating in the kind of behavior that his principles most deeply oppose.

D. The contradictions end only in the death, in some ways almost a suicide, of Bazarov. In the course of the medical practice that he decides to take up, he asks his father to cauterize a cut he received while performing an autopsy on the corpse of a peasant who had died of typhus.

E. The father grows pale at the realization that there is no way to prevent his son's infection with what was then the incurable disease of typhus. We are fated to watch the inevitable death of Bazarov, a death he could easily have avoided by following normal medical procedure at the autopsy.

F. In the midst of Bazarov's final illness, Odintsova appears, with a well-known German doctor in tow. There is nothing he can do, but we see in this scene Odintsova's strength in contrast to the physical downfall of Bazarov, together with the collapse of his dreams and plans. As always in Turgenev's work, the women turn out to be the strongest people in Russia.

V. At the end of the novel, the two old parents of Bazarov visit the grave of their son. Turgenev asks whether or not their prayers are futile, whether or not their totally devoted love has some power. He refers to a poem by Pushkin about *ravnodushnaia priroda* ("indifferent nature"), which blooms and fades without reference to our human feelings.

A. He draws the conclusion that the flowers over the grave look at us with innocent eyes, which see not only the indifference of nature but also the possibility of reconciliation and eternal life.

B. Turgenev's own reconciliation with Russia, whose regime and flaws he often castigated mercilessly, is expressed in a famous prose poem, in which he says that it is impossible to believe that the magnificent and powerful Russian language was not given to a great people.

Suggested Reading:

V. S. Pritchett, *The Gentle Barbarian: The Life and Work of Turgenev.*

Ivan Turgenev, *Fathers and Sons (A Norton Critical Edition)*, edited and translated by Ralph Matlaw, collected critical articles at the end of the Norton Critical Edition.

Questions to Consider:

1. Bazarov, the nihilist, always seems to get the better of the argument in his dialogues with Pavel Kirsanov, the elder aristocrat in Turgenev's novel. Is there nothing to be said for the defender of the best parts of our cultural traditions, represented by the aristocratic slogan *noblesse oblige*?

2. When Bazarov's old parents grieve at his graveside, Turgenev quotes Pushkin's famous line about "indifferent nature." Does nature, as depicted in this novel, truly turn out to be indifferent to human suffering and aspiration?

Lecture Twenty-Three—Transcript
The Stresses between Two Generations

In Russia, the decade of the 1860s was an extraordinarily creative time for literary prose. The most outstanding prose artists of that time were clearly Dostoevsky, Tolstoy, and Turgenev. And, of course, it might be surprising for people now to realize that in those days Turgenev had perhaps the strongest reputation. Turgenev was considered to be the outstanding member of that team; today, of course, opinions have shifted radically and sometimes Turgenev is given rather short shrift indeed—I think somewhat unjustly. It seems to me his novels were quite powerful in their own way, even though they didn't have the obvious passion and power and strength of Tolstoy and Dostoevsky.

In no small way, they were all caught up in the themes of the polemics between generations and among the political and ideological groups, which had their own various programs for the future of their very rapidly changing country. The relatively open—the relatively open—and liberal regime of Tsar Alexander II made it possible to debate many of these issues openly, and the Russian writers jumped into the fray with blazing polemical pens. One of the great themes that he dealt with, and, of course, it became the title of his most famous novel, was the theme of the change of generations, of the relationship between *Fathers and Sons*. This novel, of course, had an extraordinary influence on the people around him, most especially, by the way, on Dostoevsky.

And, of course, this whole business of fathers and sons, of how one generation gives way to another, how a second generation, in some ways, takes what it can from the previous generation but on the other hand tends to revolt against that generation is something that's been caught in many, many different kind of literature. It really goes back to the Bible—it goes back to the 22nd chapter of *Genesis*—where, as you may remember, Abraham goes out to sacrifice Isaac, his son. Now I realize that children can sometimes be annoying, particularly on a rainy day when they're in the house till five o'clock in the afternoon. But while it's okay to be angry at them, it's not really considered very good form to go out and kill them. And yet Abraham claims that he heard from God that he should take his only son and go out and kill him. As you know, it got very dangerous and very threatening until finally, at the very last moment, Isaac was saved from being killed. And you remember the appearance of the ram; and you might think that the title of the story—if we had to give it a title, we might say something like, well the "Almost Sacrifice of Isaac."

As a matter of fact, the classical side of that story tells us something very relevant to what we're talking about now. The title of that story is *Akedah*, which in Hebrew means, "Binding." Now, of course, binding obviously applies to the fact that if you're going to take a 32-year-old son—Isaac was 32 at the time—and sacrifice him, you've got to bind him somehow. Even if he doesn't want to, he's going to resist when the knife is coming down on him. So, of course, he talks about the binding of hands or the binding of feet perhaps. But it's also binding in another sense; it's the binding between generations. How does binding take place between generations? One would think that if you're talking about binding, it would be one generation taking things from the other and connecting itself with the other. But, as a matter of fact, as the story very well implies, the relationship that leads to binding also involves hostility, also involves danger; as a matter of fact, in the story, it almost involves killing. How is it that the relationship between generations involves both taking from the generation and rebelling against the generation"? And that rebelling and taking, of course, is something that's very close to the problem of *Fathers and Sons*.

Turgenev managed to straddle many of these most hotly debated issues of his day, thereby calling down upon his head intense fire from all sides of the political spectrum. As you might say, "Uneasy lies the head that wears the crown of the liberal." The novel itself takes place in the countryside on the estate of the Kirsanov family. We first observe the place through the eyes of Nikolai Kirsanov, who is excitedly awaiting the arrival of his son, Arkady, who has just come back from student life at a large Russian university. In the father's strong emotions we experience not only the delight of family reunion but also a certain trepidation for a very strong reason. After the death of his wife, Nikolai has entered into close relations with a young woman from the lower class and the two of them already have a young child, a new and unexpected brother for Arkady. And the old man, of course, doesn't know how Arkady is going to react to this. And, of course, the presence of the unexpected brother brings us back to Dostoevsky and *The Brothers Karamazov*.

Dostoevsky also talks about the bringing up of a younger generation when he has Alyosha, in *The Brothers Karamazov*, take charge of a group of young people who are very, very bright, sometimes very, very nasty and sometimes very, very rebellious. And, of course, in Dostoevsky, trying to work out the relationships between Alyosha and these children, which presumably will be better than the relationship between the brothers Karamazov and their father, you have Dostoevsky dealing with the theme of fathers and sons, a theme which he quite consciously took from Turgenev.

Now, of course, the situation in the Kirsanov house, in Turgenev's novel, is made even more complicated by the fact that Arkady has brought a guest to the house, a young man whose name, of course, has become very famous in literature, Bazarov. And clearly Bazarov is very much a model for many of the characters that Dostoevsky put in his novels. One of Turgenev's most famous characters, the young guest, represents the new radical thinking of a younger Russian generation, just coming out of the universities. It doesn't take Bazarov very long to let the older generation know, in a deliberately offensive tone, that he holds all of their most cherished convictions in deep contempt. He proudly adopts a title, a word that wasn't too well known before Turgenev wrote this novel—it's even possible that Turgenev originated it; he calls himself *nigilist* in Russian, that is to say, a "nihilist." *Nihil*, of course, in Latin means "nothing," a word rather new to the ears of Nikolai and his aristocratic brother, Pavel. It's Nikolai Kirsanov and Pavel Kirsanov.

These nihilists believe that nothing is worth preserving from the older generation. They want to deal with the world in a way that later on was described by the revolutionaries as a "*tabla rasa*," that is to say, a table which has been scraped entirely clean. Nothing, absolutely nothing, that comes from the previous generation is of any use to them. Pavel gets very angry about this. "But look, I consider myself a liberal," he says, "but, nevertheless, I realize that there are some things that we have to preserve." He talks about the English aristocracy who have the slogan, "noblesse oblige." They know their rights, but in turn they respect the rights of other people, and Pavel sees the English aristocracy as worthy of imitation. He and Bazarov get into a passionate and heated argument about the perceived worth, or rather, from Bazarov's point of view, the complete absence of worth of the most cherished convictions of the older generation.

Pavel is so upset, he says, "But you're rejecting the Russian people." And Bazarov says to him with great cynicism, "You talk about the Russian people. You aristocrats who sit in your estate and enjoy your tea and your good food and your easy life." He said, "If it comes between you and me, who is closer to the Russian peasant? I'll bet that you can't even talk to the Russian peasant. The Russian peasant easily recognizes me as someone who is very close to him. I speak his language. I know what he does. Don't talk to me about the Russian peasant." Pavel Petrovich tries to talk about law and Bazarov says, "Yes, the law that allows the landlord to whip the serf whenever he feels like it." "Well, what about family relationships?" Bazarov replies, "Well, I suppose you've never heard of the right of the first night, where the landowner thinks he has the right to sleep with the bride of the peasant." As you might imagine, this is very, very irritating to Pavel Petrovich.

Now Nikolai and, even more strongly, his brother Pavel are proud of their liberal notions and proposals for reform in Russian society. It's after all, very close, within a year of two when will occur the emancipation for all of Russia's millions of serfs. Pavel defends the notion of aristocratic noblesse oblige as well as the defined stable society where cultured and beneficent aristocrats tend to the needs of their less fortunate countrymen.

Bazarov, of course, has unconcealed contempt for aristocratic condescension and non-comprehension. He brushes aside their notions of social philanthropy, boldly boasting that he knows the country much better than any of them could possibly know and there's nothing worth preserving in the country as it now stands. All has to be destroyed and turned into *nihil,* or nothing. Only then can a better reality be conceived. In order to do this, even Russian poetry must be destroyed. Only materialist science, only the dissection of frogs, only medicine, can offer ideas and concepts of value to Russian society. Bazarov, of course, has been trained as a doctor, following in the footsteps of his father. As a matter of fact, later on, when Arkady sees his father reading Pushkin, the son gently takes the book out of the older man's hands and replaces it with a famous contemporary German materialist tract—the very title tells you something about it—"*Stoff und Kraft,*" "Material and Strength." This gesture only emphasizes the young people's utter disdain for poets and imaginative literature, whose worth they put so far below the work of scientists that Bazarov says, "One decent scientist is worth nine poets."

In a way, this reminds us of Turgenev's own statement which so infuriated Dostoevsky. You remember that he said—I've mentioned this before—that if the Crystal Palace were destroyed, containing all the useful inventions known to mankind, Russia would lose absolutely nothing because Russia has never made such contributions. And, of course, this reflected the approach of the radicals we're talking about. Well, of course, the argument breaks up. Each side goes off, Pavel, in short, to lick his wounds and Bazarov, as he readily sarcastically says, "I'm going off to dissect frogs."

In the novel, of course, we see the expression of the extreme conclusions drawn by the nihilists. And Bazarov seems to be one of the strongest male characters drawn by Turgenev. In the beginning of the novel you see a tremendous psychological and even physical strength in Bazarov. As a kind of a contrast to the atmosphere of Bazarov's polemics against the older generation, Turgenev gives us a picture of Russian feminine society in the countryside of the 1860s. He does this by a contrast between a caricature of what the Russians would have called a liberated woman and a female character who— now we're thinking that Bazarov is very strong, yet this female character turns out to be the strongest figure in the novel. And, of course, it fits very well the pattern of all of Turgenev's novels.

When the two young men leave the Kirsanov Estate, they go to visit a woman named Evdoksiia Kukshina. Now this is a rather nasty phrase on Turgenev's part. "Kukshina" is very close to a very pornographic Russian phrase and, of course, the very name is making very nasty fun of this woman and denigrating her to a very low level. She is described as a truly emancipated, progressive woman. She turns out to be the kind of person who scatters pronouncements in the air, scatters questions in the air, without the slightest intent of intelligent communication. She dismisses the notions of all serious contemporary thinkers. As a matter of fact, she even has contemptuous words for George Sand, the famous woman novelist at that time who is so widely admired by reformers in Russia. And, of course, all of this is put forward in the name of what she calls materialism and progress. And no matter what anybody says, she will put it down.

Bazarov, although you would think that, after all, what she says fits very nicely with his views, he has sense enough to take her very lightly, in spite of her seemingly materialist views which seem to agree with what he says. But he doesn't hesitate, rather cynically, to take advantage of her hospitality, particularly her good champagne. You're beginning to see that there is another element of Bazarov that's not quite so crystal clean or, we might say, squeaky clean, as Bazarov tries to present himself in the house of the Kirsanovs. He is quite willing to use other people. He is quite willing to enjoy the champagne of a woman whom he holds in utter contempt. He is quite willing to let her go on about opinions that ostensibly agree with his while secretly considering her nothing, to be a total idiot.

Furthermore, in the beginning of the novel, you think that the relationship between Arkady, the young man who has come from the university, and Bazarov is a close one. And Arkady considers himself a close friend of Bazarov; he even almost considers himself a pupil of Bazarov. But as the novel goes on, you begin to realize that Bazarov is lording it over Arkady, that, as a matter of fact, at a certain point he is even willing to engage in a physical struggle with Arkady, in which he could overcome him like he could overcome a puppy. There is a would-be tyrant in this Bazarov that is by no means attractive although, of course, when he's arguing with Pavel Petrovich, obviously Turgenev wants us to kind of enjoy the fact that he can trump the old man whenever he wants to.

The action at Kukshina's house is rather abruptly interrupted by the mention of another woman's name, Anna Odintsova. When Bazarov hears a description of this beautiful lady, he understands it would seem instinctively—he hasn't even seen her, he's only heard a description—but somehow, something inside of him—you begin to realize that there is much more to this man than he shows on the surface, that a very different person is in view. In spite of his extreme expressions of nihilism, he obviously has a genuine sensitivity for understanding people, and you see this too when he talks to peasants and even when he talks to Fenichka, the young woman whom Nikolai Kirsanov—I mentioned this in the beginning—the young woman whom Nikolai Kirsanov has gotten close to after the death of Arkady's mother, and Nikolai's wife.

After the two young friends, that is to say, Arkady and Bazarov, actually meet Odintsova, Bazarov responds to Arkady's question about the first impression made by the beautiful lady—a line that has become very famous in literature. Bazarov says, "What a delectable body, perfect for the dissecting table." Just as he would dissect frogs, so it seems anyway, at least in his imagination, he would dissect the body of this very beautiful woman. Of course, a normal person—a normal man—when he sees the body of a beautiful woman thinks of other things other than dissecting the body. But when Bazarov says this, the reader understands clearly that something rather different is happening inside Bazarov, something which the nihilist is finding rather uncomfortable. Well, the two of them decide to visit Odintsova's estate. It soon becomes obvious that Odintsova's beauty and intelligence have entered deeply into Bazarov's imagination. The nihilist is nowhere nearly so consistent as his arrogantly ejaculated arguments would make the older generation believe. Furthermore, he is intelligent enough to realize the genuine strength and intelligence of a beautiful woman who is obviously worthy of a far better position than a body on the dissecting table. Bazarov, of course, thinks that this is nonsense, that this is something that he has to fight. This is something he should reject. He has no time for such nonsensical things as close or passionate relations with women. But, obviously, the more he says this, the more we understand that he is attracted to her.

Eventually he opens up to show his passion for Odintsova. As a matter of fact, at one point he lunges towards her. But she, in spite of her attraction to his powerful personality, rejects his offer of closeness. She is not ready, she says, for the complexities of a genuinely intimate relationship. And we see that Odintsova is somebody who values her comfort, values her easy life, values everything that surrounds her in that estate at least as much as she values the possibility of any kind of a close relationship with another person, much less a love relationship with as powerful a personality as Bazarov.

Arkady, on the other hand, meets her younger sister and, of course, it soon becomes clear that Arkady and the younger sister are going to become very close; that is, the softness of Arkady is somehow reflected and attracted to the softness of that younger sister of Odintsova who is, of course, a very, very different kind of a person. At this point, Turgenev takes us to another place, a still different version of the older generation. He shows us Bazarov's parents, an old-fashioned medical doctor with his wife, a warm-hearted, plump country lady who knows how to prepare and set a marvelous traditional Russian table. Turgenev describes the two of them with obvious attraction and delight. And, of course, it's very interesting to see: here Turgenev on the one hand is clearly attracted to Bazarov and clearly exalting in the mastery that Bazarov has in the argument with the older generation and, on the other hand, when he comes to the older generation, the parents of Bazarov, he is also attracted to them. The ambivalence couldn't be more clearly stated.

The conversation between the two generations here is quite different from what it was at the Kirsanov Estate. Here the older man, that is, Bazarov's father, is trying to convince his son, who will also practice as a medical doctor, about the efficacy of medicine in previous days. You remember Bazarov puts down anything that comes from a former time. Bazarov reacts with his typical skepticism but without the arrogance he displayed earlier. We understand that he respects what his father does, in spite of the nihilist words toward medicine in general. Bazarov has a front which will immediately put down everyone who is even slightly opposed to him, particularly in the older generation, but Bazarov has intelligence and sensitivity, which makes him realize that there is something in his father to be respected.

Furthermore, it is equally clear the elder Bazarov had great respect for an earlier generation of Arkady's family, of the Kirsanov family, under whom the old man, as a doctor, had served. He brushes aside Bazarov's attempt to dismiss that generation with nihilist talk. The father is not going to listen to the son saying that, and the son, almost involuntarily, respects the father. Turgenev makes it clear in this scene that the work of the older generation can't simply be dismissed, even in the context of a younger generation that wants to change everything in the world. The doctor has respect for the force and energy of the young people, but he also has a decent amount of self-respect that's clearly reflected in his son.

But the real literary fireworks are reserved for Bazarov's mother, a genuine Russian woman of the old school who might well have lived 200 years earlier. Again, we're getting away from the nihilist. Her evening meal was incomparable, with all the flourishes of the old school of cooking. If you've ever been to a Russian table, you know what I'm talking about. She was full of the old Russian folklore, with all kinds of superstitions, expressed in marvelously spontaneous and poetic ways. She knew the devil lurked in still water, so she only washed her face in running water. You know that people who come from Russia almost never wash their face in the water in the bathtub; it's always under the faucet. Why? because devils live in that water and they don't want the devils to get to them. She wouldn't eat watermelon because, when cut in half, it reminded her of the head of John the Baptist. As Turgenev interjects, such women are increasingly harder to find. God knows if that's a good or a bad thing. The reader certainly infers the positive side of that proposition.

It is indicative of her strong influence on the subconscious of her nihilist son that her presence causes him to lose a night's sleep, thinking—guess what about? of course Odintsova and her recent rejection of his advance. The traditions which she, that is, which the mother embodies go very deeply into the character and real character of the younger generation. When the young people abruptly decide to leave the parents' house, it is she who expresses what the older generation feels in losing its younger people, with the terrible sorrow, the terrible anguish of parting with the son. Clearly Turgenev has a deep association with the feelings of this old-fashioned Russian couple.

Turgenev then plunges the reader into the internal contradictions of Bazarov's character. While upholding the stubborn consistency of his own opinions, the young nihilist manages to antagonize and even threaten physically his close friend, Arkady. When they return to the Kirsanov Estate, he even manages to get involved with Fenya, the young mistress of Nikolai Kirsanov. When Pavel, the aristocratic brother who has had bitter arguments with the nihilist, sees how warmly Fenya reacts to Bazarov—and Fenya always felt very strange and distant from Pavel—Pavel decides to take matters into his own hands. He'll provoke the young man to an old-fashioned duel. Bazarov realizes the very idea of a duel is absurd to a man of his principles, but he is also determined not to let himself be insulted by those condescending aristocrats.

The result is a duel, which, by the way, Pavel Kirsanov was ready—if Bazarov had refused a duel—Pavel was carrying a heavy stick—he was ready to beat him with the stick. Bazarov said, "If he had beaten me with that stick, I would have broken it over his head and beat him like a puppy." The result is a duel in which Bazarov wounds the brother, Pavel Kirsanov, and then insists on dealing with the wound, as a young medical doctor would. Pavel ends up by wearing the bandage set by the person whose principle the older man hates and Bazarov ends up by participating in the kind of behavior which his principles most deeply oppose. In short, what you have are the contradictions which Turgenev gloried in in the writing that he brings forth to you.

The contradictions are only ended by the death, in some ways almost a suicide, of Bazarov. In the course of the medical practice which Bazarov decides to take up, he requests his father to cauterize a cut which he had received while performing an autopsy on the corpse of a peasant who had died of typhus. Now this is a very dangerous thing. You understand that typhus, particularly in those days, was absolutely incurable. The father fails; he realizes that if the son had touched that without gloves and with any kind of even a small cut on his hand, there was no way to prevent the son's infection with the fatal disease. And we're fated to watch the inevitable death of Bazarov, a death he could easily have avoided by following the normal medical procedure at the autopsy, that is, by sterilizing the instruments and by, of course, protecting his hands. And, of course, the older generation is faced with the terrible grief of the inevitable death of their own son whom they love so much and who, in spite of all of his so-called principles, there's a very deep and strong connection with him.

In the midst of Bazarov's final illness, Odintsova appears with a well-known German doctor in tow. And, of course, German doctors were very highly respected in Russia in those days, as they probably are today. There is nothing the doctor can do, but we see in this scene Odintsova's strength in contrast to the physical downfall of Bazarov, together with the collapse of his dreams and plans. It seems almost clear that Bazarov's sloppy work as a doctor, sloppy work with the autopsy, is in part a result of his disappointment—a disappointment, of course, which he would never admit but nevertheless felt deeply—his disappointment at the refusal of Odintsova when he made his advance. Clearly her refusal has put him in what he considers to be an inferior position. She is the strong one and she is the person coming to be merciful like Caesar to those who die.

As always, in Turgenev's work, the women turn out to be the strongest people in Russia. Bazarov, of course, dies a very painful death and the parents of Bazarov are faced with a terrible necessity: first of all, watching the death of their son, burying their son, and then seeing his grave at the cemetery. And, of course, the novel ends in a very nostalgic and a very sad way, of the parents coming, the two old people, coming to a cemetery, visiting the grave of their son. And, of course, at this point Turgenev turns to Pushkin, to one of Pushkin's most powerful poems. And, of course, the way that Russian writers at that time used Pushkin is something quite extraordinary.

Pushkin tended to think about, to brood over his coming death, and tried to predict the day and the time that he would die. And in one of his most famous poems, written in 1829, he says:

Brozhu li ia vdol' ulits shumhykh,	Whether I wander along noisy streets,
Brozhu li vo mnogoliudnyi khram,	Whether I go into a crowded temple,
Sizhu l' mezh iunoshei bezumnykh,	Whether I sit among crazy youngsters,
Ia predaius' moim mechtam.	I always give myself over to my dreams.
...	…
I gde mne smert' poshlet sud'bina?	And where will death meet me? [Where will my fate come?]
V boiu li, v stranstvii, v volnakh?	In battle, in wandering, in waves?
Ili sosedniaia dolina	Or will the neighboring valley
Moi npimet okhladelyi prakh?	Receive my dust which is already cooled down?
...	…
I pust' u grobovogo vkhoda	And let it happen at the entrance to my grave
Mladaia budet zhizn' igpat',	Let young life play,
I ravnodushaia priroda	And let indifferent nature shine

Krasoiu vechnoiu siiat'.	With its internal beauty.

Ravnodushnaia priorda, "indifferent nature," which blooms and fades without reference to our human feelings! He draws a conclusion that the flowers over the grave look at us with innocent eyes, which see not only the indifference of nature but also the possibility of reconciliation and eternal life. Turgenev's own reconciliation with Russia, whose regime and flaws he often castigated mercilessly, were expressed in his famous prose poem where he said it was impossible to believe that the magnificent and powerful Russian language was not given to a great people. "...*velikii, moguchii...russkii iazyk...nel'zia verit'...takoi...ne byl dan velikomu narodu!*" "It's impossible to believe that you, oh magnificent Russian language, were not given to a great people."

Lecture Twenty-Four
Anton Pavlovich Chekhov, 1860–1904

Scope:

In the 1890s, we come to the end of what is generally called the Golden Age of Russian Literature. To be sure, the art of Chekhov is hardly, or only slightly, below the level of the writers we have already considered. If you enter the American or British world of theater, you will soon find that Chekhov is its god. Although he is famous for some outstanding short stories, *The Darling*, *Grief*, *The Lady with the Pet Dog*, which convey deep human feelings in a very economical, brief way, his plays form a kind of bedrock for the modern theater as we know it. Such plays include his early *Seagull*, an initial failure on the St. Petersburg stage but a success in the hands of Stanislavsky, the dynamo of the world-famous Moscow Art Theatre, and *The Cherry Orchard*, a clear reference to a new order coming to Russia in the 20th century. These dramatic works, in a very quiet and restrained way, define a universe of human feelings that we barely know we possess yet recognize immediately when we see them in Chekhov's theatrical art. There is one more scene that he might have written, had his hand still been in working order: It would have been that of the train car, labeled "fresh oysters," bearing him in his coffin.

Outline

I. In the years following 1883, which saw the death of Turgenev, the so-called Golden Era of Russian Literature came to an end. Starting with Pushkin, near the beginning of the 19th century, it continued to about the middle of the 1880s.

   A. Near the end of that decade, some new tendencies took hold among both Russian critics and writers, and there arose a kind of divide between those who remained attached to the earlier way of writing, often called "Realism"—although that is probably an oversimplified description of a rich and varied corpus of works—and those who sought new ways of understanding experience and its representation in literature.

B. The latter often called themselves "Decadents," or "Symbolists," to indicate that they were shoving aside the old polemics around large civic and philosophical themes. Instead, they wanted to explore a world that lay hidden somewhere beneath or beyond ordinary consciousness.

C. This period of Russian literary polemics, known as the Silver Age, involved representatives of all the arts, whose influence reached across Europe.

D. In the earlier period of these polemics, from the late 1880s up to his death in 1904, Anton Chekhov occupied a literary position not far from the traditionalists, yet his prose and drama opened new ways of thinking about theater and the art of the short story.

II. Chekhov was born into a family that had known slavery intimately. His grandfather had been a serf. The writer openly stated that he had to squeeze the slavery out of his blood slowly, deliberately, drop by drop.

A. He was educated as a doctor, and he practiced medicine for a good part of his life. In his approach to his characters, it is not hard to see the detached and observant eye of the medical examiner.

B. In an early part of his life, while still in medical school, he wrote light, humorous stories under the pseudonym of Chekhonte. He did so mainly to support his needy brothers and sisters.

C. When he had achieved a certain popularity among the reading public, he started to write stories of greater substance and developed into the Chekhov known throughout the world today. In the West, especially in England and the United States, his greatest reputation is that of a playwright. It probably would not be an exaggeration to call him the icon, if not the god, of the modern international theater.

III. As early as the 1880s, Chekhov had tried his hand at writing plays, but they did not become widely known. In 1895, he set to work on *The Seagull*, which became one of the best-known plays of its time and a formative drama of 20th-century theater.

A. *The Seagull*'s first performance in a traditional St. Petersburg theater in late 1895 was a huge flop. Chekhov was mercilessly raked over the coals by the well-known critics of the day, and the sensitive writer swore he would never write for the theater again.

B. Then he was visited by Danchenko, one of the founders of the Moscow Art Theatre, a new institution at that time, with its director, whose pseudonym, now internationally famous, was Stanislavsky. The rest is well-known theatrical history.

    1. Danchenko eventually persuaded Chekhov to let the young group perform *The Seagull*, and the new presentation captured the rapturous attention of the theater public, first in Russia, then around the world.

    2. Today, the curtain of the Moscow Art Theatre is decorated with one symbol: a seagull.

C. The plot of *The Seagull* is intensely connected with the theater, as well as the nature of the literary artist. One of its central characters is Trepliov, a young, ambitious playwright.

    1. He has written a play very much in the spirit of the new young writers at that time, who wanted a radical change in literary art, in tune with the ideology of the Symbolists and Decadents. He is on fire with new ideas.

    2. His fire also extends to Nina, the young woman who will perform his monodrama. Trepliov is passionately in love with her.

D. The opening of *The Seagull*, so typical for Chekhov, is a dialogue between a poor schoolteacher and the daughter of an estate manager.

    1. The daughter is dressed in black to indicate mourning for her life.

    2. The teacher claims not to be mourning his fate, which seems bitter enough—23 rubles a month to support a large family and a desperate love for her that she rejects in the beginning.

E. Of course, Trepliov's high hopes and ambitions are far removed from the mundane desires of the underpaid teacher and the estate manager's daughter. Yet the frustrations that each will encounter— will put them in the same Chekhovian universe of people who often talk past each other and must live their lives with great pain and minimal gratification.

    1. His play will be a miserable flop, and the young actress will seek union with another writer.

    2. The poor schoolteacher will fall into a loveless marriage with the woman who continues to mourn for her life and who nurses a secret love for the doctor in the play.

F. Chekhov calls his play a comedy. Given the high level of frustration and pain experienced by the characters, it is often hard for audiences to understand why. Certainly, Stanislavsky, the famous director, did not stage the play in a comic way. We have many statements from Chekhov himself complaining that Stanislavsky misunderstood the author's comic intent.

G. I suspect that Chekhov's notion of the comic is connected with his view as a medical observer who must remain at some emotional distance in order to understand the ailments of the patient. When one looks at human affairs from this vantage point, they can seem comic and more than a bit absurd. Such a view is very close to the one taken by Doctor Dorn, who is a character in the play.

IV. We see the theater from a very different point of view when we see the older generation in *The Seagull*.

A. Madame Arkadina, an actress with a wide reputation in the Russian theater, is the mother of Trepliov. Her affections are bound up with another writer, Trigorin, Chekhov's portrait of a popular writer at that time.

    1. Arkadina has precious little sympathy for her son and is energetic and public in her denunciation of his play and denial of his talent.

    2. Trepliov is even more deeply hurt by his mother's attraction to Trigorin, a traditional writer who has achieved the kind of popularity and recognition that Trepliov can only envy.

B. Madame Arkadina expresses genuine regret for her previous actions and manages to show real feeling for her son, but this regret does not last for more than a moment.

C. Matters become even worse when it turns out that Nina, the young actress in Trepliov's earlier play, has fallen madly in love with Trigorin. She throws herself at him, and he willingly uses her, enjoying her love, then throwing her over.

D. Near the end of the play, Nina comes back to visit Trepliov. She compares herself to the seagull, which he had previously shot and stuffed. When she flees from his attempted embrace, we realize that she will never return.

E. The famous end of the play strikes with a force built up by Chekhov's restraint. We hear a shot ring out behind the scene, and the doctor quietly takes Trigorin aside and urges him to take Madame Arkadina away; her son has just shot himself.

F. Although hardly a comedy, as Chekhov described it, *The Seagull* is an extraordinarily moving play.

V. In his short stories, Chekhov shows a similar ability to present human feeling in a special way. A good example is a story whose title is usually translated as "The Darling." In Russian, it is "Dushechka," which literally means "little soul" and is often used as a term of endearment.

A. Readers have taken the title to refer to the famous Greek legend of Psyche, whose name is the Greek word for "soul." This tale has often been interpreted as a representation of the dangers in combining the force of eros with the force of the soul.

B. In Chekhov's tale, a lady named Olga is first presented as the wife of a theater manager, who is eternally nervous about getting sufficient audiences to support his enterprise. Her every thought is devoted to the theater, and kindness and sweetness cause everyone to call her *dushechka*.

C. Unfortunately, the theater manager dies, but Olga is soon courted by and then married to a lumber merchant. Now, suddenly, the theater seems to her a senseless interest. The only important things in the world are the details connected with the manufacture and sale of lumber. And everyone calls her *dushechka*.

D. Unfortunately, the lumber merchant dies, but Olga now takes up with a veterinarian, and soon she is talking about the diseases of animals and their problems. And everyone calls her *dushechka*.

E. Then, the veterinarian leaves her, and she loses all interest in life. She has no opinions whatsoever—one can understand how painful this is! People no longer call her *dushechka*.

F. Happily, the veterinarian returns, this time with his wife and child. She rejoices, puts them up in a wing of her house, and takes over the care of the child, with all the attendant worries and problems. Once more, people call her *dushechka*. And, at the end of the story, we hear the stirring of the child in his sleep, as Olga expresses her concern about him.

G. Tolstoy interpreted this story as a retelling of the biblical tale of Balaam, the priest of a people who stood in the way of Israel on its journey out of Egypt.

    1. When Balaam was called upon to pronounce a curse on the people of Israel, he tried three times, but each time, there came out of his mouth a blessing, instead of the intended curse.

    2. He sadly realized that it was impossible to curse those whom God had blessed.

H. Tolstoy said that Chekhov, in this story, was like Balaam. He had intended to make Olga a comic character, with her light-minded adoption of different professions, but the result was only a demonstration of the power of love: She became *dushechka* only when she was deeply in love with another person, and the power of that all-giving love was the highest mark of humanity.

Suggested Reading:

Anton Chekhov, "The Darling," in *The Portable Chekhov*, with an introduction by Avrahm Yarmolinsky.

Anton Chekhov, *The Seagull*, in *Plays*, translated and edited by Eugene Bristow, Norton Critical Edition.

Paul Debreczeny and Thomas Eekman, eds., *Chekhov's Art of Writing: A Collection of Critical Essays*.

J. L. Styan, *Chekhov in Performance*.

Questions to Consider:

1. In presenting Trepliov's modernistic play, Chekhov is obviously drawing a satirically exaggerated picture. Yet is there some hint of sympathy with the style, which was new at that time? Does this affect the picture Chekhov draws of Mme. Arkadina's family, especially her ambivalent reactions to her son, Trepliov, and, in turn, his relations with the young would-be actress, Nina?

2. Is Olga, the central character in "The Darling," a comically drawn character? If so, how does our laughter fit in with whatever sympathies we may have for her and, perhaps, for her various husbands?

Lecture Twenty-Four—Transcript
Anton Pavlovich Chekhov, 1860–1904

In the years following 1883, which saw the death of Turgenev, the so-called Golden Era, or *Zolotaia Epokha*, of Russian literature came to an end. Starting with Pushkin near the beginning of the 19th century, it continued to about the middle of the 1880s. Near the end of that decade some new tendencies took hold among both Russian critics and writers and there arose a kind of divide between those who remained attached to the earlier way of writing, often called Realism—although, to tell you the truth, that's probably an over-simplified description of a rich and varied corpus of works—and those who sought new ways of understanding experience and its representation in literature. The latter often called themselves Decadents, or *dekadenty*. By the way, they called themselves that, and they were proud of the name, on the assumption that the brightest colors in the seasons always came in the fall when the trees were about to die. So the Decadents, or *dekadenty*, reflected the most beautiful things in life. They also called themselves Symbolists, meaning they didn't present directly what they were talking about, that is, the direct truth, but rather they presented symbols that represented the truth that somehow lay behind those symbols. It fit very nicely, of course, the Freudian system of psychology, when the subconscious underlay the conscious. By this then, they wanted to indicate that they were shoving aside the old polemics around large—one might say huge—civic and philosophical themes. Instead, they wanted to explore a world that lay hidden somewhere beneath or beyond ordinary consciousness.

Now we don't have a lot of time in these lectures to deal with these so-called Symbolists and Decadents—the period itself was often called the Silver Age in contrast to the term Golden Age. They include not only some very interesting poets but also musicians, artists of the dance, painters, sculptors. Almost every form of the arts was represented in the so-called Silver Age. They produced things that had tremendous effect in Europe and also went along with things that were happening in places like Paris, Rome, and even New York.

The Symbolists had a tremendous impact on literary imagination. Sometimes this happened just because people were so terribly upset. Think for just a moment about the early reactions to modern music of people like Stravinsky and Prokofiev and, to a certain extent,

Shostakovich, not to mention Bartok and Hindemith. People simply didn't understand; they thought it was some kind of cacophony or something that couldn't be comprehended. Actually, if they took the trouble to listen to it carefully and understand what the artists were getting at, you can make a great deal of sense out of it. But the sense lay behind the surface in a way that earlier classical music simply did not. The same was true of poetry and literature. If you read the works of people and poets like Blok and Bryusov and other writers of that time, which you will find is a very different kind of writing, that at first glance can seem absolutely nonsensical and totally incomprehensible, but as you get into it, as you begin to understand it and what they were trying to do, you see they were getting at a very vigorous form of art, quite different from anything we've known before.

Now Anton Chekhov occupied a literary position really not very far from the traditionalist; yet his prose and drama opened the way to very new ways of thinking about the theatre and, in addition to that, the art of the short story. In just a few moments we are going to take a look particularly at his play, *The Seagull*. We'll see how he dealt with that kind of thing. Chekhov was born into a family that had known slavery intimately; his grandfather had been a serf. The writer openly stated that in his lifetime he had to squeeze the slavery out of his blood slowly, deliberately, drop by drop. If this was the case in the life of a man who was as strong and well put together as Chekhov, imagine what it was for others to overcome the terrible legacy that was left by many centuries of years of slavery.

Chekhov reflects this very clearly, and yet, at the same time, he also reflects a kind of strength that was in the people that enabled him to overcome what he was talking about, as he put it, "drop by drop of blood." He was educated as a doctor and he practiced medicine for a good part of his life. In his approach to his characters, it's not hard to see the detached and observant eyes of the medical examiner.

In an early part of his life, while still in medical school, he was saddled with the responsibility of supporting his brothers and sisters. He wrote light, humorous stories under the pseudonym of Chekhonte. He did this mainly to get money for the support of his very needy brothers and sisters, but, at the same time, began to develop a certain style. In the beginning you might call it almost a form of, well, humor you'd find on the vaudeville stage. As he went on and began to get experiences and think ever more deeply about what he was writing, the writing became deeper and deeper. He eventually grew to be the Chekhov that we know, the man of international fame.

When he had achieved a certain popularity among the reading public, he started to write stories of greater substance and developed into the Chekhov we now know, not only today but throughout the world. As I say, that's the Chekhov that we know. However, in the West, especially in England and the United States, that is, the English-speaking world, his greatest reputation is that of a playwright. I don't think it would be an exaggeration to call him an icon, if not the God, of the modern international theatre. It's almost impossible to imagine contemporary theatre that doesn't deal with Chekhov in some way or another. Of course, this is well borne out if you go to the drama schools of America today; they are just loaded with the thought and experimentation and acting and all those things that you find in the presentations by Chekhov's plays, which are very subtle and not so easy to do. It takes a very subtle understanding to catch the characters as Chekhov tried to present them.

As early as the 1880s, Chekhov had tried his hand at writing plays, but they didn't become widely known at that particular time. However, in 1895, he set to work on what's called in Russian, *Chaika,* or *The Seagull,* which was fated to become one of the best-known plays of its time and the formative drama of 20th-century theatre. I don't think it's an exaggeration to call it that; I would even be willing to predict it will be a formative drama in 21st-century theatre as well. However, its first performance in a traditional Petersburg theatre in late 1895 was a total flop. Chekhov was mercilessly raked over the coals by the well-known critics of the day and the sensitive man swore he would never write for the theatre again. Obviously the Petersburg theatre didn't understand what Chekhov was trying to do because what he was trying to do was so tremendously different from anything they had done before. They simply didn't understand it, whereas we say—and here I like to use a slang word—they didn't dig it, a good word to use in the theatre among actors. The result was a mess which the critics lambasted—I suppose it would be fair to say—with fire and sword.

Then something very important happened in the history of the theatre as we know: Chekhov was visited by a man named Nemirovich-

Danchenko, one of the founders of the new theatre in Moscow, which took on the name of a Moscow Art Theatre, in Russian, *MKhAT*, a new institution at that time. Danchenko was more or less responsible for the literary side, and the director, whose pseudonym, now internationally famous, was sort of Godlike among actors, was Stanislavsky. The rest is well-known theatrical history. That theatre became one of the central theatres of European culture.

Danchenko eventually persuaded Chekhov to let the young group perform *The Seagull*. It took him a year to persuade Chekhov to let him have it and the new presentation captured the rapturous attention of the theatre, theatre public, that is, first in Russia, then throughout the world. Today, the curtain of the Moscow Art Theatre is decorated with one symbol that everybody recognizes, a seagull. It's worth taking some time, I think, to talk a little bit about the Moscow Art Theatre, which was centrally connected with Chekhov in those days. For anybody who cares something about theatre, and I'm certainly one of those people, it would be absolutely impossible to understand what's going on in contemporary theatre without understanding what Stanislavsky did. What he did was to construct a kind of Realism; that is, it was his idea that the actor on stage should not just represent the idea or the character or the emotion a player was trying to get across—the actor had to be in a genuinely verisimilitudinous way that character, that feeling. The actor himself or herself must go through that actual emotion; the actor must look back into his or her life to find some incident, some time, some place, or a similar emotion that was experienced or expressed. The actor must go back by a series of exercises, an emotional—you might almost say psychological trick so the actor genuinely gets himself or herself into that particular emotion.

Then, and only then, is genuine emotion taking place. And Stanislavsky was ready to work on a play that took just as long as it took to achieve that particular kind of emotion or—one is tempted to call it—Realism. It's a kind of emotional power or emotional connection, is perhaps the best way to put it. As a matter of fact, Stanislavsky wrote several famous books, one, *My Life in Art*, the other, *An Actor Prepares*, where he talks about these matters in great detail, with great subtlety and great understanding. It's clear that Stanislavsky had in mind a very creative and, of course, in his day, a very revolutionary idea about theatre. The great actors and actresses of the 19th century—in particular, I'm thinking of [Eleonora] Duse, the famous French [sic Italian] actress—acted by a system called *geste plastique*, that is to say, "plastic gestures." There were certain gestures which were appropriate to certain emotions. When you expressed that emotion as an actor or an actress, you had to do that gesture just as gracefully, beautifully, and well thought out as you could possibly could. Every part was intellectually thought out and plotted so the actor would go through certain emotions that everyone would recognize and connect it with a convention.

Stanislavsky, of course, wanted to break these conventions. He wanted to break that idea of just taking set gestures and rather getting to the actual emotion, which might require any gesture, any action, on the part of the actor or actress. The results were very impressive. It soon became clear, not only in Russia but in England and the United States, that what he was doing was producing extraordinary effects and expressions in the theatre. If you think of the most important creative forces about the theatre in this country, one is tempted to think back to a group of actors eventually called the Actors Studio in New York back in the 1940s. Later on, it came to be run by a young Greek man who had come from Turkey, a man named Elia Kazan, who, as a matter of fact, studied with Stanislavsky. He went to Moscow after Stanislavsky came to New York. In connection with this theatre and, of course, with the director's action of Kazan, you'll think of such people as Marlon Brando, Marilyn Monroe, the playwright Arthur Miller, and Eli Wallach. As a matter of fact, if you think of Russian, even Mikhoels, the famous actor in the Jewish theatre, he and all of these people were certain products of the ideas of Stanislavsky in the theatre.

In short, some of our very best theatre in this country, that is, in the USA, is a result of what was done in the theatre that Chekhov's plays made so famous. Now *The Seagull* is a play that plays a very important role in all of what I've just talked about. There's not a single name I just mentioned in the long list of names in the theatre that hasn't, in some way or another, dealt very intimately with this play. It is literally a kind of formation of contemporary theatre; I suspect it's going to be that for a long time to come. The plot of the play is intensely connected with the theatre, as well as the nature of the literary artist. One of its central characters is a young man named Konstantin Trepliov. By the way, the name implies a kind of fluttering or shaking. He is a young, ambitious playwright who is about to have the pleasure of experiencing the first performance of his work, a play written very much in the spirit of the new young writers of that time who wanted a radical change in literary art in tune with the ideology of the Symbolists and Decadents I've just been talking about a few moments ago. Trepliov is on fire with his new ideas; furthermore, he is the son of a very famous actress, [Irina] Arkadina, who has achieved great fame in the classical theatre of Russia, which is totally opposed to everything her son is doing. He is going to prove himself and to his mother in this sort of chamber theatre that takes place on her estate.

The play is going to crack the mold of modern theatre; it's going to be a tremendous revolution in the life of the theatre. His fire extends by the way, not only to the arts but also to the young actress named Nina Zarechnaia—her name means beyond or across the river—the young woman who will be performing his monodrama. Trepliov is passionately in love with her. As a matter of fact, she is probably less in love with him than she is with theatre, but, nevertheless, at the beginning of the play she seems to go along with his love. She can't quite understand all the lines or the effects he has put in the theatre; they seem completely not understandable, given the traditional nature of the theatre. But he says, "Look, it's all right. Go ahead, everything will be all right." So she agrees to go through with it.

The people attending the play, many of them relatives of Trepliov, including his mother, sit down and they can't quite understand— that's an understatement—they can't understand at all what is coming off. He raises the curtain and begins with a speech that nobody can understand. Of course, Nina is pronouncing the speech. As a matter of fact, there is some strange sort of effect with red sulfur burning and they smell the sulfur. The speech is so strange and the effects are so out of this world that nobody can understand what he is talking about and they begin to make fun of him. They say, "Well, you talk about the devil. Obviously, the devil is in the form of the sulfur we smell. You talk about ages and ages ago, when people spoke a different language. How can we know anything about that?" His self-love, he is touched to the quick; he can't stand it anymore. Furiously he yells—he rushes to the stage and yells—"Strike the curtain, strike the curtain. I see to it you people are new people who are not allowed to be in the theatre. The only people allowed to be in the theatre are those who slavishly follow the desires of old hacks like my mother." He rushes off in a fury.

Of course, the mother is somewhat abashed that she has caused this kind of reaction in her son but at the same time she feels totally justified in her reactions. She says, "Nobody could understand what he was trying to do there." Doctor Dorn, a medical man who is visiting the mother's estate has a somewhat different reaction, with some sympathy for both Trepliov and his mother. After he sees the performance and Trepliov's storming outburst, he says, "There is something in this play. Of course, it's crude and not yet worked out, not yet well worked out, but there is something in this play that has power." You understand that what I have described is a play that exists within Chekhov's play, *The Seagull*. The opening of *The Seagull*, right before we get into the play within a play, that is, a presentation of Trepliov's work that I have just described, contains very typically Chekhovian language. It's a dialogue between a poor schoolteacher and the daughter of an estate manager. She is dressed in black to indicate mourning for her life and he claims not to be mourning his fate, which seems bitter enough; 23 rubles a month to support a large family, a desperate love for her that she nevertheless rejects. The high-flown artistic aspirations of Trepliov and the mundane concerns of these two seem widely disconnected; yet the art of Chekhov brings them together in a very special way.

Of course, Trepliov's hopes and ambitions are far removed from the mundane desires of the underpaid teacher and the estate manager's daughter. Yet the frustrations which they'll meet—Trepliov's play will be a miserable flop; Nina, the young actress, will seek union with another writer; the poor schoolteacher will fall into a loveless marriage with a woman who continues to mourn for her life, and there is a secret love for Doctor Dorn—put them all in the same Chekhovian universe of people who often walk past each other and must live their lives with great pain and minimum gratification.

There is something about an absence of communication in Chekhov's plays that reminds us very much of certain aspects of everyday life. It's sometimes very hard for us to get across our feelings or ideas, our experiences, to other people because, after all, other people's feelings, ideas, and experiences are very different from ours. In the effort to make ourselves mutually understood, often we have great obstacles which are movingly and beautifully presented by Chekhov in his play.

Chekhov calls his play a comedy. Given the high level of frustration and pain I have just described and experienced by the characters, it's often hard for the readers to understand why. Certainly Stanislavsky, the famous director, did not stage the play in a comic way. We have many statements from Chekhov himself, complaining that Stanislavsky completely misunderstood the author's intent. I suspect that Chekhov's notion of the comic is connected with his view as a medical observer who has to remain at some emotional distance in order to understand the ailments of his patients. When one looks at human beings from this vantage point, they can seem comic and more than a little bit absurd, as if we're viewing from Olympus and saying in Shakespeare's words, "Oh what fools these mortals be." This is very close to the view of Doctor Dorn, the character who, nevertheless, saw something very powerful in Trepliov's play.

We see the theatre from a very different point of view when we see the older generation of *The Seagull*. Madame Arkadina, an actress with a wide reputation as the mother of Trepliov, her affections are bound up with another writer, Trigorin, who expresses a wonderful feeling about writing. He says, "I write and I write and I write. Wherever I go, I see material for writing that I can't keep myself from writing about; and what's the upshot?—well, Trigorin, a dear writer, a fine writer, but, huh, not Turgenev." This is doubly ironic when you stop to think, and today, when people often say, "Turgenev, a dear writer, a fine writer, but not Tolstoy or Dostoevsky." It's odd how these things turn in the history of literature.

Arkadina's reactions remain constant throughout this part of the play. She sees no sense in what her son has been doing. She refuses to give him any kind of encouragement in spite of the fact there are intervals in the play where she does show him some love. But they don't last long. Her emotions are all wrapped up in Trigorin. She is not going to give her son anything that he needs or requires from her. To make matters even worse, Nina, the young actress, has thrown herself at the feet of Trigorin. She tells him to use her in any way he likes and, boy, does he ever take advantage of this. He uses her and then spits her out, like a used-up orange. When Trepliov hears about this, he is quite upset, and he begins to think about his own writing and realizes he made a mistake in the way he has thought about it. It's not so much a matter of form, it's not whether you're a revolutionary in the theatre or going through the old traditions, whether you're a symbolist or not, the important thing is to express emotion as it is genuinely and truly felt, and it's clear this is close to the way that Chekhov feels.

While Trepliov has realized this, Nina comes back, and this time she visits him. As she visits him, she is in a state very close to that of insanity after what she has gone through. She compares herself, she says, "to that magnificent seagull which you once shot and put at my feet. Now I am that seagull." The seagull has obviously become the symbol of destroyed lives, the way a hunter destroys the life of an animal the hunter seeks to shoot; Nina clearly feels her life parallel to the situation of the beautiful bird that was slain. She no longer has any warm feelings for Trepliov. She runs out, and both he and we realize she'll never come back. At that point, the scene shifts to the room next door, where people are playing cards. As they are playing, they suddenly hear a pop or an explosion. Doctor Dorn goes into the next room to examine it and comes back and says, "Oh, don't worry, it's all right. It's nothing, nothing to the explosion, one of my bottles of medicine." But he says to the other characters, "Look, get Arkadina away so she can't hear. Trepliov has just committed suicide. He shot himself." Just as Trepliov killed that seagull for the good of Nina, he kills himself because he feels he can no longer make a contribution to art.

How one can interpret this as a comedy, I must admit that I'm not quite sure myself, but it's a very moving play and a play that goes into so many different aspects of human psychology and experience it's very difficult for actors to do well. But once done well, it's an extraordinarily moving play. Now Chekhov, although he's very popular in this part of the world as a playwright, was not only a playwright, he was also the writer of a series of prose stories, some of which are very moving. Furthermore, his stories don't seem to exhibit what we normally tend to think of as characteristic of Russian stories: they are short, they are brief, they make their point in a very short amount of time. We're not talking about long novels that go on for hundreds of pages. Some stories are only three or four pages, but what Chekhov manages to get across is something very powerful.

A good example of Chekhov's art in this way, although a slightly longer story, is the story whose title is usually translated as "The Darling." In Russian the title is "*Dushechka*," which literally means, "Little Soul." This is a good example of Russian diminutives. The word for soul is *dusha*, this is, "*Dushechka*." "Dear Little Soul" is often used as a term of endearment, like darling or sweetheart in English. Readers have taken it to refer to the famous Greek legend around Psyche, whose name is the Greek word for soul. This tale has often been interpreted, that is, Chekhov's tale has often been interpreted as a representation of the dangers in combining the force of eros with the force of the soul.

In Chekhov's tale, a lady named Olga is first presented as the wife of a theatre manager who is eternally nervous about getting sufficient audiences to support his enterprise. He is always yelling, "*Strashnye ubytki, strashnye ubytki*," "horrible losses, horrible financial losses." Her every thought is to go to the theatre, and her kindness and sweetness causes everyone to call her *dushechka*. The theatre manager is terribly upset; people won't come to his play. He did Faust inside out, whatever that means, by the way. But no matter what he does, people won't come. He is experiencing *strashnye ubytki*, terrible losses.

Alas, he dies. Of course, when he dies, Olga is no longer attached to the theatre and nobody calls her *dushechka* anymore. But soon enough she is courted by a lumber merchant, who then marries her. And now she says, "So what's so good about that theatre anyway? It's just a bunch of senseless vaudeville; the only important things in the world are the details connected with the manufacture and sale of lumber." She knows how to say plywood and oak wood and all the technical things that go together with lumber and she can't imagine a time when she was connected with that superficial thing called theatre, and everyone calls her *dushechka*. They come to replace the *bubliki*—I like to say they are a Russian form of bagels, but my Russian friends say they are not—and *bublichki*, and all the wonderful things that are connected with a boiling samovar and a good hot cup of tea.

Well, alas, the lumber merchant also dies. And again, nobody calls her *dushechka*. There is a wonderful little intermezzo in the story where she sits, and because she is not connected with anybody she has no opinions, no opinions whatsoever. And what a terrible thing it is not to have any opinions at all about anything in this world, and the reader is almost lulled, perhaps to sleep, by this. But now, lo and behold, a veterinarian comes to her. Soon she takes up with the veterinarian and soon she is talking about diseases of animals and their problems and what she'd have to do to keep the cattle and pets alive and how very good veterinarians are for the animal world and the human world; and again everybody calls her *dushechka.* And the veterinarian is no fool; he knows that the two previous men that have been connected to this woman have died. There is something about her that seems to bring on death; so he leaves, and she loses all interest in life, no opinion whatsoever, and one can again understand how painful it is, and no one calls her *dushechka.* But happily, the veterinarian returns, this time with his wife and child. He had taken up with her before but obviously not married her. She rejoices, puts them up in a wing of her house and takes over the care of the child, with all its attendant worries and problems. And once more people call her *dushechka.*

At the end of the story, the child goes off to school. She follows. He says, "Look, Auntie, don't follow me. I want to go on my own." He comes home and the two of them worry over his homework. Oh, my God, what is an island? An island is a body of land, completely surrounded by water. How difficult it is to learn. How hard they are on the young people. "All these poor young people," she says, "they have such hard things to learn." She reverberates to every feeling of the young child. As a matter of fact, at the end of the story, he's a real kid. We hear the stirrings, "Get out of my way." He's stirring in his sleep; he's dreaming. "Get out of my way. I'm going to give it to you. I'm going to get into a fight. Watch out, watch out." She sits there just praying and exalting in the fact she is once more connected with a human being.

By the way, Tolstoy did not like Chekhov's plays very much. And he would tell him and he would talk to Chekhov, whose name in patronymic is Anton Pavlovich. He said, "Anton Pavlovich, I love you very much. You're a wonderful man and I love your stories. But your plays, they are impossibly bad. They are worse than Shakespeare's." Tolstoy couldn't stand Shakespeare. Maybe it was out of professional jealousy but then again maybe he felt there was too much violence. In any case, the same Tolstoy interpreted the story I've just told you about as a retelling of a Biblical tale of Balaam, the priest of a people who stood in the way of the people of

Israel on their journey out of Egypt toward the Promised Land. These people, that is, who were meeting the people of Israel, were getting rather nervous about meeting them because rumors had been going around that they had been conquering people here, they had been conquering people there. The people of Israel seemed to have some extraordinary force on their side. Of course, the Israelites claimed it was God. So in order to neutralize this force, Balaam, the prophet of the people, was ordered to go out and pronounce a curse on the people of Israel. He went out on his donkey. As a matter of fact, the donkey had sense enough to try and stop him. But he beat the donkey, so the donkey, in order to avoid the beating, went ahead. Balaam came out to proclaim a curse. He opened his mouth and, instead of a curse, out came a blessing. "What the devil is going on? I meant to curse and a blessing came out of my mouth." He went back; he reinforced himself. Again he went out on the donkey, again the donkey didn't want to go out, and again he beat the donkey. And again he tried to pronounce a curse and out came a blessing. He did it a third time, and again he tried to curse and out came a blessing.

Finally he understood, and this is Biblical language: it was impossible to curse those whom the Lord God had blessed. Tolstoy said that Chekhov, in the story, was like Balaam. He had intended to make Olga *dushechka*, a comic character, with her like-minded adoption of different professions, but the result was only a demonstration of the power of love. She became *dushechka*, that is, a living soul, only when she was deeply in love with another person. And the power of that all-giving love was the highest mark of humanity. In short, as Tolstoy points out, of course as the Bible implies, true love is blind. It gives itself to those whose feelings arouse our feelings and to whose love we respond with our love.

Timeline

863 ....Cyril and Methodius devise an alphabet for a common Slavic language.

988 ....Prince Vladimir brings Byzantine Christianity to Kiev.

1185 ....Kievan epic poem "The Lay of the Host of Prince Igor" is composed.

1237–1240 ....Tatar heirs of Genghis Khan conquer Kiev; the "Tatar yoke" begins and lasts more than 200 years.

1547 ....Ivan IV ("the Terrible") is crowned as the first "tsar" in Moscow.

1703 ....Peter I orders construction of St. Petersburg, to be the capital of his empire.

1799 ....Birth of Aleksandr Pushkin, Russia's greatest poet.

1811 ....Aleksandr I establishes the Lycée, which educates Pushkin and a brilliant group of contemporaries.

1812 ....The Napoleonic armies invade Russia.

1815 ....The Russian army, with many French- speaking officers, occupies Paris.

1825 ....Decembrist Uprising (includes friends of Pushkin) in St. Petersburg.

1837 ....Pushkin's duel with D'Anthès results in the poet's death.

1842	Gogol's *Dead Souls* leads to wide fame for the author.
1845	Dostoevsky's first novel, *Poor Folk*, creates instant fame for the young author.
1849	Arrest and sentencing of Dostoevsky, ostensibly to execution, actually to shackled Siberian imprisonment.
1852	Death of Gogol', as he lay with leeches hanging from his nose.
1854–1855	Crimean War, disastrous for Russia, with one exception: It provided material for Tolstoy's first published work, *Tales of Sevastopol'*.
1856	Death of Tsar Nikolai I; ascension to the throne of Aleksandr II, most liberal of all Russian tsars.
1859	Dostoevsky, released from Siberian exile, returns to European Russia.
1860s	Most liberal and creative time in tsarist Russian culture and politics.
1861	Liberation of Russian serfs, a huge majority of Russia's Slavic population.
1862	Beginning of great polemical novels, including Turgenev's *Fathers and Sons*, and resulting polemics between liberals and conservatives.
1866	Dostoevsky's *Crime and Punishment*.
1865–1869	Tolstoy's *War and Peace*.
1876–1877	Tolstoy's *Anna Karenina*; polemics arise over issues of women's rights

and their rightful position in Russian society.

1881 ....Dostoevsky's final novel, *The Brothers Karamazov*, followed shortly by the author's death.

1881 ....Tsar Aleksandr killed by a revolutionary terrorist's bomb; succeeded by his son, Aleksandr III, a far more conservative ruler.

1880s...Growing political unrest in Russia, with resulting violence and corresponding acts of governmental repression.

1882–1885 ....Series of repressive, often bloody acts of violence; pogroms against religious minorities, particularly against Jews; dissension within the government about how to deal with them.

1891 ....Unexpected death of Aleksandr III; ascension to the throne of his son, Nikolai II, a young man not well prepared to rule the country.

1892 ....End of the Golden Age of Russian Literature; proclamations of new trends in Russian literature, away from realism, and away from Romanticism in Russian music.

1892 ....Maxim Gorky begins to attract attention as the voice of the urban lower classes, previously unrepresented in Russian literature.

1896 ....Chekhov's play *The Seagull*, after a disastrous performance in St. Petersburg, becomes a great success in Moscow, thanks to Stanislavsky's direction at the Moscow Art

Theatre; Chekhov and Stanislavsky become a worldwide theatrical force.

1901 ....Nascent political parties begin to take on form in literature: Marxist group expresses radical ideas; group of poets and writers concentrates on aesthetic issues; conservative group feels frightened by strong changes taking place in Russian life and culture.

1901 ....Tolstoy, around whom a group of pacifist and reforming Christians had formed, is excommunicated from the Russian Orthodox Church.

1903 ....Large and violent anti-Jewish pogrom, in the southern city of Kishinev, observed and condemned around the world; Tolstoy claims it is a result of government policy, not an expression of popular Russian feeling.

1904 ....Death of Chekhov abroad; his body brought back to Russia in a freight car marked "fresh oysters"; described by Gorky.

1904–1905 ....Russo-Japanese War is disaster for Russia, large part of Russia's navy sunk; calls for reform result in tsarist manifesto granting some elected representation in the government.

1905 ....First Marxist political uprising to establish a socialist state; put down by tsarist police; arrest and exile of Lenin, Trotsky, and Stalin.

1906 ....Gorky's disastrous visit to the United States—thrown out of a New York hotel for traveling with his mistress.

1906–1913 ....Large emigré groups of anti-tsarist Russian politicians and revolutionaries active in Western Europe and the United States.

1910 ....Tolstoy runs away from famous country home at Iasnaia Poliana and dies in a railway stationmaster's room; church refuses Christian prayers at funeral; buried in famous grave at home estate.

1914 ....Beginning of World War I; agrarian Russia, with little help from England and France, fights industrialized powers of Germany and Austria/Hungary; some initial successes against Austrian army, soon overborne by huge losses of soldiers in battles against Germans.

February/March 1917..................Popular uprisings against tsar result in abdication of Nikolai II; a range of Russian political parties clumsily tries to govern through parliament (Duma).

October/November 1917............Bolshevik party, led by Lenin and Trotsky, takes power through successful coup d'état, ostensibly in the name of the working class; legislative body called *Soviet* ("council") forms.

1918 ....New Bolshevik government signs peace treaty with Kaiser's Germany, ceding many Western territories to foe.

1918–1922 ....Bloody civil war within the territory of the previous Russian Empire, eventuating a new state called the Union of Soviet Socialist Republics; government determined to bring on socialism quickly and thoroughly; period called "War Communism."

1920–1922 ....Huge number of intellectuals and artists find it very difficult to work under the Soviets; they undergo repression; many emigrate to Western Europe and the United States; Gorky, who had been close to Lenin, among them.

1923–1928 ....A period of ideological retrenchment, when government pulls back some of its forces under a program called the New Economic Policy (NEP); political police force ("Cheka") remains in power.

1924 ....Death of Lenin; beginning of a bloody struggle for power within the USSR.

1920s..Many literary and cultural movements struggle for position under the Soviet regime; Maiakovsky lays claim to the title of Revolution's Tribune; Sholokhov begins to write a major novel about the fate of the Cossacks; Zoshchenko observes it all with a sharp eye for parody and humor.

1928–1929 ....Consolidation of Stalin's power; beginning of collectivization of Soviet agriculture; beginning of five-year plans for the whole Soviet society.

1928–1933 ....Gorky returns to USSR; works with Soviet authorities to establish central line in literature and culture: socialist realism.

1930 ....Suicide of Maiakovsky sends shock wave among Soviet writers.

1933–1934 ....Millions of deaths from starvation resulting from clumsy and crude policies connected with collectivization of agriculture.

1936 ....Death of Gorky; beginning of mass Stalinist purges—widespread arrests and millions of deaths.

1933–1940 ....Pasternak, like many other poets and writers, concentrates on artistic translations and works, which keeps him out of political trouble.

1939 ....Stalin and Hitler sign the Pact of Mutual Assistance; World War II begins with occupation of western Poland by Nazi Germany and eastern Poland by the Soviet Union; soon, Soviets also occupy Baltic countries.

1941 ....Nazi invasion of the USSR and Soviet alliance with England and free France; soon followed by alliance with the United States.

1945 ....Allied victory over Nazi Germany; hopes for a peaceful, cooperative postwar world defeated by the growing reality of the Cold War between the East and West.

1946 ....Soviet government publicly attacks Zoshchenko, together with other highly respected cultural figures;

postwar policy of cultural repression begins in earnest.

1953 .... Death of Stalin; hopes for some easement in cultural policy.

1956 .... Khrushchev's famous speech denounces some of Stalin's crimes; release of millions of political prisoners from forced labor camps.

1958–1964 .... "The Thaw," new policy under Khrushchev, allows slightly more freedom for literature.

1958 .... Publication abroad of Pasternak's *Doctor Zhivago*; awarded Nobel Prize; author forced to turn it down.

1962 .... Khrushchev authorizes publication of Solzhenitsyn's novel describing a day in one of the Soviet forced labor camps, whose existence had previously been officially denied.

1964 .... Khrushchev peacefully removed from power and allowed to live; among intellectuals, continuing hopes for gradually increasing freedom.

1968 .... Soviet invasion of Czechoslovakia; end of intellectuals' hopes for increasing feeedom.

1970s and early 1980s .... Era under the leadership of Brezhnev, who held back threats of governmental terror but kept a tight public rein on freedom; era of covert self-publishing (*samizdat*) on typewriters with many carbon copies.

1974 .... Solzhenitsyn is expelled from the Soviet Union; his residence becomes Vermont in the United States.

1985 ....Gorbachev comes to power with slogans of restructuring and open public expression of opinion.

1991 ....End of the Soviet Union after attempted *putsch*; proclamation of a new Russian Federal Republic, free from one-party control.

1994 ....Solzhenitsyn returns to the new Russian Republic.

2000 ....Election of Putin as president of the Russian Republic; new policy of consolidating power; wide and free expression of public opinion remains.

Glossary

Bolshevik: Literally, "member of the majority," the faction of the Russian Marxist Revolutionary Party under Lenin's leadership that sought and achieved a violent uprising to overthrow the Russian monarchy and establish a socialist state.

Cap of Monomakh: Headpiece presumably worn by a famous prince of Kiev, Vladimir Monomakh, during his coronation. Later, the tsars used the cap at their own coronation ceremonies.

Church Slavic: Written form of the language used by all Slavic peoples during the 9th century. The language received an alphabet devised by the brothers Cyril and Methodius, Christian monks and professors at the University of Constantinople. Church Slavic is now used in prayer services in the Slavic branches of the Eastern Orthodox Christian Church.

Cossack: Originally runaway serfs in the 15th and 16th centuries, the Cossacks formed their own independent territory. In the 17th century, they signed a treaty of alliance with the Muscovite tsar and became the crack cavalry troops of the Russian army.

Cyrillic alphabet: Alphabet constructed some decades after the death of St. Cyril (869), using some Greek and some Roman letters, plus a few derived from other sources. It accurately reflects, with few exceptions, the phonetics of the Russian language even today.

Decembrist Uprising (1825): A group of aristocrats, many of whom were officers in the Russian army when it occupied Paris right after Napoleon's fall, naively hoped to bring a parliamentary republic to Russia after a political coup in St. Petersburg with almost no support from the population at large.

Dvoeverie: Literally "two faiths intermixed." In the late 10th century, when Vladimir, prince of Kiev, returned with the Eastern Orthodox Christian faith, he decreed that the population should become Christian. Under pressure, people agreed, although large numbers of peasants retained elements of the old faith for many centuries. These elements eventually found their ways into Christianity.

Eastern Slavs: People who, in the 10th century, spoke a dialect of the common Slavic language. As the centuries went by, their dialects developed into the Eastern Slavic languages: Russian, White Russian, and Ukrainian.

Forest Brotherhood and the White Army: The Forest Brotherhood is typical of the groups that fought in Siberia to establish Soviet control over the region. The White Army was organized by a wide coalition of parties that did not want to live under the Soviet regime. The Whites included a wide range of political opinions, from traditional monarchists to democratic parties that wanted to establish a Russian parliamentary democracy.

Futurists, imagists, acmeists: Groups of poets who used new kinds of artistic effects deemed revolutionary. Such artistic developments continued through much of the 1920s, only to be quashed in the Stalinist crackdown of the 1930s.

GULAG: Russian abbreviation for the State Administration of (Forced Labor) Camps (*Gosudarstvennoe Upravlenie Lagerei*). Solzhenitsyn's novel saw such camps as a huge archipelago spread throughout the USSR.

Infernal'nitsa: Literally, "infernal woman." Dostoevsky used the term to describe his notion of the woman who controlled men by her violent and attractive passions.

Inspector general: The Russian Empire covered an enormous territory, with many different peoples and ethnic groups. Communication and transportation were slow, often requiring weeks. When news of local malfeasance reached St. Petersburg, the authorities would often send out such a seasoned inspector to analyze the local situation and root out the trouble.

Iurodivyi: Often rendered as "a fool in Christ"; such a person, often a poor wanderer, would mouth expressions that would seem senseless, although they supposedly contained great depth and holiness. Such people enjoyed great respect among East Slavic peasants, and the holy fools could often safely say things that others would not dare to express.

Kenotic saint: In Greek, *kenosis* literally means "emptying out"; in one of Paul's epistles, Jesus empties himself out of godliness and takes on the form of a suffering human being. The kenotic saints tried to emulate Jesus and would never resist evil with violence.

KGB: Literally, "Committee for State Security" (*Komitet Gosudarstvennoi Bezopasnosti*). Successor to previous political police groups, the KGB acquired the reputation, well deserved, for repressive, rigorous, sometimes murderous action against all opponents to the regime, as well as those who *might* become opponents of the regime.

Moscow Art Theatre: Founded by Stanislavsky and Nemirovich-Danchenko to reform what they regarded as worn-out conventions of the theater. The theater acquired a worldwide reputation and enormous prestige, closely connected with the work of Chekhov and Gorky.

Novella (Russian: *povest'*): A work of literary prose, longer than a short story but shorter than a novel. The Russian writers of the 19th century developed the form to a high artistic level.

Optina Pustyn': Famous monastery in 19th-century Russia, to which many troubled people went in search of help from its famous church elders, who were perceptive psychologists. A certain Father Amvrosii evidently brought great help and care to the troubled Dostoevsky. Many of the priest's words turn up on the lips of Father Zosima in Dostoevsky's last novel.

Polovetsians: National group who occupied a territory to the south and east of the 13th-century East Slavs. Despite the fact that the Polovetsians were allies, an East Slavic armed force, under the leadership of Prince Igor, tried to conquer them, with disastrous military results (but good literature for the East Slavs).

Rus': Territory extending in all directions from the city of Kiev in the 10th through the 12th centuries. Rus' was established by the East Slavs and produced the cultural basis for the Russian form of Eastern Orthodox Christianity.

Serf: East Slavic agricultural peasants were forced into slavery, or serfdom, from the end of the 15th through the middle of the 19th centuries. A serf was subject to the authority of aristocratic landowners, backed by the power of the tsar.

Soul: Russian popular and legal term used to refer to a serf (*dusha*); an aristocrat's economic status was often measured by how many souls he or she possessed.

Tatars: Turkic-speaking people who spread westward from the edges of Mongolia through the territories of the Slavs in the 14th and 15th centuries. They possessed a military and economic technology very advanced for that time. Their military power was nearly invincible, and they ruled over Slavic territories for more than 200 years.

Troika: Vehicle attached to three horses, whose positions were arranged in a way to obtain the maximum possible speed. For many centuries, it was the fastest available vehicle, especially useful in the vast expanses of the Russian Empire. The word—literally, "the three of them"—is often used to indicate a triumvirate, a powerful combination of three elements, or a playing card with the number 3.

Biographical Notes

Biographies are provided for those whose lives are not already described in the lectures. These people, mainly historical political figures, with the addition of the French writer Stendhal, played very important roles in the development of Russian literature.

Aleksandr II (1818–1881). Most liberal and open of all the tsars. Under his regime, the serfs were liberated, and writers and intellectuals found it much easier to express their views in the 1860s and 1870s. Radicals arranged to kill him with a bomb in 1881 because they believed his reforms did not go far enough.

Aleksandr III (1845–1894). A much more repressive and conservative ruler than Aleksandr II, his reputation among the liberals and reformers was bad because he tried to preserve order by highly repressive means. Yet he was a great patron of the arts and of intellectual life.

Khrushchev, Nikita Sergeevich (1894–1971). Politician who maneuvered successfully under Stalin and managed to win out in the succeeding power struggle after the dictator's death. He was responsible for a mild anti-Stalinist liberalization called "The Thaw," and he was also responsible for the bloody repression of uprisings in communist East Germany and Hungary. Mercurial and dramatic in temperament, he captured the imagination of the world and inspired the caricatures of its most prominent cartoonists.

Lenin (pseudonym for Vladimir Il'ich Ul'anov, 1870–1924). Brother of an executed revolutionary and founder of the Bolshevik faction of the Communist Party. He was a politician of inexorable will and aggressiveness, who presided over the Bolshevik Revolution and the first year of the young Soviet regime. A would-be assassin's bullet did not kill him but undoubtedly shortened his life.

Nikolai II (1868–1918). Last of the Romanov dynasty, he tried to continue the conservative policies of his father, Aleksandr III, but he lacked the stern will and strength of his predecessors. He foolishly allowed himself to be drawn into World War I, and he agonized over the breakdown of the traditional Russian social order. The democratic parties deposed him, but the later Bolshevik government exiled him to the Urals and then butchered him, together with his whole family and retinue.

Stalin (pseudonym for Iosif Vissarionovich Dzhugashvili, 1879–1953). Born in the Caucasus and educated in an Eastern Orthodox Christian seminary, he rose to power as an efficient and wily executor of Lenin's directives and used his position to gain control of the Soviet bureaucracy and the whole government and society. Absolutely ruthless in crushing and killing all possible opponents (and many non-opponents), he successfully administered a defeat to Hitler by means of the most bloody possible tactics. Over time, his regime also murdered close to 20 million Soviet citizens. He inspired both extraordinarily wide reverence and immeasurably deep hatred among his subjects.

Stendhal (pseudonym for Mari Henri Beyle, 1783–1842). French writer who served in Napoleon's army, which invaded Russia. Throughout his life, Stendhal retained a love for Napoleon, which plunged him into political hot water during the French restoration. Despite his attraction to the invader of their country, Russian writers, especially Tolstoy, found Stendhal's work and approach to life both compatible and inspiring. He, in turn, greatly admired the Russian aristocracy.

Sviatoslavich, Igor (1151–1202). Protagonist of the East Slavic medieval epic poem *The Tale of Prince Igor*. He led an army against the Polovician (sometimes called "Kuman") khan, Konchak, with whom he had previously arranged an alliance. He was defeated and his army was destroyed. He managed to escape, and his son married the daughter of the khan.

Sviatoslavich, Vladimir (son of Sviatoslav, d. 1015). Prince of Kiev who married the sister of the Byzantine emperor and brought Christianity to Kiev and the Eastern Slavs; considered a saint by the Russian Orthodox Church.

Trotsky (pseudonym for Lev Davidovich Bronstein, 1879–1940). Powerful orator and writer who lent his considerable talents to the Bolshevik uprising and presided over the formation of the victorious Red Army. He was unable to resist the rise of Stalin and went into exile, ending up in a fortress in Mexico. His later writing castigated Stalin and his regime. He became the victim of an assassin's alpine axe, which was guided by Stalin's political police.

Bibliography

Babel, Isaak. *The Collected Stories.* Edited and translated by Walter Morison. Introduction by Lionel Trilling. New York: World Publishing Co., 1961. Stories by a popular Soviet writer who saw the Cossacks from the Jewish point of view, with a mixture of fear and admiration—a contrast to Sholokhov's account of Cossack reality.

Bayley, John. *Pushkin: A Comparative Commentary.* Cambridge: Cambridge University Press, 1971. More general commentary by one of the most respected contemporary observers of Russian Literature.

————. *Tolstoy and the Novel.* London: Chatto and Windus, 1966. An interpretation by a highly respected and original British scholar.

Bearne, C. G. *Sholokhov.* Edinburgh: Oliver and Boyed, 1969. An account of Sholokhov and some of the literary and political turbulence he lived through and, to a certain extent, caused.

Belknap, Robert. *The Genesis of the Brothers Karamazov.* Evanston, Ill.: Northwestern University Press, 1990. Published in a series by Columbia University's Harriman Institute, by a fine and highly respected specialist in Russian literature.

Berlin, Isaiah. *The Hedgehog and the Fox.* New York: Simon and Schuster, 1970. This Latvian-born Oxford scholar held colleagues and readers spellbound, both by his incisive brevity and his brilliant and effervescent conversational powers.

Binyon, T. J. *Pushkin: A Biography.* New York: Alfred A Knopf, 2003. An excellent new biography: reliable, authoritative, level-headed, and intelligently written.

Brown, Edward J. *Literature Since the Revolution.* New York: Collier, 1971. Edward Brown was one of the most prominent American academic observers of Soviet cultural life; his comments are the result of extensive knowledge about the situation in the Soviet Union.

Cain, T. G. S. *Tolstoy.* London: Paul Elek, 1977. Comments by an excellent British specialist in Russian literature.

Chekhov, Anton. *Plays.* Translated and edited by Eugene Bristow. Norton Critical Edition. New York: W.W. Norton, 1977. Part of a useful series of critical editions concerning Russian literature.

————. *The Portable Chekhov.* Introduction by Avrahm Yarmolinsky. New York: Viking Portable Library, 1973. An excellent selection of Chekhov's stories by a great American popularizer of Russian literature.

Christian, R. F. *Tolstoy: A Critical Introduction.* Cambridge: Cambridge University Press, 1969. A work by another highly respected British scholar.

Cross, Samuel Hazard, and Olgerd P. Sherbowitz-Wetzor, eds. *The Russian Primary Chronicle.* Cambridge, Mass: Medieval Academy of America, 1953. Year-by-year events as seen by monks who were the historians in medieval times.

Debreczeny, Paul, and Thomas Eekman, eds. *Chekhov's Art of Writing.* Columbus, Ohio: Slavica Publishers, 1977. Includes some fascinating articles put together by Paul Debreczeny, one of the best American specialists on Chekhov and other Russian writers.

Dostoevsky, Fedor. *Poor Folk.* Translated and with an introduction by David McDuff. London: Penguin, 1988. A competent translation of Dostoevsky's first novel.

————. *Notes from the Underground. Three Short Novels of Dostoevsky.* Translated by Constance Garnett. Revised by Avrahm Yarmolinsky. New York: Doubleday Anchor Books, 1960. A good revision of the translation by the most faithful and assiduous 19th-century translator of Russian literature.

————. *Crime and Punishment.* Edited by George Gibian and translated by Jessie Coulson. Norton Critical Edition. New York: W.W. Norton, 1989. Contains the novel and a remarkable collection of critical commentary from American, Russian, and other sources.

————. *The Brothers Karamazov.* Translated by Constance Garnett and extensively revised by Ralph Matlaw. New York: W.W. Norton, 1976. Includes the novel, plus a large selection of Dostoevsky's letters and a collection of critical essays. This volume contains a careful revision of a standard translation, an interesting view of Dostoevsky's correspondence, and some excellent critical articles.

Erlich, Victor, ed. *Pasternak—A Collection of Critical Essays.* Englewood Cliffs, N.J.: Prentice Hall, 1978. A collection by a beloved emigré professor from a famous Jewish intellectual family in pre-revolutionary Russia.

Fleishman, Lazar. *Boris Pasternak: The Poet and His Politics.* Cambridge: Harvard University Press, 1990. A work by an esteemed Russian emigré in the United States.

Frank, Joseph. *Dostoevsky—The Miraculous Years, 1865–71.* Vol. 4. Princeton: Princeton University Press, 1995. The fourth volume of a huge and fascinating scholarly work devoted to Dostoevsky's life and work; written by a highly respected scholar.

———. *Dostoevsky—The Mantle of the Prophet, 1871–81.* Vol. 5. Princeton: Princeton University Press, 1998. The final volume of Frank's colossal series, it has justly attracted wide attention.

Gogol', Nikolai. "The Inspector General," in *A Treasury of Russian Literature.* Translated and with commentary by Bernard Guerney. New York: Vanguard Press, 1943. A brilliant translation by a real enthusiast.

———. *The Nose, The Overcoat, Diary of a Madman and Other Stories.* Translated and with an introduction by Ronald Wilks. London: Penguin, 1972. Gives a clear version of the stories.

———. *Dead Souls.* Edited by George Gibian and translated by George Reavey. Norton Critical Edition. New York: W.W. Norton and Co., 1985. Translation by a good poet. The commentary by an eminent scholar cites good American critics and excellent Russian scholars seldom read in the United States; many critical articles included.

Gorky, Maxim. *Autobiography of Maxim Gorky.* Translated by Isidore Schneider. New York: Citadel Press, 1949. A competent presentation of Gorky's style to American readers.

Hingley, Ronald. *Pasternak—A Biography.* New York: Knopf, 1983. A reliable account of Pasternak's life and works by a knowledgeable specialist.

Jackson, Robert L. *The Art of Dostoevsky.* Princeton: Princeton University Press, 1981. A work by one of the most eminent American specialists on Russian literature.

———, ed. *A New Word on the Brothers Karamazov.* Evanston, Ill.: Northwestern University Press, 2004. An excellent collection of articles by some of the best contemporary American specialists on Dostoevsky.

Kataev, Vladimir. *If Only We Could Know: An Interpretation of Chekhov.* Translated by Harvey Pitcher. Chicago: Ivan R. Dee, 2002. A gentle yet penetrating examination of varying interpretations of Chekhov, presented by the contemporary chairman of the Moscow State University Department of Classical Russian Literature.

Kaun, Alexander. *Maxim Gorky and His Russia.* New York: Benjamin Blom, 1968. An interesting work by a scholar who met the writer while he lived in Italy.

Kozintsev, Grigorii. *Hamlet.* 140 min., 1964. Music by Dmitry Shostakovich. A famous film version of *Hamlet* using Boris Pasternak's translation.

Kutik, Ilya. *Writing as Exorcism—The Personal Codes of Pushkin, Lermontov, and Gogol.* Evanston, Ill.: Northwestern University Press, 2005. A stimulating and provocative approach to Pushkin and literary perception, by a very original contemporary Russian poet. He will make your ears sting and your mind and imagination race.

Maiakovsky, Vladimir. *The Bedbug and Selected Poetry.* Translated by Max Hayward and George Reavey. Introduction by Patricia Blake. Bloomington: Indiana University Press, 1975. Translation and commentary by some of the best known and most penetrating American critics who lived and agonized in Soviet times.

———. *Plays.* Translated by Guy Daniels, with an introduction by Robert Payne. Evanston, Ill.: Northwestern University Press, 1968. The plays show other aspects of Maiakovsky's art and political positions; part of an interesting literary series.

———. *Vladimir Majakovskij—Memoirs and Essays.* Edited by Beng Jangfeldt and Nils Ake Nilsson. Stockholm: Almqvist and Wiksell, Intl., 1975. Various approaches to the poet; gets behind the simplistic view promoted by Soviet propaganda.

Mann, Robert, trans. *The Song of Prince Igor.* Eugene, Ore.: Vernyhora Press, 1979. The clearest English-language rendition of the famous East Slavic epic, with clear explanations and commentary; available through the Northwestern University bookstore.

Marshall, Herbert. *Mayakovsky.* New York: Hill and Wang, 1965. Memoirs of a British writer and critic who was personally close to Maiakovsky and his world.

Medvedev, Roy. *Problems in the Literary Biography of Mikhail Sholokhov.* Cambridge: Cambridge University Press, 1977. A Russian publicist, well known in Soviet intellectual circles, examines the accusations of plagiarism often raised against Sholokhov.

Mirsky, D. S. *A History of Russian Literature.* Edited by Francis J. Whitfield. New York: Knopf, 1966. A work by a well-known and sensitive Russian aristocrat and scholar who worked in England, then met a tragic fate when he returned to the USSR.

Mochulsky, Konstantin. *Dostoevsky: His Life and Work.* Princeton: Princeton University Press, 1967. A beautifully written work, with an emphasis on the religious aspect of Dostoevsky's art and psychology.

Morson, Gary Saul. *Hidden in Plain View: Narrative and Creative Potentials in "War and Peace."* Palo Alto, Calif.: Stanford University Press, 1987. A perceptive work by one of the best Russian literary scholars in the United States.

Moser, Charles A., ed. *Cambridge History of Russian Literature.* Cambridge: Cambridge University Press, 1989. Like all the handbooks in the series, this one is useful and totally reliable for quick reference to the history of Russian literature.

Mussorgsky, Modest. *Boris Godunov.* London: Decca Records, 1998. Conducted by Herbert Von Karajan. Mussorgsky's brilliant musical and dramatic adaptation of Pushkin's tragedy; one of the world's greatest operas.

Nabokov, Vladimir. *Lectures on Russian Literature.* Edited and with an introduction by Fredson Bowers. New York: Harcourt Brace Jovanovich, 1981. As always, Nabokov is provocative, representing his own often contrarian opinions. He intensely dislikes the work of Dostoevsky.

———. *Nikolai Gogol.* Norfolk, Conn.: New Directions, 1944. The brilliant, sparkling book that introduced Nabokov as a critic to the American reading public.

Orwin, Donna Tussing, ed. *The Cambridge Companion to Tolstoy.* Cambridge: Cambridge University Press, 2002. A kind of Tolstoy handbook done by past masters of the academic world.

Pasternak, Boris. *Doctor Zhivago.* Translated by Max Hayward, Manya Harari, and Bernard Guerney. New York: Pantheon Books, 1958. A carefully prepared translation of the novel by well-respected specialists in the field of Soviet studies; well done, despite the mistaken attacks by Edmund Wilson.

Pritchett, V. S. *The Gentle Barbarian: The Life and Work of Turgenev*. London: Chatto and Windus, 1977. An approach by a very individual British writer and critic.

Pushkin, Aleksandr. *Eugene Onegin*. Translated by James E. Falen. London: Oxford University Press, 1998. A highly readable attempt to render verse that is very difficult to translate.

———. *Eugene Oenegin—A Novel in Verse*. Translated with commentary by Vladimir Nabokov. 4 vols. New York: Bollingen Series, Pantheon Books, 1964. A literal translation, highly accurate but clumsy and, in places, difficult to read; brilliant, provocative, with sometimes maddening commentary and criticism, by one of the 20th century's outstanding literary personalities.

———. "Boris Godunov," in *The Poems, Prose, and Plays of Alexander Pushkin*. Edited by Avrahm Yarmolinsky. New York: Random House, Modern Library, 1964. An English rendition of Pushkin's tragedy; gives some idea of the original.

———. "Mozart and Salieri," in *The Poems, Prose, and Plays of Alexander Pushkin*. Edited by Avrahm Yarmolinsky. New York: Random House, Modern Library, 1964. An English rendition of the play; reasonably accurate.

———. "Egyptian Nights," in *Aleksandr Pushkin—Complete Prose Fiction*. Translated and with commentary by Paul Debreczeny. Palo Alto, Calif.: Stanford University Press, 1983. Debreczeny is one of the outstanding Pushkin scholars in the United States.

———. "The Bronze Horseman," in *Pushkin Threefold*. Translated by Walter Arndt (bilingual edition). New York: E. P. Dutton, 1972. This translator totally captures Pushkin's rhythm and rhyme schemes, necessarily changing many of the words and phrases; Nabokov savagely criticized the work, giving chapter and verse about the mistakes. I cannot help but sympathize with Arndt, although I must acknowledge his mistakes.

Randall, Francis B. "Belinsky's Letter to Gogol'," in *Vissarion Belinskii*. Newtonville, Mass.: Oriental Research Partners, 1987. An interesting and discursive discussion of the famous letter, with the author's own interpretations.

Riasanovsky, Nicolas. *History of Russia*. New York: Oxford University Press, 2000. Widely regarded as one of the best and most balanced accounts of one of the world's most exciting histories.

Scammell, Michael. *Solzhenitsyn: A Biography*. New York: Norton, 1984. A widely recognized, authoritative work on the writer.

Schaffer, Peter. *Amadeus*. Los Angeles, Calif.: The Saul Zaentz Company, 1984. A play and a film based on Pushkin's play *Mozart and Salieri*. Although it departs a great deal from the original play, the film brilliantly captures Pushkin's frolicsome yet penetrating mood and intent.

Schapiro, Leonard. *Turgenev: His Life and Times*. New York: Random House, 1978. A fascinating examination of Turgenev's life.

Shakespeare, William. *Complete Works*. Edited by W. J. Craig. London: Oxford University Press, 1969. *Richard II, Henry IV, Part One, Henry IV, Part Two, Henry V*. Shakespeare's history plays, which interpret the guilt-ridden monarch in contrast to the great monarch, stimulated Pushkin's imagination as a dramatist.

Sholokhov, Mikhail. *And Quiet Flows the Don*. Translated by Stephen Garry. New York: Hill and Wang, New American Library, 1959. This is the standard English translation; reasonably competent, although it leaves out some sections of the original published text.

Solzenitsyn, Alexandr. *One Day in the Life of Ivan Denisovich*. Translated by H. T. Willetts. With an introduction by Katherine Shonk. New York: Farrar, Straus, and Giroux, 2005. A new translation of the most famous work, done with the approval of the writer.

————. *And Quiet Flows the Don*. Translated by Robert Daglish. Revised and edited by Brian Murphy. New York: Carroll and Graf, 1996. This is a new version of the entire text of the novel, previously published in two separate volumes, under two titles. It is thoroughly revised by Brian Murphy, a British specialist, who spent considerable time in the USSR.

Stahlberger, Lawrence. *The Symbolic System of Majakovskij*. The Hague: Mouton and Co., 1964. Written under the influence and guidance of R. Jakobson, a scholar who knew the poet well.

Styan, J. L. *Chekhov in Performance*. Cambridge: Cambridge University Press, 1978. Written by a British scholar who often crossed the line between literary criticism and theatrical performance.

Tchaikovsky, P. I. *Eugene Onegin.* Germany: Philips Classics sound recording, 1993. A chance for English speakers to get some of the rhythms of Pushkin, as adapted and changed by Tchaikovsky.

Thomas, D. M. *Aleksandr Solzhenitsyn—A Century in His Life.* New York: St. Martin's Press, 1998. Another approach to the issues of politics and literature that surround the writer's life.

Tolstoy, Lev. *Childhood, Boyhood, and Youth.* Translated and edited by Michael Scammell. New York: Random House, Modern Library, 2002. Translation and commentary by an eminent American specialist in Russian literature.

———. *Tales of Army Life.* Translated by Louise and Aylmer Maude. London: Oxford University Press, 1963. Translation by two of the best-known early British translators of Russian literature.

———. *War and Peace.* Translated by Ann Dunnigan, with an introduction by John Bayley. New York: Signet, 1968. Competent translation with an insightful introduction by one of England's best specialists on Russian literature.

———. *Anna Karenina.* Translated by Louise and Aylmer Maud, with an introduction by W. Gareth Jones. London: Oxford University Press, 1995. Translation by two of the best-known early British translators of Russian literature.

Trotsky, Leon. *Literature and Revolution.* Ann Arbor: University of Michigan Press, 1960. A fascinating essay by the man who, after Lenin, did most to establish the USSR.

Turgenev, Ivan. *First Love and Other Stories.* Translated and with an introduction by Richard Freeborn. New York: Oxford University Press, 1989. A translator with a good feeling for Turgenev's fine style.

———. *Fathers and Sons (A Norton Critical Edition).* Edited and translated by Ralph Matlaw. New York: W.W. Norton, 1966. An interesting collection of various views concerning Turgenev, both in and out of Russia.

Wasiolek, Edward. *Tolstoy's Major Fiction.* Chicago: University of Chicago Press, 1978. A work by an original and challenging American critic.

————, ed. *Critical Essays on Tolstoy*. Boston: G.K. Hall, 1986. Commentary by a highly original American critic who knows Russia from firsthand experience.

Weil, Irwin. *Gorky: His Literary Development and Influence on Soviet Intellectual Life*. New York: Random House, 1966. I shall let the reader arrive at his or her own conclusions about the early work of this enthusiast of Russian literature.

Zenkovsky, Sergei. A., ed. *Medieval Russia's Epics, Chronicles, and Tales*. New York: Dutton and Co., 1963. The best English-language collection of old Russian literature, organized by an excellent scholar.

Zoshchenko, Mikhail. *Nervous People and Other Stories*. Translated by Maria Gordon and Hugh McLean, with an introduction by Hugh McLean. Bloomington: Indiana University Press, 1975. A good selection of the stories, with a very intelligent and knowledgeable account of the literary and political context.